Awake O Harp

A Devotional Commentary on the Psalms

WILLIAM VARNER

Scripture quotations are from The Holy Bible, English Standard Version® (ESV®), copyright © 2001 by Crossway, a publishing ministry of Good News Publishers. Used by permission. All rights reserved.

Scripture quotations marked HCSB are taken from the Holman Christian Standard Bible®, Copyright © 1999, 2000, 2002, 2003, 2009 by Holman Bible Publishers. Used by permission. Holman Christian Standard Bible®, Holman CSB®, and HCSB® are federally registered trademarks of Holman Bible Publishers.

Scripture quotations taken from the New American Standard Bible®, Copyright © 1960, 1962, 1963, 1968, 1971, 1972, 1973, 1975, 1977, 1995 by The Lockman Foundation. Used by permission." (www.Lockman.org)

Copyright © 2011, 2014, 2017 William Varner

All rights reserved. No part of this book may be reproduced or transmitted in any form or by any means, electronic or mechanical, including photocopying and recording, or by any information storage and retrieval system, without permission in writing from the publisher.

Cover design and typesetting by Greg Wright (DiamondPointMedia.com)

Printed in the United States of America

2017—Updated Edition

ISBN-13: 978-1548743789
ISBN-10: 154874378X

This commentary is dedicated to
Bob King

Bob is my fellow laborer in the ministry of
the Sojourners Fellowship at Grace Community Church.
More than anyone I have ever known, Bob exemplifies
the righteous man who is described in Psalm One
and he prays like the Psalms teach us to pray.

Contents

Acknowledgements xiii
Introduction...1
Psalm 1—Only Two Ways..11
Psalm 2—The Father and His Son................................13
Psalm 3—Advice for Insomniacs.................................15
Psalm 4—A Prayer for Compline 17
Psalm 5—Encouragement for the Slandered 19
Psalm 6—Sickness and Sin 21
Psalm 7—How to Handle Bad News 23
Psalm 8—The Crown of Creation...............................26
Psalm 9—Groaning about the Goyim 28
Psalm 10—When Good Things Happen to Bad People 31
Psalm 11—When to Flee and When to Stick it Out 34
Psalm 12—The Flatterers and the Faithful 36
Psalm 13—From Questions to Quietness 38
Psalm 14—The Practical Atheist 40
Psalm 15—Getting Dressed for Church 42
Psalm 16—Messiah Lives!.......................................44
Psalm 17—An Honest Plea......................................46
Psalm 18—Hind's Feet on High Places 48
Psalm 19—God's Three Books...................................52
Psalm 20—Messiah Prays for You 55

Psalm 21 — When We Receive Our Heart's Desire 57
Psalm 22 — A Song of the Singing Sufferer 59
Psalm 22 (part 2) — Of Whom Does David Speak? 62
Psalm 23 — Our Forever Shepherd 64
Psalm 24 — The King of Glory 66
Psalm 25 — The Holy Alphabet 68
Psalm 26 — A Claim to Integrity 71
Psalm 27 — One Thing 73
Psalm 27 (part 2) — Forsaken But Not Abandoned 75
Psalm 28 — Answered Prayer 77
Psalm 29 — Orientation 79
Psalm 30 — Joy in the Morning 81
Psalm 31 — Into Your Hands 83
Psalm 32 — Forgiven 86
Psalm 33 — Maker and Monarch 88
Psalm 34 — Thriving in Crisis 90
Psalm 35 — A Cry for Help 93
Psalm 36 — Hesed Forever! 96
Psalm 37 — Meek Shall Inherit 98
Psalm 37 (part 2) — He Shall Not Fall 101
Psalm 38 — A Penitent 103
Psalm 39 — Lament 105
Psalm 39 (part 2) — O Lord 107
Psalm 40 — Up from the Bog 109
Psalm 40 (part 2) — "To Do Your Will" 111
Psalm 41 — When You're Down 113
Psalms 42&43 — Drought and Deliverance 115
Psalms 42&43 (part 2) — Drought and Deliverance 118
Psalm 44 — A National Lament 120

Psalm 45—The King in His Beauty...............123
Psalm 46—City of the King...................126
Psalm 47—I'm the King of the World!.........128
Psalm 48—Zion, City of God..................130
Psalm 49—Ransomed From Sheol................132
Psalm 50—Here Comes the Judge...............135
Psalm 51—Have Mercy.........................138
Psalm 52—A Really Bad Dude..................141
Psalm 53—Salvation for Israel...............143
Psalm 54—My Helper..........................145
Psalm 55—Betrayed!!.........................147
Psalm 56—When I am Afraid...................150
Psalm 57—In the Cave with Dave..............152
Psalm 58—Retribution and Reward.............154
Psalm 59—Night and Morning..................156
Psalm 60—Trouble Back Home..................158
Psalm 61—Messiah and Me.....................160
Theme of the Psalms—Hesed Va'emet...........162
Psalm 62—Absalom, Again!....................164
Psalm 63—General Patton.....................166
Psalm 64—Bad and Good Fear..................168
Psalm 65—Now Thank We All Our God...........170
Psalm 66—The Many and the One...............172
Psalm 67—Let the Nations be Glad............174
Psalm 68—The Most Difficult of All..........176
Psalm 69—Persecuted But Not Forsaken........179
Psalm 70—Hurry Up, God!.....................182
Psalm 71—Growing Old Gracefully.............184
Psalm 72—The Perfect King...................187

Psalm 73—Whom Do I Have But You? 190
Psalm 74—When Heaven Seems Silent........................193
Psalm 75—The Just Judge 196
Psalm 76—Resplendent, Majestic, Awe-Inspiring 198
Psalm 77—Asaph's Autobiography...........................200
Psalm 78—Don't Know Much About History 202
Psalm 79—The Psalms and Jeremiah 206
Psalm 80—A Flock and a Vine..............................208
Psalm 81—The Shofar Blows 211
Psalm 82—God and the Gods 213
Psalm 83—Let's Wipe Them Out! 215
Psalm 84—Longing For God 217
Psalm 85—Revival!! 85....................................219
Psalm 86—In The Day of My Trouble 221
Psalm 87—Glorious Things of Thee Are Spoken 223
Psalm 88—"Song Sung Blue" 225
Psalm 89—Sure Mercies of David 228
Psalm 90—O God Our Help in Ages Past 231
Psalm 91—Under His Wings.................................233
Psalm 92—How to Thrive...................................235
Psalm 93—The Lord Reigns! 237
Psalm 94—How Do They Get Away With It?...................239
Psalm 95—The Way to Worship 241
Psalm 96—Tell His Glory Among the Gentiles...............243
Psalm 97—Reigning and Ruling 245
Psalm 98—King and Savior.................................247
Psalm 99—Holy Is He! 249
Psalm 100—Is It Thanksgiving Yet? 251
Psalm 100 (part 2)—"The Old Hundredth" 253

Psalm 101—The Ruler and the Ruled 255
Psalm 102—"But You..." 257
Psalm 103—"Don't You Forget It!" 260
Psalm 104—Creator – Sustainer 262
Psalm 105—Faithful! 265
Psalm 105 (part 2)—Faithful 105 268
Psalm 106—Nevertheless! 270
Psalm 107—"They Cried...He Saved" 273
Psalm 108—"We Shall Do Valiantly" 276
Psalm 109—With Yahweh at Hand 278
Psalm 110—The LORD and My Lord 281
Psalm 111—A Student's Psalm 283
Psalm 112—A God-Fearer 285
Psalm 113—Hallel! 287
Psalm 114—The Exodus and Us 289
Psalm 115—Soli Deo Gloria 291
Psalm 116—How Can I Say Thanks? 293
Psalm 117—Let's Hear It For the Goyim! 295
Psalm 118—Luther's Favorite 297
Psalm 118 (part 2)—An Overlooked Messianic Text 299
Psalm 119 Overview—The Golden Alphabet 301
Psalm 119 vv. 1–24—Aleph, Bet, Gimel 303
Psalm 119 vv. 25–48—Dalet, Hay, Vav 306
Psalm 119 vv. 49–72—Zayin, Het, Tet 308
Psalm 119 vv. 73–96—Yod, Kaf, Lamed 310
Psalm 119 vv. 97–120—Mem, Nun, Samek 313
Psalm 119 vv. 121–144—Ayin, Pe, Tsade 315
Psalm 119 vv. 145–168—Qof, Resh, Shin 317
Psalm 119 vv. 169–176—"Tav and the Sof" 319

Psalm 119—What is the *Sof*?...................................320
Psalms 120-134—Introduction to the Psalms of Ascent.........321
Psalm 120—Depressed In the Diaspora 322
Psalm 121—The Keeper 324
Psalm 122—Let's Go 326
Psalm 123—Desiring God's Favor............................328
Psalm 124—What If The Lord Wasn't There?..................330
Psalm 125—Mountains Around The City 332
Psalm 126—From Joy to Tears to Joy........................334
Psalm 127—A Quiver Full of Arrows 336
Psalm 128—Kids as House Plants............................338
Psalm 129—Anti-Semitism, Then and Now 340
Psalm 130—Out of the Depths...............................342
Psalm 131—A Calm and Quiet Soul...........................344
Psalm 132—David – Messianic King 346
Psalm 133—Unity, O to Dwell In Unity......................348
Psalm 134—Blessings 24/7..................................350
Psalm 135—God Is Great, God is Good.......................352
Psalm 136—First the Boys, Then the Girls 354
Psalm 137—By The Rivers of Babylon........................356
Psalm 138—Goodness Beyond Measure.........................358
Psalm 139—The Omni Psalm 360
Psalm 140—"That's Not True"...............................363
Psalm 141—Set a Guard for My Mouth 365
Psalm 142—In The Cave With Dave, Again!...................367
Psalm 143—In Your Righteousness 369
Psalm 144—A King's Song...................................371
Psalm 145—Who He Is and What He Does 373
Psalm 146—Faith, Hope, Love 376

CONTENTS

Psalm 147—No Other Nation.................................378
Psalm 148—A Choir of Creation 380
Psalm 149—Sing Along...382
Psalm 150—What a Way to End!............................384
What I've Learned During My Journey Through The Psalms......386

Acknowledgements

I would like to express my deep appreciation to Warren Wiersbe and Roger Ellsworth, whose books inspired me to make my own contribution to the writings on the Psalms. The influence of Wiersbe's *With the Word* commentary and Ellsworth's *Opening up Psalms* can be seen throughout this book. I would also like to thank the readers of my blog, DrIBEX Ideas, for their encouraging responses to my original posts on the Psalms over the course of a year. Those posts were expanded and now appear in this form. In that regard, deep appreciation is also expressed to a former student, Yvette Fox, who laboriously transferred those blog posts into a Word document and also inserted the appropriate Bible texts from three English versions. Two current students, Rafael and Sarah Montoya-Ortega, proofed the manuscript and made some valuable suggestions. My dear wife, Helen, assisted with typing and proofing the manuscript as well as with many other editorial decisions. "Your wife will be like a fruitful vine within your house" (Psa. 128:3).

Introduction

The Psalms and Us

I have been reading the Psalms for years and have been praying them regularly for the past few years. It is out of my own personal involvement with this prayer and praise book of Israel that this devotional commentary on the Psalms has been birthed.

Why should we concern ourselves with the Book of Psalms? There are many answers to that question and I will list a number of them below, but consider just the following reasons that are unique to the Psalter. First, the Book of Psalms comprises the longest book in the Bible—much longer than its closest competitors, Jeremiah and Isaiah. Second, it is the only book of the Bible that was written by many authors. Third, it contains both the longest and shortest chapters of the Bible, 119 and 117 respectively. Fourth, it is the Old Testament book most frequently quoted by New Testament writers.

These are some of the features that lend interest and fascination to the book, but these are only formal features. The true significance of the Psalter lies in its timeless message, both for ancient Israel and also for all believers today.

And what is that message? The Book of Psalms, as is the case with every other book of the Bible, is ultimately a message about the Messiah, our Lord Jesus. We find Jesus here because he found himself here. As he walked with two of his disciples on the day of his resurrection, Jesus 'expounded to them in all the Scriptures the things concerning himself ' (Luke 24:27). Later that day he appeared to other disciples and said: 'These are the words which I spoke to you while I was still with you, that all things must be fulfilled which were written in the Law of Moses and the Prophets and the **Psalms** concerning Me' (Luke 24:44).

All of Scripture is about Jesus the Messiah, His ineffable Person and His saving work, and that includes the Psalms! The above passages indicate that it is not just individual verses that are about Him (one author calls these individual "prophecies" the tips of a very large iceberg!), but the Old Testament *as a whole* is also about Him!

But where do we find our Messiah in the Psalms? There are more prophecies and allusions and types of the Messiah in the Psalms than in any other book of the Old Testament! Some of these, as we shall see, are so very detailed and precise that they appear to be the descriptions of those actually viewing the events instead of foretelling them hundreds of years before. The table on the next page is a suggested list, although I do not intend it to be exhaustive.

We need the Psalms, then, because they point us to Jesus, who is the source of our salvation. But we also need them because they describe what the lives of Jesus-followers should look like—that is, the qualities that those who have faith in the Messiah are to seek and to practice. More specifically:

The Psalms teach us to be deeply occupied with our God. They magnify and exalt Him as the Sovereign Creator and Ruler of the universe. What is it to be much occupied with God? It is to treasure His Word, to delight in His worship, to reflect on His glorious attributes, to rehearse His great acts in history, to trust in His care, to glory in His gospel and to anticipate His final victory. The more we are occupied with God, the more strength we find for living.

The Psalms teach us to praise our God and also show us how to praise Him. There are few lessons that we need more. So very often we mumble mechanical praise from hearts that are crowded with unworthy loves and occupied with earthly concerns. The need is for robust praise from hearts that are deeply schooled in the stunning truths of the Sovereign Lord who not only made us but pours from his bounty countless blessings, the chief of which is eternal salvation through his Son.

The Psalms teach us how to trust our God during afflictions and how to receive comfort from Him. They express every human emotion and address every human need. John R. W. Stott writes: "The reason why Christian people are drawn to the Psalms is that they speak the universal language of the human soul ... Whatever our spiritual mood may be, there is

Messianic Reference		New Testament "Fulfillment"
2:7	God declares Him to be His Son.	Matthew 3:17
8:6	All things will be put under His feet.	Hebrews 2:8
16:10	He will be resurrected from the dead.	Mark 16:6, 7
22:1	God will forsake Him in His hour of need.	Matthew 27:46
22:7, 8	He will be scorned and mocked.	Luke 23:35
22:16	His hands and feet will be pierced.	John 20:25, 27
22:18	Others will gamble for His clothes.	Matthew 27:35, 36
34:20	Not one of His bones will be broken.	John 19:32, 33, 36
35:11	He will be accused by false witnesses.	Mark 14:57
35:19	He will be hated without a cause.	John 15:25
40:7, 8	He will come to do God's will.	Hebrews 10:7
41:9	He will be betrayed by a friend.	Luke 22:47
45:6	His throne will be forever.	Hebrews 1:8
68:18	He will ascend to God's right hand.	Mark 16:19
69:9	Zeal for God's house will consume Him.	John 2:17
69:21	He will be given vinegar and gall to drink.	Matthew 27:34
72:1–19	He will be a worldwide king.	Revelation 19:11–20:6
109:4	He will pray for His enemies.	Luke 23:34
109:8	His betrayer's place will be filled by another.	Acts 1:20
110:1	His enemies will be made subject to Him.	Matthew 22:44
110:4	He will be a priest like Melchizedek.	Hebrews 5:6
118:22	He will be the chief cornerstone.	Matthew 21:42
118:26	He will come in the name of the Lord.	Matthew 21:91

sure to be a psalm which reflects it—whether triumph or defeat, excitement or depression, joy or sorrow, praise or penitence, wonder or anger." We might say the Psalms show us how to respond to every conceivable situation that life throws at us. In the Psalms we can pour out our hearts before Yahweh. Examples of repentance, communion, hope, faith, love, and lament abound. There are psalms for every occasion in life and for every spiritual condition in which we find ourselves. The Psalter is simply universal in its appeal to believing hearts.

The Psalms show us how to be zealous for the cause of our God. From hearts flooded with love for God, the various psalmists expressed fervent desires to see the advancement of God's truth, the vindication of His name, the acknowledgement of His glory and the triumph of His kingdom. All of this requires, as the imprecatory psalms so wonderfully comprehend, the defeat of evil and the judgment of evil-doers.

The Psalms show us how to worship our God both publicly and privately. The Psalms throb with both kinds of worship. The former is vigorously endorsed in the pilgrimage psalms, as well as in other types. And the latter is modeled by individual psalmists who, even in the midst of heart-wrenching circumstances, find their hearts going out after God in praise and adoration.

Types of Psalms

There is little agreement among Bible scholars on the various types of psalms. Some see eight categories, while others see nine or ten or more. Another problem is that some psalms fit into more than one category. An example of this is Psalm 40 which has been classified as a psalm of individual lament, individual thanksgiving and imprecatory. A few of the pilgrimage psalms—127, 128, and 133—are placed by some in the "wisdom" category. While clear-cut genre typing is not possible for every psalm, different psalms can be grouped by similarities of form, content, and pattern. Yet, variations do occur, and each psalm is unique in both message and content. Even if the lay reader cannot undoubtedly discover what type of psalm he is reading, I guarantee you that blessing will not be lost to that reader!

While categorization is imprecise, it is still helpful. Consider the following types: wisdom, laments, pilgrimage, thanksgiving, praise, imprecatory, messianic, and royal psalms.

I invite you, then, to join me on a spiritual journey through the Psalms. It must of necessity be brief. There is still so much that we will not be able to see! But those sights which we do see will certainly make the journey worthwhile. So be sure to bring a mind that is ready to ponder the glories of God and a heart that is ready to stand in awe of Him.

Laymen have profited from the Psalms without knowing any of the preceding or subsequent information. If the following is not interesting or helpful to you, at this point you can proceed to Psalm One and be blessed!

There are a few further matters, however, that will be helpful to many as you look at the Psalms as a whole before you start to examine them individually.

The Title

The name "Psalms" means "songs to the accompaniment of a stringed instrument." It is taken from the Greek translation of the Old Testament, which used the title "Psalmoi." The Hebrew title for the book was "Tehillim," which means "praise songs."

Authorship

The Psalms were composed over a period of approximately 900 years, with the earliest being written by Moses (Ps. 90) and the latest written by various authors after the Babylonian Captivity (Ps. 126 and 147).

The Psalms are primarily associated with David because he wrote most of them as the following breakdown indicates:

David—seventy-three (Psalms 3–9, 11–32, 34–41, 41–65, 68–70, 86, 101, 103, 108–110, 122, 124, 131, 133, 138–145)
Asaph—twelve (Psalms 50, 73–83)
Descendants of Korah—ten (Psalms 42, 44–49, 84–85, 87)
Solomon—two (Psalms 72 and 127)
Ethan—one (Psalm 89)
Heman—one (Psalm 88)
Moses—one (Psalm 90)
Anonymous—fifty (Many of these may also have been written by David. For example, Acts 4:25 attributes Psalm 2 to David.)

Divisions

The Psalms fall into five "books":
Book I: 1–41 (41 psalms)
Book II: 42–72 (31 psalms)
Book III: 73–89 (17 psalms)
Book IV: 90–106 (17 psalms)
Book V: 107–150 (44 psalms)

Each of these 'books' ends with a triumphant burst of praise (Ps. 41:13; 72:18–19; 89:52; 106:48; and 150:6).

Some have suggested that each division corresponds to the first five books of the Bible—the books of Moses. Because Book I emphasizes the themes of creation, sin and salvation, it supposedly corresponds to Genesis which prominently displays those same themes. Furthermore, because the psalms of Book II are weighted with the theme of redemption, it is said to correspond to the Book of Exodus. This arrangement connects Book III with Leviticus because of their common emphasis on the sanctuary, Book IV with Numbers because of the prominence in each of Moses and Israel's wandering in the wilderness and Book V with Deuteronomy because of the emphasis in each on the Word of God. This last explanation, however, has the appearance of being brought *into* the Psalms instead of being been drawn out of them. It may be useful as an illustration, but it seems a bit forced.

Superscriptions

A good number of psalms—116 to be exact—include either a historical or a musical heading. The former gives us the situation in which the Psalmist found himself when he sat down to write. The first of these is Psalm 3, which says, 'A Psalm of David when he fled from Absalom his son.' The latter gives instructions on how the Psalm was to be played. The first musical heading is found in Psalm 4: "To the Chief Musician. With stringed instruments. A Psalm of David."

Were these "titles" part of the original compositions? Probably not, but what we do know is that the earliest copies of the Psalms that we have (the Septuagint and the Dead Sea Scrolls) contain them! Another interesting thought is that when the New Testament writers referred to their authoritative "Scriptures," namely the Old Testament, they were referring to the Psalms along with their titles! Thus, from a canonical viewpoint, the Psalms along with their titles, were part of the Jewish canon and a part of the New Testament writer's Old Testament canon as well. Thus, I am hesitant to doubt the veracity of the contents of the titles.

Selah Psalms

The word "Selah" appears seventy-four times in forty psalms. This word signifies a pause or interlude. It may have been used to inform musicians to change instruments or to call for both musicians and listeners to ponder the truth that had been sung. In the public reading of the Psalms, we should honor each "Selah," not by actually saying the word, but rather by pausing.

Types of Poetry

The Psalms display primarily four types of poetry. **Synonymous parallelism** is on display when the second line of a poem uses similar words to express the same thought as the first line. An example of this is:

> O LORD, do not rebuke me in your anger,
> > Nor chasten me in your hot displeasure
>
> (Ps. 6:1).
>
> Show me your ways
> > O Lord.
> Teach me your paths
> (Ps. 25:4)

Antithetical parallelism takes us to the other end of the spectrum. Here the second line expresses the opposite of the first and is usually introduced by the word "but":

> The wicked borrows and does not repay,
> **but**
> the righteous shows mercy and gives
> (Ps. 37:21).

Synthetic parallelism occurs when the second line carries further or expands the first line:

> God is our refuge and strength,
> A very present help in trouble
> (Ps. 46:1).

Climactic parallelism takes place when succeeding lines repeat some words from the first line and complete the thought:

> Our fathers **trusted** in you;
> They **trusted**, and you
> delivered them.
> They cried to you, and were
> delivered;
> They **trusted** in you, and were
> not ashamed.
> (Ps. 22:4–5).

Helpful Resources

We are about ready to launch into the Psalms themselves, but first I want to add a few words about additional resources on the Psalms, especially for those who want to go "deeper." Here are a few recommendations for "average" folks.

There is a plethora of good academic and expository commentaries on the Psalms. In my opinion, the most accessible is the one by Derek Kidner in the *Tyndale OT Commentary*. Kidner gives you enough of the technical aspects of each psalm (the literary features, the parallelism, and the Hebrew words) to help you appreciate both the Psalm's literary beauty and also its theological significance. Kidner also recognizes the intensely practical meaning of the Psalms and I have benefited from his comments in many ways that show up in my own comments.

I discovered the marvelous commentary on the Psalms by the British academic, John Eaton, late in my preparation of this manuscript. I am sure the work would have been better if I had been able to study more closely his *Psalms: A Historical and Spiritual Commentary*. Few scholarly commentaries draw out both the academic and the spiritual/Messianic meaning of the Psalms, but Eaton does! I have also adapted some of his excellent prayers.

A Guide to the Psalms, by Graham Scroggie, is also very helpful. Scroggie was Pastor of Spurgeon's Tabernacle, London, when the church was destroyed in the great air raids of May, 1941. You may have to search for this book, but when you find it, it will be like finding a treasure of practical and spiritual minded comments.

Introduction

While it is not technically a commentary on the Psalms, Warren Wiersbe's outlines and observations on the Psalms have often helped me to get at the spiritual message of each psalm. These are found in his *With the Word* commentary. It is Wiersbe who actually inspired me to write this commentary. When I directly quote him, I acknowledge him by name, but he has influenced me often by sometimes simply becoming part of my own words. The same can be said of the concise insights gained from John Sailhamer in his *NIV Compact Bible Commentary*.

An often-overlooked resource is *Reflections on the Psalms* by the great English literature scholar and author of *Mere Christianity*, C. S. Lewis. This is the only book by Lewis that is a direct treatment of the Bible, and what better scholar to handle the sublimest poetry ever penned than an authority on poetry? Although Lewis constantly acknowledges that he is not a Biblical scholar, readers at any level can benefit from his sensitive handling of all issues related to the Biblical Psalms.

When I quote or borrow directly from one of the above authors, I will simply place his name in a parenthesis, e.g.: (Kidner). The reference is back to his volume mentioned above.

Another small but helpful resource for reading the Psalms devotionally is *Psalms: The Prayer Book of the Bible*, by Dietrich Bonhoeffer, Augsburg Publishing House, 1970. While this German pastor-theologian was not fully within our evangelical camp, he did reject the German critical attitude toward the Bible and fed his soul on the Scriptures. Following his guidance will also help to feed our own souls!

Academic commentaries on the Psalms usually fall short of the purpose for which they were written, namely as an expression of worship and prayer! If you would like to pray the Psalms, you can do it simply with an open English Bible. If you would like a convenient presentation of the Psalms for this purpose, I suggest *The Paraclete Psalter* that arranges the Psalms for prayer at three times during the day. If you consistently use this guide, you will pray through all the Psalms in a month! If you like to pray the daily offices – four times a day – *The Divine Hours*, edited by Phyllis Tickle, is about 95% composed of selections from the Psalms. I have been using the last two resources daily for four years now, and my prayer life has been revitalized in so doing.

The Psalms were originally written to be prayed AND to be sung, and no one does that better than the Australian group, the Sons of Korah. As I write this, I am listening to their rendition of Psalm 42. Spiritual dynamite! Their beautiful arrangements are available on iTunes.

Enough introductory information about these precious compositions has been shared. Let's get to the Psalms themselves!

How Best to Use This "Commentary"

I suggest a daily use of this devotional guide to the Psalms. I have included the Biblical text so this book can serve as a "one-stop shopping center" for your experience of this priceless body of sacred literature. For the sake of legitimate diversity, I have included the text of each psalm in one of three excellent modern versions. Psalms 1–50 are from the English Standard Version text (ESV); Psalms 51–100 contain the Holman Christian Standard Bible text (now CSB), and Psalms 101–150 have the New American Standard Bible text (NASB). My comments that follow the Bible text will only be valuable if you read the Biblical text along with them. When you have read the Psalm, my advice is to then try to slowly visualize my main points that are usually in the form of an outline. You may also want to turn the Psalm into a prayer. Don't rush. It is better to pour over an individual psalm through a few days than just to finish it quickly. It is not as important that you go *through the Psalms*, as that *the Psalms go through you*! Finally, I have included a personal prayer with its contents drawn from the words and ideas of that psalm. Some prayers were adapted from those in Eaton's commentary. Praying the Psalm and then praying words drawn from the Psalm will be a great devotional practice.

Since this is a devotional commentary and because the psalms are mostly prayers, I recommend that you also pray before reading each psalm. There is no better prayer than the one provided by the Psalmist:

"Open my eyes, that I may behold wonderful things out of Your law." (Psalm 119:18)

Happy reading, praying, meditating, and singing the Psalter! Oh yes—Psalm 57:8 provided the title for this commentary, "Awake O harp and lyre! I will awake the dawn!"

Only Two Ways

This Psalm of the "Two Ways" draws on a Jewish teaching paradigm shared by the Wisdom Literature (Pr. 1–9), Him who is Incarnate Wisdom (Matt. 7:13–14), and THE Wisdom writing of the NT (Jas. 3:13–18).

> 1:1 Blessed is the man who walks not in the counsel of the wicked, nor stands in the way of sinners, nor sits in the seat of scoffers;
> 2 but his delight is in the law of the LORD, and on his law he meditates day and night.
> 3 He is like a tree planted by streams of water that yields its fruit in its season, and its leaf does not wither. In all that he does, he prospers.
> 4 The wicked are not so, but are like chaff that the wind drives away.
> 5 Therefore the wicked will not stand in the judgment, nor sinners in the congregation of the righteous;
> 6 for the LORD knows the way of the righteous, but the way of the wicked will perish.
>
> (Psalm 1, ESV)

The way of blessing (vv. 1–3). God will bless your life, but you must be "blessable." That means being first of all, *separated from the world* (v. 1). This means avoiding the steps that lead to sin: considering sin (walking), contemplating sin (standing), and being comfortable in sin (sitting). Watch your step!

Blessing also involves being *saturated with the Word* (v. 2) The Word guides your walk and rejoices your heart (Jer. 15:16). Meditation is to your inner person what digestion is to your outer person. Feed inwardly and outwardly and you will grow accordingly!

Blessing also involves being *situated by the water* (v. 3). Do the above (vv. 1–2) and your spiritual roots will go deep beside the river of God's grace, and you will bear fruit because the power of His grace will course through your branches!

The way of perishing (vv. 4–6). When Jesus offers abundant life, how tragic that some still perish! Contrast the tree and the chaff if you want to see the difference between the godly and the ungodly. Those who choose this way are *unstable* (v. 4); they are *unprepared* (v. 5); and they are *unknown* (v.6). The godly receive blessing (v. 3) while the ungodly receive judgment (v. 6).

Psalm One begins with "blessed" and ends with "perish." This introduces you to the Psalms as a whole, but it also presents you with a choice between two paths in life. As previously mentioned, the "two ways" appear throughout the Scriptures as the choices that each of us face in life (Josh. 24:15; 1 Kings 18:21).

Which "way" will you choose to walk?

> *O, LORD, grant that through my study of Your word and through the nourishment of Your grace, that I may know the happiness of walking that good way where You are ever at my side. AMEN.*

Psalm 2

The Father and His Son

There are psalms that portray Israel's ideal ruler as a King. Sometimes the language about this King goes beyond the power and influence of even a David or Solomon. These are known as the **Messianic Psalms**, of which the first is here in Psalm Two. These psalms speak about the future "anointed one" (Ps. 2:2) and often portray Him as Ruler and Judge. On the other hand, some of them portray him as a righteous sufferer (Ps. 22; 69). Here he is portrayed as a King who is also God's Son (Ps. 2:7, 12). Whether as Sovereign or as Sufferer, Jesus told us that He is in the Psalms (Luke 24:44).

2:1 Why do the nations rage and the peoples plot in vain?
2 The kings of the earth set themselves, and the rulers take counsel together, against the Lord and against his Anointed, saying,
3 "Let us burst their bonds apart and cast away their cords from us."
4 He who sits in the heavens laughs; the Lord holds them in derision.
5 Then he will speak to them in his wrath, and terrify them in his fury, saying,
6 "As for me, I have set my King on Zion, my holy hill."
7 I will tell of the decree: The Lord said to me, "You are my Son; today I have begotten you.
8 Ask of me, and I will make the nations your heritage, and the ends of the earth your possession.
9 You shall break them with a rod of iron and dash them in pieces like a potter's vessel."
10 Now therefore, O kings, be wise; be warned, O rulers of the earth.
11 Serve the Lord with fear, and rejoice with trembling.
12 Kiss the Son, lest he be angry, and you perish in the way, for his wrath is quickly kindled. Blessed are all who take refuge in him.

(Psalm 2, ESV)

God the Father, along with His Son, is described as performing four actions in this Psalm:

The Lord hears the scoffers (vv. 1–3). God hears the ravings of the nations and the plots of their rulers. What is it that they really want? Freedom from God! But the way to real freedom is by submission, not by rebellion. To throw off God's will is to invite bondage and destruction.

The LORD laughs at the scoffers (v. 4). Man does not worry God by all his noise and threats (the New Atheists?). He is on His throne and has everything in control. When the noise from the world frightens you, turn to the Lord and let Him take over. See how the early church did just this by referring to this Psalm (Acts 4:23–31).

The LORD speaks to His Son (vv. 5–9). *God the Father* announces that His King now sits enthroned in the Heavenly Zion where the raving nations can't touch Him. *God the Son* announces that the nations will be His, so their rebellion is futile (v. 7–9). Psalm 2:8 is not a prayer request for missions; it is a statement of judgment on those who reject the Son (Rev. 19:15). David here affirms his faith in the promise of the Davidic Covenant (2 Sam. 7:16).

The LORD commands us to trust His Son (vv. 10–12). *God the Spirit* invites all rebels to submit to the Son and be blessed instead of destroyed (v. 10–12). To kiss the Son means to do homage to Him as Sovereign Lord. All those who trust Him are safe and blessed. (The rare word for "son" is also used in Pr. 31:2).

✡ **I call Psalm 2:12 the John 3:16 of the OT.** ✡

Above the noise of the nations and their rantings, listen for the firm and assuring voice of the Living God. As was earlier promised in Psalm 1, you will be blessed if you put your trust in His Son (Ps. 1:1, 2:12).

> *O LORD, speak Your mighty word to the nations that they may turn back from the ways of destruction, and find peace and happiness through their reverence for You and Your Son. AMEN.*

Psalm 3

Advice for Insomniacs

If worry keeps you from getting a good night's sleep, Psalms 3 and 4 were written for you. Psalms 3–7 were evidently composed when David was exiled from Jerusalem because his son Absalom had stolen the kingdom (2 Sam. 15–18 and see the Titles of Psalms 3 and 7).

> *A Psalm of David, when he fled from Absalom his son.*
> 3:1 O LORD, how many are my foes! Many are rising against me;
> 2 many are saying of my soul, there is no salvation for him in God.   Selah
> 3 But you, O LORD, are a shield about me, my glory, and the lifter of my head.
> 4 I cried aloud to the LORD, and he answered me from his holy hill.   Selah
> 5 I lay down and slept; I woke again, for the LORD sustained me.
> 6 I will not be afraid of many thousands of people who have set themselves against me all around.
> 7 Arise, O LORD! Save me, O my God! For you strike all my enemies on the cheek; you break the teeth of the wicked.
> 8 Salvation belongs to the LORD; your blessing be on your people!   Selah
> (Psalm 3, ESV)

Psalm 3 is a morning psalm (Ps. 3:5), and
Psalm 4 is an evening psalm (Ps. 4:8).

How was David able to sleep when he was in such danger? The enemy was *against* him (vv. 1, 6) but David knew that God was *for* him. When people discourage you (v. 2), God lifts up your head and keeps you going (v. 3).

God **surrounds** you like a shield (v. 3).
God **sustains** you by your sleep (v. 5).
God **secures** you with His salvation (v. 7–8).

While others say that there is no **salvation** (deliverance) for him (v. 2), David knows that his **salvation** is secure because it "belongs to the Lord."

Like Psalm 2, David again shows his faith in the Davidic Covenant Promise (2 Sam. 7:27–29).

Therefore, you will NOT be afraid even if you are surrounded and outnumbered! (v. 6).

God never sleeps (Ps. 121:3–4), so why should you stay awake and worry?

 "If you can't sleep, don't count sheep—talk to the Shepherd!"

> *Almighty God and Father, when my enemies are all around me, help me to trust in Your promises, to know that Your love and power are a shield about me, and that nothing can separate me from the salvation which You have given me in Your Son Jesus. AMEN.*

Psalm 4

A Prayer for Compline

Among liturgical Christians who pray the "offices," the prayer before retiring for the night is called "Compline." Psalm 4 is prayed during this very personal quiet time before sleep. You may not pray the "hours" but this one surely is appropriate at night–or for anytime when darkness enters the soul!

> *To the choirmaster: with stringed instruments. A Psalm of David.*
>
> 4:1 Answer me when I call, O God of my righteousness! You have given me relief when I was in distress. Be gracious to me and hear my prayer!
> 2 O men, how long shall my honor be turned into shame? How long will you love vain words and seek after lies? *Selah*
> 3 But know that the Lord has set apart the godly for himself; the Lord hears when I call to him.
> 4 Be angry, and do not sin; ponder in your own hearts on your beds, and be silent.
> 5 Offer right sacrifices and put your trust in the Lord.
> 6 There are many who say, "Who will show us some good? Lift up the light of your face upon us, O Lord!"
> 7 You have put more joy in my heart than they have when their grain and wine abound.
> 8 In peace I will both lie down and sleep; for you alone, O Lord, make me dwell in safety.
>
> (Psalm 4, ESV)

David wrote this psalm as he was about to retire for the night (Ps. 4:8), and it follows another psalm associated with the rest of sleep. He could not do much about the war *around* him, but he could do something about the war *within* him. He did not want to lie in bed and worry, so he committed himself and his situation to the Lord. That is easily said, but to those who lie awake at night because of anxiety, real relief requires real answers. Here they are.

He requested help (vv. 1–3). Asking the Lord for help seems so simplistic, but it is the simple solution that we often forget or ignore. Asking has always been the best way to deal with inner turmoil (Phil. 4:6–7, read it!). "*Ask* and you will receive; *seek* and you will find; *knock* and it will be opened to you" (Matt. 7:7). Remember that Acronym: A S K.

He rested his heart (vv. 4–5). He faced his anger honestly and turned it over to the Lord (Eph. 4:26). Instead of lying in bed and thinking about your problems, meditate on the Lord and offer Him sacrifices of praise. Have you ever tried to worry when you were praising? It can't be done!

He received hope (vv. 6–8). In the darkness, he saw the face of God and received light. "In your light do we see light" (Ps. 36:9). In his sorrow, he discovered the gift of gladness. In the time of battle, he received peace.

It is important to realize that God did not immediately change David's situation. Absalom continued to rebel and pursue his father into the very wilderness where David was trying to sleep out in the open air. He did not immediately change David's circumstances, but He did change David! This psalm makes that abundantly clear.

He can do the same for you. While circumstances are always different, if you follow the Son of David, his God is the same then and now.

Psalm 4:8 is prayed every evening in the Compline Prayer. Pray it with me now and also tonight!

> "Lighten our darkness, we beseech you, O Lord; and by your great mercy, defend us from all perils of this night; for the love of your only Son, our Savior, Jesus Christ." AMEN.
> (Book of Common Prayer).

Psalm 5

Encouragement for the Slandered

When he served in King Saul's court, David was often attacked by some of Saul's officers who flattered the king and lied about David (vv. 4–6, 9). King Saul wrongly believed that David was trying to steal his throne. Because of this he acted out his sad paranoia and eventually destroyed himself, not David!

To the choirmaster: for the flutes. A Psalm of David.

5:1 Give ear to my words, O Lord; consider my groaning.
2 Give attention to the sound of my cry, my King and my God, for to you do I pray.
3 O Lord, in the morning you hear my voice; in the morning I prepare a sacrifice for you and watch.
4 For you are not a God who delights in wickedness; evil may not dwell with you.
5 The boastful shall not stand before your eyes; you hate all evildoers.
6 You destroy those who speak lies; the Lord abhors the bloodthirsty and deceitful man.
7 But I, through the abundance of your steadfast love, will enter your house. I will bow down toward your holy temple in the fear of you.
8 Lead me, O Lord, in your righteousness because of my enemies; make your way straight before me.
9 For there is no truth in their mouth; their inmost self is destruction; their throat is an open grave; they flatter with their tongue.
10 Make them bear their guilt, O God; let them fall by their own counsels; because of the abundance of their transgressions cast them out, for they have rebelled against you.
11 But let all who take refuge in you rejoice; let them ever sing for joy, and spread your protection over them, that those who love your name may exult in you.
12 For you bless the righteous, O Lord; you cover him with favor as with a shield.

(Psalm 5, ESV)

When people slander you, follow David's example and pray about the matter, rather than stew–or sue!

Note his **four** specific prayer requests:

Listen to me (vv. 1–6). David began the day with his heart lifted up to God. Psalm 5:3 is included in all prayer books as part of the morning prayers as well as Isa. 26:9: "My soul yearns for you in the night; in the morning my spirit longs for you." He then shifts from his believing praise to his recognition of the slander against him (vv. 4–6). God knew about the sinful words of the liars, but He also heard the believing prayers of His servant.

Lead me (vv. 7–8). The Lord's *hesed* (v. 7 "steadfast love" or "lovingkindness") overcomes the schemes of the liars. David had to be very careful because Saul and his "posse" were watching him and his life was always in danger. He both worshiped God and asked for His daily direction. Verse 8b sounds like the familiar promise of Pr. 3:6 ("make my paths straight").

Protect me (vv. 9–10). David did not take up arms against Saul or Saul's men. He left those battles to the Lord (see 1 Sam. 24:2–7, 26:6–12). He trusted God to care for him, and God did not fail. It is important in reading these "imprecatory" psalms to recognize that David always left the judgment of his slanderers to God. He did not take personal vengeance on them.

Provide for me (vv. 11–12). "Taking refuge" recalls Psalm 2:12. The blessing for the righteous person recalls Ps. 1:1–3. Protection is described by the metaphor of a shield (v. 12). Isn't that what God told Abram that He was (Gen. 15:1)? Because he had God as King and Shield, David was blessed with joy, confidence, and an even deeper love for the Lord.

I heard a theologian comment that in this psalm David has reached a balance between absolute transcendence and elitist immanence. To us mortals that means that he knows the One who is lofty and high and who also dwells with the lowly (Isa. 57:15).

Times of suffering can be times of growing if we just allow the Lord to finish what He has started.

O Lord, help me to believe that You who began a good work in me WILL complete it in the day of Jesus Christ (Phil. 1:6). AMEN.

Psalm 6

Sickness and Sin

This psalm grew out of an experience of sickness and pain, when David thought he was going to die. Besides his pain, he had to put up with the attacks of his enemies who wanted him to die. It is part of those psalms (Psalms 3–7) that were composed during the Absalom Rebellion. It was a time of deep personal anguish for David. How tragic for him and also for parents today who suffer distress over an estranged child. In spite of all this, he did not waver in his faith. How can parents in such pain survive? This Psalm shows us how.

To the choirmaster: with stringed instruments; according to The Sheminith. A Psalm of David.

6.1 O Lord, rebuke me not in your anger, nor discipline me in your wrath.
2 Be gracious to me, O Lord, for I am languishing; heal me, O Lord, for my bones are troubled.
3 My soul also is greatly troubled. But you, O Lord—how long?
4 Turn, O Lord, deliver my life; save me for the sake of your steadfast love.
5 For in death there is no remembrance of you; in Sheol who will give you praise?
6 I am weary with my moaning; every night I flood my bed with tears; I drench my couch with my weeping.
7 My eye wastes away because of grief; it grows weak because of all my foes.
8 Depart from me, all you workers of evil, for the Lord has heard the sound of my weeping.
9 The Lord has heard my plea; the Lord accepts my prayer.
10 All my enemies shall be ashamed and greatly troubled; they shall turn back and be put to shame in a moment.

(Psalm 6, ESV)

David asked for mercy for his body (vv. 1–2) and he then asked for mercy for his soul (vv. 3–5). Mercy means that God does not give us what we deserve, and grace means that He gives us what we do not deserve. What a loving God He is! That rich word *hesed* (God's *covenant love* or *mercy*) again appears (Ps. 6:4). It is the Lord's *hesed* that saves and sustains us. "It is of the LORD's mercies (*hesed*) that we are not consumed, because his compassions fail not" (Lam. 3:22 KJV).

David asked God about his tears of repentance and confession (vv. 6–7). His bed should have been a place of rest, but it had become a place of trial as God chastened him. Sickness can lead to greater sanctification but it can also lead to greater sin! Tears of pain can become tears of repentance. "Put my tears into your bottle. Are they not in your book?" (Ps. 56:8).

David was assured and his enemies would be ashamed (vv. 8–10)! God heard and answered his prayers! When the night is dark and long, keep on trusting, and the dawn will come in God's good time. "Weeping may tarry for the night, but joy comes with the morning" (Ps. 30:5). Here we see David again clinging to the promises of the Davidic Covenant (2 Sam. 7:14–15). What a lesson for us to **cling to the promises even when they don't appear to be active in our everyday experiences!**

The age-old query, "How long" (v. 3) is a perennial question with which Moses (Ps. 90:13) and Asaph (Ps. 74:10) also struggled. As we shall see later in the "Lament Psalms," it is better to ask the Lord that question than complain about it to others.

The Penitential Psalms

Psalms 6, 32, 38, 51, 102, 130, and 143 are known as the "Penitential Psalms." You may use these psalms as your own prayers when you want to confess sin and ask for God's forgiveness (1 John 1:9). More about these when we get to Psalms 32 and 38.

My Faithful LORD, have pity on those of us who are sorely troubled and wasted with grief. Hear the voice of our weeping, and drive away all that troubles us, so that we may bear witness to Your salvation as we live in Your light. AMEN.

How to Handle Bad News

Don't conclude that I am an Anglican because I refer to the *Book of Common Prayer*. I just think that the saintly theologian, Thomas Cranmer, knew how to carefully and creatively turn the scriptures into prayer, as in the following Bible-soaked "Prayer Before Reading Scripture."

"Blessed Lord, who has caused all Holy Scriptures to be given us for our learning, grant that I may so hear them, read them, learn them, and inwardly digest them, that by patience and comfort of Your Holy Word I may embrace and ever hold fast the blessed hope of eternal life, which You have given me in Your Son, my Savior, Jesus Christ. Amen."

Psalm 7. "A *Shiggaion* of David which he sang to the Lord concerning Cush, a Benjamite." Perhaps Cush was one of the "court liars" who flattered Saul and made life difficult for David (1 Sam. 24:9). It is also possible this person was the Cushite who brought the bad news to David about Absalom's death (2 Sam. 18:21–23). When you have a "Cush" in your life, do what David did.

A Shiggaion of David, which he sang to the LORD concerning the words of Cush, a Benjaminite.

7:1 O LORD my God, in you do I take refuge; save me from all my pursuers and deliver me,

2 lest like a lion they tear my soul apart, rending it in pieces, with none to deliver.

3 O LORD my God, if I have done this, if there is wrong in my hands,

4 if I have repaid my friend with evil or plundered my enemy without cause,

5 let the enemy pursue my soul and overtake it, and let him trample my life to the ground and lay my glory in the dust. Selah

6 Arise, O LORD, in your anger; lift yourself up against the fury of my enemies; awake for me; you have appointed a judgment.

7 Let the assembly of the peoples be

gathered about you; over it return on high.
8 The LORD judges the peoples; judge me, O LORD, according to my righteousness and according to the integrity that is in me.
9 Oh, let the evil of the wicked come to an end, and may you establish the righteous—you who test the minds and hearts, O righteous God!
10 My shield is with God, who saves the upright in heart.
11 God is a righteous judge, and a God who feels indignation every day.
12 If a man does not repent, God will whet his sword; he has bent and readied his bow;
13 he has prepared for him his deadly weapons, making his arrows fiery shafts.
14 Behold, the wicked man conceives evil and is pregnant with mischief and gives birth to lies.
15 He makes a pit, digging it out, and falls into the hole that he has made.
16 His mischief returns upon his own head, and on his own skull his violence descends.
17 I will give to the LORD the thanks due to his righteousness, and I will sing praise to the name of the LORD, the Most High.

(Psalm 7, ESV)

So, how do you handle bad news?

Be honest with the LORD (vv. 1–5). David did not say that the enemy was telling the truth, but he was willing for God to examine him and punish him. He had nothing to hide. How rarely do we take off our masks and talk honestly with the Lord in prayer? The Psalms introduce us to people who poured out their souls in sometimes brutal honesty.

Let the LORD be the judge (vv. 6–13). It is wise to let God be the judge because His judgment is always right (1 Cor. 4:3–5). We do not see ourselves and others as He sees, so it is best to turn the matter over to Him. David was careful to maintain his integrity (v. 8) and let God be his defense (v. 10).

Wait on the LORD (vv. 14–16). Sin has a way of bringing its own punishment if we wait long enough. It is like giving birth in pain and trouble (v. 14; Jas. 1:14–15), falling into a pit (v. 15), or getting back the trouble that they tried to impose on others (v. 16).

Give the LORD thanks (v. 17). What does it matter that men slander us, so long as the righteousness of God prevails and the name of the Lord is glorified?! The Psalm moves from the intensely personal plea of a man who is betrayed and hounded, to the conviction that God is judge of all the earth, and that wickedness is self-defeating. So it ends with confidence and praise.

The last few psalms have been "downers" reflecting David's darkness over Absalom's rebellion. This ending of praise and thanksgiving, however, prepares us for the brighter rays in Psalm Eight! (Ps. 8:1).

NOTE: Another treatment of this psalm stresses "David's confidence in the divine Judge as the backbone of Psalm 7:
1. David's concern as he begs attention of the Judge (vv. 1–5)
2. David's court appearance as he argues his case with the Judge (vv. 6–16)
3. David's composure as he awaits the verdict of the Judge (v. 17)" (MacArthur)

> *See the prayer that begins this psalm and pray it at the end as well! O LORD my God, in You do I take refuge. Save me from all my pursuers and deliver me. AMEN.*

The Crown of Creation

This psalm is an example of what a hymn should be, celebrating the glory and grace of God, rehearsing who He is and what He has done, and relating us and our world to Him. All this is done with a masterly economy of words, and in a spirit of mingled joy and awe. It picks up where Psalm 7 ended, by praising the "name" of the Lord (Ps. 7:17) (Kidner).

> *To the choirmaster: according to The Gittith. A Psalm of David.*
>
> 8:1 O LORD, our Lord, how majestic is your name in all the earth! You have set your glory above the heavens.
> 2 Out of the mouth of babies and infants, you have established strength because of your foes, to still the enemy and the avenger.
> 3 When I look at your heavens, the work of your fingers, the moon and the stars, which you have set in place,
> 4 what is man that you are mindful of him, and the son of man that you care for him?
> 5 Yet you have made him a little lower than the heavenly beings and crowned him with glory and honor.
> 6 You have given him dominion over the works of your hands; you have put all things under his feet,
> 7 all sheep and oxen, and also the beasts of the field,
> 8 the birds of the heavens, and the fish of the sea, whatever passes along the paths of the seas.
> 9 O LORD, our Lord, how majestic is your name in all the earth!
>
> (Psalm 8, ESV)

The universe is vast and full of grandeur, yet **God pays attention to weak and insignificant men and women** (vv. 1–4). He can use the weakness of little ones to reveal His great strength (Matt. 21:16) and to defeat the enemy (1 Sam. 17:47). If He can use children and shepherd boys, surely He can use you!

"What is man?" can be asked with varying nuances. In Ps. 144:3, the question mocks the arrogance of the rebel. In Job 7:17, it is a sufferer's plea for respite. In Job 25:6, it shudders at human sin. But here it has no tinge of pessimism - only wonder that God is mindful and cares (Kidner).

Dear child, you are significant because **God made you in His image** (v. 5; Gen. 1:26–28). Sin has marred that image, but in Jesus Christ, that image can be restored (2 Cor 3:18; Col. 3:10). The use of this language in Heb. 2:5–8 indicates that Jesus is the ideal "Man" who has begun to restore Adam's commission to be the lord over God's creation and which he forfeited in the fall.

Dear child, you are privileged because **God has shared His dominion with you** (vv. 6–8). The language used clearly recalls the creation account with Adam as head of the created order. Since Messiah Jesus restores that forfeited role, can you think of specific occasions when Jesus proved that He had dominion over beasts, birds, and fish? List the incidents.

Verses 1 and 9 form an *inclusio* that brackets the Psalm and focuses our attention on the unrivaled majesty of the Divine name.

Yes, you are cared for by God; you are significant to Him; and you have been privileged by Him. He thus has a purpose for you to fulfill and Jesus has begun to fulfill your calling in His incarnation and resurrection. The Father wants you to "reign in life" through His Son (Rom. 5:17), for you are enthroned in the heavenlies with Him (Eph. 2:6).

Why groan like a slave when you can glory like a sovereign?

> *O LORD, glorious in heaven and earth, by Your grace You make the praises of the humble a stronghold against evil, and have appointed human beings to be Your royal ministers on earth. Grant that we may rule with love, until we are made perfect in joyful submission to THE ultimate Son of Man, our Lord Jesus Christ. AMEN.*

Psalm 9

Groaning about the Goyim

This is a devotional commentary on the Psalms that does not deal with technical aspects of language and academic issues. Occasionally I will share with you some of these issues that affect the interpretation of the Psalm. The **psalm titles** that precede about half of the Psalms mention the author, musical directions for singing the Psalm, and sometimes relate historical events that provide the original context of the Psalm. These psalm titles precede verse one in our English Bibles, but comprise the first verse in the Hebrew Bible. Although not part of the authors' original words, they must be ancient because they are found in the oldest copies of the Hebrew Bible (Dead Sea Scrolls) and in the pre-Christian Septuagint (Greek translation of the Old Testament). The expression preceding Psalm 9 is *Almut Laben* which means "Concerning the Death of a Son" (see note in the NASB and the NIV translation). While this could be a dirge composed at Absalom's death, it may also have a Messianic meaning, recalling the *Son of Man* in the previous Psalm 8. It is fascinating to note how the "glory and honor" with which the Son of Man is crowned (Ps. 8:5) is associated in Heb. 2:9 with the death of Jesus the ultimate Son of Man (Sailhamer).

The close connection of this Psalm to the one following will be mentioned in the commentary on Psalm 10.

This is the first Psalm that deals with the nations apart from Israel. Some of the Psalms deal with the *salvation* of the **goyim** (Gentiles—see Psalms 67 and 96), but this one deals with their righteous *judgment*.

To the choirmaster: according to Muth-labben. A Psalm of David.

9:1 I will give thanks to the LORD with my whole heart; I will recount all of your wonderful deeds.
2 I will be glad and exult in you; I will sing praise to your name, O Most High.
3 When my enemies turn back, they stumble and perish before your presence.
4 For you have maintained my just cause; you have sat on the throne, giving righteous judgment.
5 You have rebuked the nations; you have made the wicked perish; you have blotted out their name forever and ever.
6 The enemy came to an end in everlasting ruins; their cities you rooted out; the very memory of them has perished.
7 But the LORD sits enthroned forever; he has established his throne for justice,
8 and he judges the world with righteousness; he judges the peoples with uprightness.
9 The LORD is a stronghold for the oppressed, a stronghold in times of trouble.
10 And those who know your name put their trust in you, for you, O LORD, have not forsaken those who seek you.
11 Sing praises to the LORD, who sits enthroned in Zion! Tell among the peoples his deeds!
12 For he who avenges blood is mindful of them; he does not forget the cry of the afflicted.
13 Be gracious to me, O LORD! See my affliction from those who hate me, O you who lift me up from the gates of death,
14 that I may recount all your praises, that in the gates of the daughter of Zion I may rejoice in your salvation.
15 The nations have sunk in the pit that they made; in the net that they hid, their own foot has been caught.
16 The LORD has made himself known; he has executed judgment; the wicked are snared in the work of their own hands. Higgaion Selah
17 The wicked shall return to Sheol, all the nations that forget God.
18 For the needy shall not always be forgotten, and the hope of the poor shall not perish forever.
19 Arise, O LORD! Let not man prevail; let the nations be judged before you!
20 Put them in fear, O LORD! Let the nations know that they are but men! Selah

(Psalm 9, ESV)

Praise in presence of the nations (vv. 1–6). God had won a victory for David, so he sang a song of praise to the Lord. It was not a personal battle. Because David was doing God's will, the Lord maintained his cause. Although in your Christian battle you do not fight with human beings (Eph. 6:12–13), you should still praise the Lord for the spiritual victories He has graciously given you.

Promise to judge the nations (vv. 7–12). David looked ahead to the time when God would finally judge sin and establish His righteous kingdom.

God's people do not need to worry; He is their refuge and will never forsake them (Heb. 13:5). The Father forsook His Son on the cross, but because of that very action, He will not forsake you.

Prayer for the nations (vv. 13–20). From considering the past and the future, David turned to his present need as he prayed for God's help. His need was for mercy and his motive was that he might praise the Lord and tell others of His salvation. Why? Because there is a place called hell (Ps. 9:17) and God's salvation is the only escape from that terrible place.

Paul advised, "Knowing, therefore, the terror of the Lord, we persuade men" (2 Cor. 5:11).

> "The safest road to hell is the gradual one—the gentle slope, soft underfoot, without sudden turnings, without milestones, without signposts." C. S. Lewis

See the end of Psalm 10 for a prayer that covers this psalm as well.

Psalm 10

When Good Things Happen to Bad People

I mentioned in our discussion of Psalm 9 that there are certain technical things about the Psalms that are helpful to know for those who read them today. There I briefly described their occasional "titles." Here I mention the **close relationship between Psalms 9 and 10**. Hebrew manuscripts combine these two psalms into one composition. The ancient Septuagint Greek version combines the two as well. Therefore, beginning with this psalm, the numbering of the Psalms in our English Bibles is one off from the Hebrew Bible. For example, next we will look at Psalm 11 which is Psalm 10 in the Hebrew Bible. Their content, however, is the same.

A further indication that these psalms were originally one is that the two together form an **acrostic**, with successive verses beginning with the letters of the Hebrew alphabet. Obviously, this cannot be seen in a translation, whether it be the Septuagint or our modern English versions. The most famous acrostic in the Bible is Psalm 119. This arrangement was originally done as an aid to memorization, but English readers will not miss anything in the content, I assure you.

Because of this introduction, my thoughts on the message of Psalm 10 will be briefer than usual. Three questions are of concern to the Psalmist as he considers the prosperity of bad people.

> 10:1 Why, O Lord, do you stand far away? Why do you hide yourself in times of trouble?
>
> 2 In arrogance the wicked hotly pursue the poor; let them be caught in the schemes that they have devised.
>
> 3 For the wicked boasts of the desires of his soul, and the one greedy for gain curses and renounces the Lord.
>
> 4 In the pride of his face the wicked does not seek him; all his thoughts are, "There is no God."

⁵ His ways prosper at all times; your judgments are on high, out of his sight; as for all his foes, he puffs at them.
⁶ He says in his heart, "I shall not be moved; throughout all generations I shall not meet adversity."
⁷ His mouth is filled with cursing and deceit and oppression; under his tongue are mischief and iniquity.
⁸ He sits in ambush in the villages; in hiding places he murders the innocent. His eyes stealthily watch for the helpless;
⁹ he lurks in ambush like a lion in his thicket; he lurks that he may seize the poor; he seizes the poor when he draws him into his net.
¹⁰ The helpless are crushed, sink down, and fall by his might.
¹¹ He says in his heart, "God has forgotten, he has hidden his face, he will never see it."
¹² Arise, O Lord; O God, lift up your hand; forget not the afflicted.
¹³ Why does the wicked renounce God and say in his heart, "You will not call to account"?
¹⁴ But you do see, for you note mischief and vexation, that you may take it into your hands; to you the helpless commits himself; you have been the helper of the fatherless.
¹⁵ Break the arm of the wicked and evildoer; call his wickedness to account till you find none.
¹⁶ The Lord is king forever and ever; the nations perish from his land.
¹⁷ O Lord, you hear the desire of the afflicted; you will strengthen their heart; you will incline your ear
¹⁸ to do justice to the fatherless and the oppressed, so that man who is of the earth may strike terror no more.

(Psalm 10, ESV)

Does God sometimes hide (vv. 1–4)? "Why do the wicked prosper?" is a perennial question God's people ask. As they consider the suffering of the godly and the security of the ungodly, they may feel that God has forgotten and forsaken His people. He is hiding. If God blesses the righteous and punishes the wicked, why do we not see that NOW? Psalm 73 is the most famous Psalm that deals with this question. Rabbi Kushner wrote a book titled "When Bad Things Happen to Good People." In a different vein, the Psalmists together have written a book that could be titled "When Good Things Happen to Bad People."

Does God always hear (vv. 5–13)? Note the repetition of "He has said in his heart" (vv. 6, 11, and 13). God hears what ungodly people say and He does not approve of their pride and rebellion. The ungodly person may announce, "I shall not be moved! God does not see what I do! Even if He does, He will never judge me!" What arrogance! The so-called *New Atheism* is the most recent manifestation of this rebellious spirit.

PSALM 10

Does God ever help (vv. 14–18)? Of course He does! He sees the trouble of His people, feels their grief, and helps them in the right way at the right time. After all, the Lord is King! It may look as though the ungodly are winning the day, but the Lord will triumph in the end. Asaph, the author of the similar Psalm 73 mentioned above, recounted the outcome of his own questioning when he described his crucial encounter: "Until I went into the sanctuary of God; then I discerned their end" (Ps. 73:17).

> "... their foot shall slide in due time ..." (Deut. 32:35 KJV). This was the text for Jonathan Edward's famous sermon, "Sinners in the Hands of an Angry God."

O God Most High, I praise and thank You for Your marvelous works and for the sure hope of the triumph of Your kingdom. I also commend to Your mercy those who are crushed by this present world. Save them from evil people and lift them up with Your Son Jesus from the gates of death. AMEN.

Psalm 11

When to Flee and When to Stick it Out

David was in great difficulty. Around him, the archers were getting ready to shoot. Under him, the foundations of society were shaking. What should he do? What would you do? Well-meaning friends had advised him to flee for refuge to the many mountains that surround Jerusalem. But David wanted to stay in the Temple, not run from it!

> *To the Choirmaster. Of David*
> 11:1 In the Lord I take refuge; how can you say to my soul, "Flee like a bird to your mountain,
> 2 for behold, the wicked bend the bow; they have fitted their arrow to the string to shoot in the dark at the upright in heart.
> 3 If the foundations are destroyed, what can the righteous do?"
> 4 The Lord is in his holy temple; the Lord's throne is in heaven; his eyes see, his eyelids test the children of man.
> 5 The Lord tests the righteous, but his soul hates the wicked and the one who loves violence.
> 6 Let him rain coals on the wicked; fire and sulfur and a scorching wind shall be the portion of their cup.
> 7 For the Lord is righteous; he loves righteous deeds; the upright shall behold his face.
>
> (Psalm 11, ESV)

When you are in that kind of situation, your first thought may be to get away as fast as you can. It is right to flee from temptation (Gen. 39:11–13) but not from duty (Neh. 6:10–11; Luke 13:31–32). Instead of flying away like a frightened bird, you should trust God and "mount up with wings like eagles" (Isa. 40:31).

If the foundations are destroyed, lay the foundations again! That is what Ezra did (Ezra 3:8) and what each new generation may have to do. David became king of Israel and laid the foundations for a godly society. After all,

God is still on His throne (v. 4) and will one day judge the wicked (vv. 5–6), If you love righteousness, God is on your side (v. 7).

"... **the upright shall behold his face**" (v. 7). This simple statement, affirmed by the Lord Jesus (Matt. 5:8), describes what medieval theologians called the *beatific vision*. But unlike what Roman Catholicism teaches, this vision is not reserved for those "saints" who have progressed from purgatory to heaven. This vision is the blood-bought right of every child of God (Rev. 22:4). What was forbidden and impossible to do on earth—to physically behold His glory (Ex. 33:20)—will be our blessed privilege for all eternity.

> "The humblest praise most, while cranks and malcontents praise least. Praise almost seems to be inner health made audible." C. S. Lewis

---

Lord, we know there is a time to flee, but when we must stand and face the enemy, help us to find shelter in You and not flee away in fear. May we trust in Your rule and not despair, and being found true, may we behold the beauty of Your face. Amen.

Psalm 12

The Flatterers and the Faithful

James reminds us that with the same tongue we can bless God and curse people! (Jas. 3:9–10). We usually recognize the badness of lying and boasting, but flattering words can easily deceive us. This Psalm reminds us to be wise in using our tongue and discerning in how we hear the tongues of others!

> To the choirmaster. According to the Sheminith. A Psalm of David.
>
> 12:1 Save, O LORD, for the godly one is gone; for the faithful have vanished from among the children of man.
> 2 Everyone utters lies to his neighbor; with flattering lips and a double heart they speak.
> 3 May the LORD cut off all flattering lips, the tongue that makes great boasts,
> 4 those who say, "With our tongue we will prevail, our lips are with us; who is master over us?"
> 5 "Because the poor are plundered, because the needy groan, I will now arise," says the LORD; "I will place him in the safety for which he longs."
> 6 The words of the LORD are pure words, like silver refined in a furnace on the ground, purified seven times.
> 7 You, O LORD, will keep them; you will guard us from this generation forever.
> 8 On every side the wicked prowl, as vileness is exalted among the children of man.
>
> (Psalm 12, ESV)

David's Words are Fervent (vv. 1–2). In the previous Psalm, David saw the foundations failing. In this Psalm, the faithful were vanishing from the earth (v. 1). The godly remnant was getting smaller and smaller, and David was feeling very much alone. No wonder he cried out, "Help, Lord!"

Man's Words are Flattering (vv. 3–5). What made David conclude that godliness was on the decline? The way people spoke. David heard flattering words, proud words, and oppressive words, and he knew that God was displeased. In our "age of communication," are you able to discern what is true and right? When you speak, is it communication or manipulation?

David's concern for the poor and needy is a theme that continues through the Psalms (Ps. 35:10), the Prophets (Amos 5:11), and the New Testament (Jas. 1:27). Who today will be an advocate for the most vulnerable in our church and society?

God's Words are Faithful (vv. 6–8). God's Word is pure, proved, and preserved, and you can depend on it. So much of what man says is cheap and temporary, but God's Word is like pure silver that is valuable and lasting. The Bible holds out hope in the *future*, but this psalm also comforts us with the *present* assurance that He keeps us (v. 7). Although the psalm ends with outward *things* unchanged (vv. 1, 8), that does not mean that *we* are unchanged. His word remains faithful!

Let your words be controlled by His words and God will make your words valuable (Pr. 10:20; 25:11). "Heaven and earth will pass away, but My words will not pass away" (Matt. 24:35).

> *O Lord, save Your little ones who are exploited when vileness is exalted. And help me to receive Your words and hold them fast in a pure heart, that I may be defended from the devious speech of the deceiver. AMEN.*

From Questions to Quietness

A rabbi's students were frustrated because he always answered their questions with a question in return! Finally, one of them asked, "Rabbi, why is it that when we ask you a question, you then reply with a question?" To which the rabbi wisely replied, "So what's wrong with asking questions?"

The psalmist begins with a series of questions addressed to the LORD. He then wonders how his concerns fit into what he knows of God's character. He ends with a trusting affirmation of God's *hesed*. This psalm fits perfectly the pattern of a **Lament Psalm**:

(a) The *address* (**v. 1**, "O Lord");
(b) The *complaint*, with the subject "I" (**v. 2a**), "thou" or "they" (**v. 2c**);
(c) The *request for help* (**vv. 3–4**);
(d) The *affirmation of trust* (**v. 5**);
(e) The *vow to praise God* when the crisis is past (**v. 6**).

13:1 **How long**, O LORD? Will you forget me forever?
How long will you hide your face from me?
2 **How long** must I take counsel in my soul and have sorrow in my heart all the day?
How long shall my enemy be exalted over me?
3 Consider and answer me, O LORD my God; light up my eyes, lest I sleep the sleep of death,
4 lest my enemy say, "I have prevailed over him," lest my foes rejoice because I am shaken.
5 But I have trusted in your steadfast love (*hesed*); my heart shall rejoice in your salvation.
6 I will sing to the LORD, because he has dealt bountifully with me.

(Psalm 13, ESV)

Asking God why? (vv. 1–2). Four times David asked, "How long?" He had prayed, but God had hidden Himself and not answered. David had examined his heart and knew of no reason why God should abandon him. The longer God waited, the more the enemy would succeed. When you have this same feeling, do what David did and talk to God with an honest and humble heart.

Arguing God's ways (vv. 3–4). Would God be glorified by David's defeat? Would God's cause be helped by David's death? Should the enemy rejoice while God's people suffer? David reasoned with God but did not try to tell God what to do. Sometimes prayer means wrestling. It is better to complain to God than to complain to others.

Affirming God's Word (vv. 5–6). Faith does not always give answers, but it does give encouragement. No matter how successful the enemy appears to be, you can trust the Lord, rejoice in the Lord, sing to the Lord and know that He will always deal bountifully with you.

"It is faith's work to claim and challenge loving-kindness out of all the roughest strokes of God." Samuel Rutherford

"To live above with saints we love—O that will be glory! But to live below with saints we know—well, that's another story!" Have you noticed how David really complains a lot about the people he encounters! What keeps him from being just another whiner? It is better to complain to God than to others!

> Look with pity, LORD, on Your servants who see no end to their sufferings. Give light to their teary eyes, and help them to trust in Your faithful love. Assure them that the song of thanksgiving can still be sung and that their hearts can still rejoice in Your salvation.
> AMEN.

Psalm 14

The Practical Atheist

I recently purchased *The Christian Atheist: Believing in God but Living as If He Doesn't Exist* by Craig Groeschel. The subjects of the book, as well as those mentioned in this psalm, are not theoretical atheists who deny God in their logic; they are practical atheists who deny God in their lives.

> *To the choirmaster. Of David.*
> 14:1 The fool says in his heart, "There is no God." They are corrupt, they do abominable deeds, there is none who does good.
> 2 The LORD looks down from heaven on the children of man, to see if there are any who understand, who seek after God.
> 3 They have all turned aside; together they have become corrupt; there is none who does good, not even one.
> 4 Have they no knowledge, all the evildoers who eat up my people as they eat bread and do not call upon the LORD?
> 5 There they are in great terror, for God is with the generation of the righteous.
> 6 You would shame the plans of the poor, but the LORD is his refuge.
> 7 Oh, that salvation for Israel would come out of Zion! When the LORD restores the fortunes of his people, let Jacob rejoice, let Israel be glad.
> (Psalm 14, ESV)

The contrast in the psalm is between the generation of the wicked and the generation of the righteous (v. 5). The latter group is made up of those who have trusted the Lord and seek Him and His will (Ps. 24:6).

1. The generation of the wicked is composed of people who are "practical atheists." God is not in their hearts, no matter what they may say and do outwardly. The Hebrew for fool in this Psalm is *nabal*, a word which implies an aggressive perversity, epitomized in the Nabal of 1 Samuel 25:25. The assertion, There is no God, is treated in Scripture not as a sincere if misguided conviction, but as an proud act of defiance (Kidner). These fools disobey God and exploit people made in the image of God. They are corrupt (v. 1), and so they do corrupt things. The folly of evil is now seen as failure to discriminate (v. 4) and failure to foresee (vv. 5–6). There is an animal complacency about the unconcerned exploiters and secularists of verse 4. It is more impenetrable than the bluster of verse 1. While this well describes contemporary mankind, it also portrays everyone all the time (See Rom. 3:10–12).

2. **The generation of the righteous** calls on the Lord and He answers (v. 4). God dwells with these people (v. 5), protects them (v. 6), and gives them joyful hope (v. 7). This group may not be large, but it is precious to God, and the future of God's program rests with it. The Christian is taught by Romans 8:19–25 to pray just such a prayer, in the context of the whole creation's "eager longing" for liberty (Kidner).

Of which group are you a member? Have you made your allegiance known?

Who is a greater fool? The one who says in his heart, "there is no God," or the one who knows in his heart that there is a God, yet lives as if there is no God?

> "I pray because the need flows out of me all the time, waking and sleeping. It doesn't change God, it changes me" (C. S. Lewis).

O Word of the Father, and Savior of the humble, I pray that all may know You, as Your salvation goes out to turn earth's corruption to the beauty of life in Your presence. AMEN.

Getting Dressed for Church

When I was saved 46 years ago, people dressed up when they went to church. I will not comment on what I think we ought to specifically wear in church today, but we should always prepare diligently for the public gathering of God's people before the Lord. The Psalmist says here that we should "wear" some special spiritual garments when we come before Him.

> *A Psalm of David*
> 15:1 O Lord, who shall sojourn in your tent?
> Who shall dwell on your holy hill?
> 2 He who walks blamelessly and does what is right and speaks truth in his heart;
> 3 who does not slander with his tongue and does no evil to his neighbor, nor takes up a reproach against his friend;
> 4 in whose eyes a vile person is despised, but who honors those who fear the Lord; who swears to his own hurt and does not change;
> 5 who does not put out his money at interest and does not take a bribe against the innocent. He who does these things shall never be moved.
>
> (Psalm 15, ESV)

David loved God's house and longed to dwell there and fellowship with Him (Ps. 27:4–5). He yearned to be like the priests who lived in the tabernacle and had constant access to holy things. David wished he could even be a guest and pay God a visit, but did he qualify? Does anybody qualify? This Psalm is not a test for who can get into God's worship center, but instead it is a warning to worshippers to come prepared.

God's children have open access into His presence through the work of Jesus Christ (Heb. 10:19–25). He is our High Priest and Advocate in heaven, and He welcomes us. We come on the basis of His righteousness, not our own. But we should be sure we have experienced the cleansing of Heb. 10:22 before we rush into His presence.

PSALM 15

This Psalm helps us examine our **walk**, our **works**, and our **words** (v. 2). The inventory includes our relationship with others (vv. 3–4), how we keep our promises, and how we use our money (v. 5). Meditating on this Psalm and pondering these "qualifications" will help you deepen your relationship with God.

Isaiah tells us that the garments that God has provided for us to wear to worship are these: "To give them a beautiful headdress instead of ashes, the oil of gladness instead of mourning, the garment of praise instead of a faint spirit; that they may be called oaks of righteousness, the planting of the LORD, that he may be glorified" (Isa 61:3).

"For a day in your courts is better than a thousand elsewhere. I would rather be a doorkeeper in the house of my God than dwell in the tents of wickedness" (Ps. 84:10).

> *LORD, as I desire to cross the threshold to come and rest before Your face, grant that I may take to heart Your will for me to love my neighbour as myself. AMEN.*

Messiah Lives!

You have taken a giant step toward true Christian maturity when you can say to the Lord and also mean it, "I have no good apart from you" (v. 2).

A Miktam of David.

16:1 Preserve me, O God, for in you I take refuge.
2 I say to the Lord, "You are my Lord; I have no good apart from you."
3 As for the saints in the land, they are the excellent ones, in whom is all my delight.
4 The sorrows of those who run after another god shall multiply; their drink offerings of blood I will not pour out or take their names on my lips.
5 The Lord is my chosen portion and my cup; you hold my lot.
6 The lines have fallen for me in pleasant places; indeed, I have a beautiful inheritance.
7 I bless the Lord who gives me counsel; in the night also my heart instructs me.
8 **I have set** the Lord always before me; because he is at my right hand, I shall not be shaken.
9 Therefore my heart is glad, and my whole being rejoices; my flesh also dwells secure.
10 For **you will not abandon my soul to** Sheol, or let your holy one see corruption.
11 You make known to me the path of life; in your presence there is fullness of joy; at your right hand are pleasures forevermore.

(Psalm 16, ESV)

This Psalm records David's own reflections on the Davidic promise (2 Sam. 7:16). At the center of his thoughts is his confidence in his own resurrection. David (and his anointed *Son*!) is confident of three unchanging realities to which he testifies in this Psalm:

He has good fellowship (vv. 3–4). God's people are not perfect, but we should delight in their fellowship and not in the fellowship of the world's crowd (2 Cor. 6:14–16). The world needs our witness, but we must take care not to start loving the world (1 John 2:15–17).

He has a good heritage (vv. 5–6). Not just God's gifts, but God Himself! What a joy it is to let God choose your inheritance for you instead of acting like the world and fighting for your "place in the sun."

He has good counsel (vv. 7–8). God gives wisdom if you will ask Him (Jas. 1:5). God teaches you in the darkness as well as in the light. These verses are summarized in Matthew 6:33. Psalm 16:8 is a familiar verse to many Jewish people today. Most Jewish homes have a *Sheviti* plaque on a wall. *Sheviti* means "I have set." I pray that the verses following about the Messiah will also become familiar to them.

He has a good hope (vv. 9–11). This passage is one of the few in the Old Testament dealing with resurrection (Ps. 49:15; Isa. 26:19; Dan. 12:2). It was applied by Peter to the resurrection of the Messiah in an argument that is hard to refute (Acts 2:22–32). A resurrected Messiah is what gives us our hope (1 Cor. 15:19–20; 1 Pet. 1:3). That David's descendant had such confidence in his own resurrection is furthered by the fact that the next psalm also lays great stress on the resurrection (Ps. 17:15).

> "How sweet all at once it was for me to be rid of those fruitless joys which I had once feared to lose! ... You drove them from me. You who are the true, sovereign joy. You drove them from me and took their place, You who are sweeter than all pleasure, though not to flesh and blood, You who outshine all light, yet are hidden deeper than any secret in our hearts, You who surpass all honor, though not in the eyes of men who see all honor in themselves. ... O Lord my God, my Light, my Wealth, and my Salvation" (Augustine).

Psalm 17

An Honest Plea

David's first concern in Psalm 17 is to honestly plead his innocence, opening himself to God's scrutiny. This is the prelude to a call for protection, which dominates the second half of the Psalm. The first mention of his danger is in verse 7, which leads into a vivid account of the encircling enemies and a strong plea for their overthrow. The final verse leaves these earthly preoccupations behind. Night will give way to a cloudless morning (Kidner).

A prayer of David.

17:1 Hear a just cause, O Lord; attend to my cry! Give ear to my prayer from lips free of deceit!
2 From your presence let my vindication come! Let your eyes behold the right!
3 You have tried my heart, you have visited me by night, you have tested me, and you will find nothing; I have purposed that my mouth will not transgress.
4 With regard to the works of man, by the word of your lips I have avoided the ways of the violent.
5 My steps have held fast to your paths; my feet have not slipped.
6 I call upon you, for you will answer me, O God; incline your ear to me; hear my words.
7 Wondrously show your steadfast love, O Savior of those who seek refuge from their adversaries at your right hand.
8 Keep me as the apple of your eye; hide me in the shadow of your wings,
9 from the wicked who do me violence, my deadly enemies who surround me.
10 They close their hearts to pity; with their mouths they speak arrogantly.
11 They have now surrounded our steps; they set their eyes to cast us to the ground.
12 He is like a lion eager to tear, as a young lion lurking in ambush.
13 Arise, O Lord! Confront him, subdue him! Deliver my soul from the wicked by your sword,
14 from men by your hand, O Lord, from men of the world whose portion is in this life. You fill their womb with treasure; they are satisfied with children, and they leave their abundance to their infants.
15 As for me, I shall behold your face in righteousness; when I awake, I shall be satisfied with your likeness.

(Psalm 17, ESV)

Although "God is Spirit" (John 4:24), Scripture sometimes refers to Divine body parts to describe God's activities with respect to His people. This figure of speech is called an anthropomorphism. David refers to four of these "parts" to describe God's attributes.

God's ears (vv. 1–2). The enemy opposed David's just cause, so he cried out to God for vindication. David's prayer was not self-serving but simply sincere, and he wanted God to judge righteously.

God's eyes (vv. 3–5). David had nothing to hide. His heart was right and his walk was righteous. You must be able to say the same of your heart and walk if you expect God to answer your prayers (Ps. 66:18).

God's hand (vv. 6–14). David trusted not his own hand but the hand of God to protect him and to defeat the enemy. The pride of the enemy grieved David because he wanted God alone to be glorified. The "apple of the eye" is the pupil (Ps. 17:8; Pr. 7:2; Zec. 2:8). This figure of speech is followed by that of the protective wings also in the song of Moses (Deut. 32:10–11). Elsewhere it is a standard way to express God's protection (Ruth 2:12; Ps. 36:7, 57:1, 63:7, 91:4).

God's face (Ps. 17:15). This verse clearly is linked with **the promise of resurrection** in the preceding Psalm (Ps. 16:11). Also, the word "awake" refers to the resurrection in Isaiah 26:19 and Daniel 12:2. "It is safe to tell the pure in heart that they shall see God, for only the pure in heart want to" (C.S.Lewis).

The promise, however, can also be applied to **contentment in life today**. While his enemies may find temporal satisfaction in their children (v. 14), David finds endless satisfaction in God's future promise and current presence (v. 15). Our Lord goes with us into the furnace so that we may be more like Him when we come out of it (Dan. 3:19–25).

(Wiersbe suggested the above outline that utilizes the anthropomorphic parts of God's "body").

Eternal Father, receive me through the righteousness of Jesus Your Son. Keep me then as the little one mirrored in Your eye. Hide me under the shadow of Your wings, and grant that, through the vision of You in all my darkness, I may be satisfied with Your everlasting peace. AMEN.

Psalm 18

Hind's Feet on High Places

Psalm 18 is a victor's song of gratitude to God for all that He had accomplished through David's efforts. He sang this song **after God delivered him** from his enemies and established him as the king of Israel (2 Samuel 22 repeats this Psalm within a historical narrative). Keep in mind that he often sang to God **in the midst of his trials** as well. It is easier to sing after the victory; it takes faith to sing during the conflict. As David looked back on those difficult years, what attributes of God did he most remember?

To the choirmaster. A Psalm of David, the servant of the L ORD, who addressed the words of this song to the L ORD on the day when the L ORD rescued him from the hand of all his enemies, and from the hand of Saul. He said:

18:1 I love you, O L ORD, my strength.
2 The L ORD is my rock and my fortress and my deliverer, my God, my rock, in whom I take refuge, my shield, and the horn of my salvation, my stronghold.
3 I call upon the L ORD, who is worthy to be praised, and I am saved from my enemies.
4 The cords of death encompassed me; the torrents of destruction assailed me;
5 the cords of Sheol entangled me; the snares of death confronted me.
6 In my distress I called upon the L ORD; to my God I cried for help. From his temple he heard my voice, and my cry to him reached his ears.
7 Then the earth reeled and rocked; the foundations also of the mountains trembled and quaked, because he was angry.
8 Smoke went up from his nostrils, and devouring fire from his mouth; glowing coals flamed forth from him.
9 He bowed the heavens and came down; thick darkness was under his feet.
10 He rode on a cherub and flew; he came swiftly on the wings of the wind.
11 He made darkness his covering, his canopy around him, thick clouds dark

PSALM 18

with water.
12 Out of the brightness before him hailstones and coals of fire broke through his clouds.
13 The LORD also thundered in the heavens, and the Most High uttered his voice, hailstones and coals of fire.
14 And he sent out his arrows and scattered them; he flashed forth lightnings and routed them.
15 Then the channels of the sea were seen, and the foundations of the world were laid bare at your rebuke, O LORD, at the blast of the breath of your nostrils.
16 He sent from on high, he took me; he drew me out of many waters.
17 He rescued me from my strong enemy and from those who hated me, for they were too mighty for me.
18 They confronted me in the day of my calamity, but the LORD was my support.
19 He brought me out into a broad place; he rescued me, because he delighted in me.
20 The LORD dealt with me according to my righteousness; according to the cleanness of my hands he rewarded me.
21 For I have kept the ways of the LORD, and have not wickedly departed from my God.
22 For all his rules were before me, and his statutes I did not put away from me.
23 I was blameless before him, and I kept myself from my guilt.
24 So the LORD has rewarded me according to my righteousness, according to the cleanness of my hands in his sight.
25 With the merciful you show yourself merciful; with the blameless man you show yourself blameless;
26 with the purified you show yourself pure; and with the crooked you make yourself seem tortuous.
27 For you save a humble people, but the haughty eyes you bring down.
28 For it is you who light my lamp; the LORD my God lightens my darkness.
29 For by you I can run against a troop, and by my God I can leap over a wall.
30 This God—his way is perfect; the word of the LORD proves true; he is a shield for all those who take refuge in him.
31 For who is God, but the LORD? And who is a rock, except our God?—
32 the God who equipped me with strength and made my way blameless.
33 He made my feet like the feet of a deer and set me secure on the heights.
34 He trains my hands for war, so that my arms can bend a bow of bronze.
35 You have given me the shield of your salvation, and your right hand supported me, and your gentleness made me great.
36 You gave a wide place for my steps under me, and my feet did not slip.
37 I pursued my enemies and overtook them, and did not turn back till they were consumed.
38 I thrust them through, so that they were not able to rise; they fell under my feet.
39 For you equipped me with strength for the battle; you made those who rise against me sink under me.
40 You made my enemies turn their backs to me, and those who hated me I destroyed.
41 They cried for help, but there was none to save; they cried to the LORD, but he did not answer them.

⁴² I beat them fine as dust before the wind; I cast them out like the mire of the streets.
⁴³ You delivered me from strife with the people; you made me the head of the nations; people whom I had not known served me.
⁴⁴ As soon as they heard of me they obeyed me; foreigners came cringing to me.
⁴⁵ Foreigners lost heart and came trembling out of their fortresses.
⁴⁶ The LORD lives, and blessed be my rock, and exalted be the God of my salvation—
⁴⁷ the God who gave me vengeance and subdued peoples under me,
⁴⁸ who delivered me from my enemies; yes, you exalted me above those who rose against me; you rescued me from the man of violence.
⁴⁹ For this I will praise you, O LORD, among the nations, and sing to your name.
⁵⁰ Great salvation he brings to his king, and shows steadfast love to his anointed, to David and his offspring forever.

(Psalm 18, ESV)

God's faithfulness (vv. 1–3). God saved David, protected him, and strengthened him when Saul and his men were out to kill him. Is God your refuge and your strength (Ps. 46:1)?

God's righteousness (vv. 4–27). Those had been stormy years for David, yet God rescued him and upheld His dedicated servant. (Read these verses!). David describes his deliverance in the form of a theophany—an awesome display of God's power as Creator. When the storm comes, remember that God is greater than the storm and will help you to wait for the rainbow.

God's gentleness (vv. 28–38). God did many things to make David a great soldier, but His gentleness made David what he was (Ps. 18:35). God was doing more than winning wars; He was building character. It humbled David to think that God would condescend to call him, equip him, and help him (Ps. 8:3–5, 113:5–6; Isa. 57:15–16).

God's sovereignty (vv. 37–50). David did not take credit for his victories; he gave all the glory to the Lord. Whatever David had, God gave it to him; whatever he was, God made him; whatever he did, God enabled him. He even casts himself as a figure of the promised Messiah, the "anointed." His victories provide a portrait of his eternal descendant (v. 50 and 2 Sam. 7:12–16).

PSALM 18

The KJV of Psalm 18:33 inspired Hannah Hurnard's *Hind's Feet on High Places*. Those of us who have observed the Nubian ibex carefully maneuvering the cliffs at En Gedi like to think that David himself, while fleeing from Saul, observed this nimble creature and immortalized it in this Psalm.

> *O Great Father, who rescued Your faithful Son from the waters of death, give me through Him the desire of loving You. May the hearts of my spiritual enemies be turned, and may we together make melody to Your name. And, dear LORD, keep my feet steady in my walk with You. AMEN.*

Psalm 19

God's Three Books

Three major psalms stress the revelation of God's will in His Word (Psalms 1, 19, and 119). Each is then followed by a distinctly messianic psalm (Psalms 2, 20, and 120). This suggests that within the Psalter, the arranger intended to balance the theme of *God's Word*, with that of *God's Anointed*, the Messiah. The Written Word and the Living Word are thus represented as God's two primary means for bringing salvation (Sailhamer).

The beauty and power of this "Word about the Word" can be adequately experienced only when read aloud.

To the choirmaster. A Psalm of David.

19:1 The heavens declare the glory of God, and the sky above proclaims his handiwork.
2 Day to day pours out speech, and night to night reveals knowledge.
3 There is no speech, nor are there words, whose voice is not heard.
4 Their voice goes out through all the earth, and their words to the end of the world. In them he has set a tent for the sun,
5 which comes out like a bridegroom leaving his chamber, and, like a strong man, runs its course with joy.
6 Its rising is from the end of the heavens, and its circuit to the end of them, and there is nothing hidden from its heat.
7 The law of the Lord is perfect, reviving the soul; the testimony of the Lord is sure, making wise the simple;
8 the precepts of the Lord are right, rejoicing the heart; the commandment of the Lord is pure, enlightening the eyes;
9 the fear of the Lord is clean, enduring forever; the rules of the Lord are true, and righteous altogether.
10 More to be desired are they than gold, even much fine gold; sweeter also than honey and drippings of the honeycomb.
11 Moreover, by them is your servant warned; in keeping them there is great reward.
12 Who can discern his errors? Declare me innocent from hidden faults.
13 Keep back your servant also from

> presumptuous sins; let them not have dominion over me! Then I shall be blameless, and innocent of great transgression.
> 14 Let the words of my mouth and the meditation of my heart be acceptable in your sight, O Lord, my rock and my redeemer.
>
> (Psalm 19, ESV)

In this *Wisdom Psalm* (like Psalms 1 and 119), David declares that God reveals Himself **in creation** (vv. 1–6); **in the Scriptures** (vv. 7–11), and **in your heart** as you worship Him (vv. 12–14).

To be properly educated, you must seek to master three books: the **book of nature, the book of God, and the book of humanity**. A scientist specializes in the book of nature and a psychologist specializes in the book of human nature, but if they ignore God's Book, their conclusions may be wrong. Keep balanced as you grow in knowledge, for all truth is God's truth.

The goal of all study is a knowledge of Jesus Christ and of yourself. Psalm 19:7–11 tells you what the Bible can do for you if only you will read it, meditate on it, and obey it. Notice, for example, the beautiful symmetry of the six parallel statements about (1) **the Word,** (2) **what it is**, and (3) **what it does**:

> "The law of the Lord is perfect, reviving the soul.
> The testimony of the Lord is sure, making wise the simple.
> The precepts of the Lord are right, rejoicing the heart.
> The commandment of the Lord is pure, enlightening the eyes.
> The fear of the Lord is clean, enduring forever.
> The rules of the Lord are true, and righteous altogether."

> No wonder that the Word is more valuable than gold and sweeter than honey (v. 10). "In science we have been reading only notes to a poem; in Christianity we find the poem itself." (C. S. Lewis).

The explicit effects of seriously exposing yourself to the written Word are graphically described in verses 12–14. If you like your life the way it is, don't seriously read your Bible, because the results for your life will be serious! These words are very personal statements about the forgiveness of **"hidden sins"** (v. 12), the prevention of **"presumptuous sins"** (v. 13a), and the avoidance of the **"great transgression"** (v. 13b).

Open each day beholding God's glory both in Creation and in Christ (v. 1; 2 Cor. 3:18). Live each day with the devotion of a bridegroom and the determination of an athlete (vv. 4–5). Close each day with the satisfaction that your attitudes and actions have pleased Him (v. 14).

> *Each morning I conclude my private prayer time with the final request of this marvelous psalm: "Let the words of my mouth and the meditation of my heart be acceptable in your sight, O Lord, my rock and my redeemer." Amen.*

Messiah Prays for You

David, the Messianic King (v. 6, 9), prays for those who follow Him (vv. 1–4). Verse 5 then moves to the first person plural ("we") as He anticipates the shared victory. Verses 6–9 then display the fulfillment of the promises to David as described in Psalm 2 and 2 Samuel 7. Note the references to "the anointed one" (v. 6) and to the "king" (v. 9). Psalm 21 then continues David's reflection on his own Messianic role (Ps. 21:1–7). His psalms are often a theological expansion of God's promises to him in 2 Samuel 7:12–16 (Luke 24:44).

> *To the choirmaster. A psalm of David.*
> 20:1 May the LORD answer you in the day of trouble! May the name of the God of Jacob protect you!
> 2 May he send you help from the sanctuary and give you support from Zion!
> 3 May he remember all your offerings and regard with favor your burnt sacrifices! Selah
> 4 May he grant you your heart's desire and fulfill all your plans!
> 5 May we shout for joy over your salvation, and in the name of our God set up our banners! May the LORD fulfill all your petitions!
> 6 Now I know that the LORD saves **his anointed**; he will answer him from his holy heaven with the saving might of his right hand.
> 7 Some trust in chariots and some in horses, but we trust in the name of the LORD our God.
> 8 They collapse and fall, but we rise and stand upright.
> 9 O LORD, save **the king**! May He answer us when we call.
>
> (Psalm 20, ESV)

A day of trouble (vv. 1–3). David was going out to battle, and he and his people gathered to pray. His secret of victory was the name of the Lord (v. 1), the One he worshiped sincerely and sacrificially. Have you ever wondered what to pray for someone when you don't know any specific requests? Like

Paul's prayer in Ephesians 1:15–23, consider praying Psalm 20:1–4 for someone—and also for yourself!

A day of triumph (vv. 4–6). Again, it is in the name of the Lord that you fight the forces of evil (v. 5). God hears and answers prayer and sends you the help you need. The beautiful prayer of verse 4 echoes in Psalm 37:4, where it says that God will grant the desires of our hearts when we delight in Him. I often append verse 4 to the end of my emails and letters.

A day of trust (vv. 7–9). David had a great name, but the name of the Lord is much greater. Some people have names that cannot be trusted, but God's name has never failed. Your days of trouble can become days of triumph if you trust in the name of Yahweh.

What's in a Name?

This psalm begins and ends with a prayer to the LORD, God's personal *name* (*Yahweh*). It is in that *name* that we trust. In the Bible, *names* are important because one's *name* represents the person. When somebody had a life-changing experience, their *name* was often changed. For example, Abram became *Abraham* and Sarai became *Sarah,* and Simon was given the name *Peter*. The Bible records many *names* of God, and all of them can be trusted (Ps. 9:10, 33:21).

> *Answer me, O LORD, in the day of my troubles. Send me help from the sanctuary and accept my sufferings as an offering to You. Breathe into my heart Your counsels, and save me by the mighty name of Your Son, my Savior, the Lord Jesus Christ. AMEN.*

Psalm 21

When We Receive Our Heart's Desire

If Psalm 20 is a prayer before the battle, Psalm 21 is the praise after the victory. Too often we forget to praise God when He answers prayer and gives us what we requested (Luke 17:11–19).

To the choirmaster. A psalm of David.

21:1 O LORD, in your *strength* the **king** rejoices, and in your salvation how greatly he exults!
2 You have given him his heart's desire and have not withheld the request of his lips.
3 For you meet him with rich blessings; you set a crown of fine gold upon his head.
4 He asked life of you; you gave it to him, length of days forever and ever.
5 His glory is great through your salvation; splendor and majesty you bestow on him.
6 For you make him most blessed forever; you make him glad with the joy of your presence.
7 For the **king** trusts in the LORD, and through the steadfast love of the Most High he shall not be moved.
8 Your hand will find out all your enemies; your right hand will find out those who hate you.
9 You will make them as a blazing oven when you appear. The LORD will swallow them up in his wrath, and fire will consume them.
10 You will destroy their descendants from the earth, and their offspring from among the children of man.
11 Though they plan evil against you, though they devise mischief, they will not succeed.
12 For you will put them to flight; you will aim at their faces with your bows.
13 Be exalted, O LORD, in your *strength*! We will sing and praise your power.

(Psalm 21, ESV)

Psalm 21 has an evident inner texture (within the psalm) and a remarkable intertexture (outside the psalm). References to God's *strength* for the **king** at the beginning (v. 1) and at the end (v. 13) bind the psalm together with an *inclusio*. David's reference to God's granting him his heart's desire (v. 3) recalls Psalm 20:4, while his reference to being in the Lord's presence (v. 6) recalls Psalm 16:11. This underlines the Messianic theme of the preceding psalms and leads into the Messianic trilogy of Psalms 22–24.

Yahweh and the king (vv. 1–7). God gave David strength to win the battle and then gave him honor and majesty from the victory. Before the battle, David asked God to spare his life, and God gave him his request. God responded to David's faith by protecting him, and David responded to God's blessings by praising Him. David rejoiced in God's strength and salvation (v. 1) and in His presence with him (v. 6).

Yahweh and the enemy (vv. 8–12). These were the enemies of God because they wanted to destroy His people Israel. David fought the Lord's battles, and the Lord gave victory. We have tried to point out the many connections in the Psalms to the Davidic Covenant, but this time the connection goes further back to the Abrahamic Covenant (Gen. 12:1–3).

Yahweh and the nation (v. 13). Now the whole congregation praises the Lord. Individual praise in private is important, but we should share the joy with others and let them praise God with us. The congregation's praise of God's strength and power is not simply an outward exercise. It is an acknowledgment that our strength is found in His strength (Phil. 4:13).

Psalm 21 focuses our attention on the future of the house of David instead of on its past. For the Davidic king, the fulfillment of the hope expressed in the Psalms still lies in the future, the hope of the Messiah's coming.

> *O Yahweh Almighty, Who raised up Your Son and crowned Him with glory and honor, rise up now against everything and everyone who would attempt to spoil Your glory. Hasten the victory of Your coming kingdom, that I may live and sing Your praise forever. AMEN.*

A Song of the Singing Sufferer

Psalms 22, 23, and 24 are sometimes called the "Shepherd Psalms" because they speak of Jesus the Messiah in His shepherding ministry. In Psalm 22, the Good Shepherd dies for the sheep (John 10:11). In Psalm 23, the Great Shepherd lives for the sheep (Heb. 13:20–21). In Psalm 24, the Chief Shepherd returns for the sheep (1 Pet. 5:4). Another way to view this trilogy is that the Messiah is portrayed as "Sufferer" in Psalm 22, as "Shepherd" in Psalm 23, and as "Sovereign" in Psalm 24.

To the choirmaster: according to The Doe of the Dawn. A Psalm of David.

22:1 My God, my God, why have you forsaken me? Why are you so far from saving me, from the words of my groaning?

2 O my God, I cry by day, but you do not answer, and by night, but I find no rest.

3 Yet you are holy, enthroned on the praises of Israel.

4 In you our fathers trusted; they trusted, and you delivered them.

5 To you they cried and were rescued; in you they trusted and were not put to shame.

6 But I am a worm and not a man, scorned by mankind and despised by the people.

7 All who see me mock me; they make mouths at me; they wag their heads;

8 "He trusts in the Lord; let him deliver him; let him rescue him, for he delights in him!"

9 Yet you are he who took me from the womb; you made me trust you at my mother's breasts.

10 On you was I cast from my birth, and from my mother's womb you have been my God.

11 Be not far from me, for trouble is near, and there is none to help.

12 Many bulls encompass me; strong bulls of Bashan surround me;

13 they open wide their mouths at me, like a ravening and roaring lion.

14 I am poured out like water, and all my bones are out of joint; my heart is like wax; it is melted within my breast;

15 my strength is dried up like a potsherd, and my tongue sticks to my jaws; you lay me in the dust of death.

16 For dogs encompass me; a company of evildoers encircles me; they have pierced my hands and feet
17 I can count all my bones they stare and gloat over me;
18 they divide my garments among them, and for my clothing they cast lots.
19 But you, O Lord, do not be far off! O you my help, come quickly to my aid!
20 Deliver my soul from the sword, my precious life from the power of the dog!
21 Save me from the mouth of the lion! You have rescued me from the horns of the wild oxen!
22 I will tell of your name to my brothers; in the midst of the congregation I will praise you:
23 You who fear the Lord, praise him! All you offspring of Jacob, glorify him, and stand in awe of him, all you offspring of Israel!
24 For he has not despised or abhorred the affliction of the afflicted, and he has not hidden his face from him, but has heard, when he cried to him.
25 From you comes my praise in the great congregation; my vows I will perform before those who fear him.
26 The afflicted shall eat and be satisfied; those who seek him shall praise the Lord! May your hearts live forever!
27 All the ends of the earth shall remember and turn to the Lord, and all the families of the nations shall worship before you.
28 For kingship belongs to the Lord, and he rules over the nations.
29 All the prosperous of the earth eat and worship; before him shall bow all who go down to the dust, even the one who could not keep himself alive.
30 Posterity shall serve him; it shall be told of the Lord to the coming generation;
31 they shall come and proclaim his righteousness to a people yet unborn, that he has done it.

(Psalm 22, ESV)

If Psalm 16 could be called the Easter Psalm, then Psalm 22 could be called the Good Friday Psalm. But this psalm actually covers the entire *weekend that changed the world.* Three great redemptive acts of the Messiah are portrayed in Psalm 22:

His crucifixion (vv. 1–21). Because he was a prophet (Acts 2:30), David was able to write about the Messiah centuries before He came. Crucifixion was not a Jewish form of capital punishment, yet David described it accurately. As you read, see Jesus at Calvary: His cry to the Father (v. 1; Matt. 27:46); the period of darkness (v. 2; Matt. 27:45); the ridicule of the people (vv. 6–8; Matt. 27:39–44); His thirst and pain (vv. 14–15; John 19:28); His pierced hands and feet (v. 16; Luke 24:39); and the gambling for His clothes (v. 18; John 19:23–24). Remember, He endured all of these things as an innocent sufferer on your behalf (2 Cor. 5:21).

His resurrection (vv. 22–26). In these verses the Messiah no longer is suffering but is alive and in the midst of His people, leading them in praise for the mighty victory God has won (Heb. 2:11–12). Note that the Singing Savior joins us in worship! The first day of the week is the memorial to His resurrection, and we follow His example by meeting with God's people along with Jesus as we praise Yahweh together. Resurrection day is victory day!

His coronation (vv. 27–31). The Messiah shares the resulting blessings of His obedient suffering with His church (v. 22), with Israel (v. 23), and now with the whole world (vv. 27–31). The psalm even contains an exhortation that we must get the message out to every nation that Messiah Jesus is Savior and King (v. 27). "May all peoples be blessed in him and all nations call him blessed" (Ps. 72:17).

IMPORTANT: This psalm is Messianic but that does not exclude suffering believers from also finding solace in His words. It is exactly because the Messiah is the sufferer *par excellence* that His sufferers can be comforted here. Psalm 22:1–5 thus provides some two-fold guidance drawn from the example of the Messianic Sufferer. What did He do in the face of the greatest suffering ever experienced by anyone? And what should you do?

1. Express your feeling (vv. 1–2).
2. Confess your faith (vv. 3–5). (Brant Reeves)

O Jesus my Messiah, who understood the hour of forsakenness and the sharpness of death, do not be far from me in my sorrows. Come quickly to my help, that I may offer myself as a living sacrifice of thanksgiving, and then tell of Your goodness to all around me.
AMEN.

Of Whom Does David Speak?

Although this is a devotional commentary, it is necessary occasionally to explore some academic-interpretive issues surrounding the Psalms. If we wrongly interpret the Psalms, we will wrongly apply them. Therefore, we must get right our hermeneutics in the Psalms!

The title of our continued study of this psalm adapts a similar question asked by the Ethiopian Eunuch to Philip about Isaiah 53 (Acts 8:34). In Psalm 22 does David refer only to himself, or is he describing someone else, namely the Messiah? I argue that the psalm is Messianic and what follows, with a little help from John Sailhamer, defends that interpretation.

The first part (vv. 1–22) is a lament for "the afflicted one" (v. 24). Though David is the author, he is not the one speaking in the major part of the psalm. David begins to speak only at verse 23, where he addresses the congregation about the suffering of the "afflicted one" which was recorded in the first part of the psalm. David affirms that God has listened to his cry for help (v. 24), and in verse 25 he turns to address that sufferer: "From you comes my praise in the great congregation." By speaking *about* the Lord, not *to* him in verses 25–26, he shows that he is addressing the Afflicted One. Continuing to address him, David says that "all nations shall worship before you" (v. 27), using an image recalling Psalm 2:12 and anticipating the "Son of Man" in Daniel 7:13–14. Looking into the distant future, David concludes, "Posterity shall serve him ... they will proclaim his righteousness" (vv. 30–31).

The psalm thus represents David's proclamation about the suffering of "the afflicted one" and his ultimate victory over death. Therefore, the detailed description of his suffering (Ps. 22:7–18) has for good reason been interpreted as describing the crucifixion of Jesus (John 19:24).

PSALM 22

FINAL NOTE: The Hebrew Masoretic Text of Psalm 22:16 as it stands means "like a lion my hands and feet" and not "**they pierced my hands and feet**"—as traditional English translations render it. What is overlooked is the fact that two ancient translations, the *Septuagint* Greek and the *Vulgate* Latin, do render the expression as "they pierced," thus recognizing their pre-Christian Hebrew text in the way that the later English versions render it. The Masoretic text, however, is later (9th century AD) and reflects editing by its Hebrew scribes who slightly changed this verse to avoid the "Christian" understanding of its meaning. Furthermore, a few Hebrew manuscripts not in the Masoretic tradition actually preserve the ancient reading "they pierced." No one should have any doubt that our English translations faithfully convey what David wrote!

> *Thank You, Lamb of God, that being slain from the foundation of the world in Your Father's purpose, You did not shirk Your appointed role as You faced Gethsemane and Calvary. Thank You for doing that for me. AMEN.*

Our Forever Shepherd

The middle psalm of the Messianic Trilogy portrays the Messiah as "Shepherd." A "Christian" reading of Psalm 23 is quite appropriate since Jesus portrayed himself as the shepherd of his sheep (John 10:11) and other New Testament writers joined this chorus. He is the Good Shepherd, the Great Shepherd, and the Chief Shepherd (Heb. 13:20; 1 Pet. 2:24, 5:4).

Depth and strength underlie the simplicity of this Psalm. Its peace is not escape and its contentment is not complacency. It displays a readiness to face deep darkness and imminent attack, and the climax reveals a love focused on no material goal but rather the Lord Himself (Kidner).

While I normally use the ESV translation, the Authorized Version is simply too familiar and beloved to be replaced by any newer version.

> *A Psalm of David.*
> 23:1 The LORD is my shepherd; I shall not want.
> 2 He maketh me to lie down in green pastures: he leadeth me beside the still waters.
> 3 He restoreth my soul: he leadeth me in the paths of righteousness for his name's sake.
> 4 Yea, though I walk through the valley of the shadow of death, I will fear no evil: for thou art with me; thy rod and thy staff they comfort me.
> 5 Thou preparest a table before me in the presence of mine enemies: thou anointest my head with oil; my cup runneth over.
> 6 Surely goodness and mercy shall follow me all the days of my life: and I will dwell in the house of the LORD forever.
>
> (Psalm 23, KJV)

Although Psalm 23 is often read at funerals, its message applies to the days of your life right now (v. 6). The Savior who died for you also lives for you and cares for you, the way a shepherd cares for the sheep (John 10:1–18). If you can say, "The LORD is my Shepherd," you can also say, "I shall not want." The word "want" is simply Old English for "lack." The NT equivalent promise is found in Philippians 4:19.

The Shepherd feeds us and leads us. Sheep must have grass and water to live, and the shepherd finds those essential elements for them. God meets the everyday needs of your life as you follow Him (Ps. 37:25; Phil. 4:18). Never worry!

If we wander, **the Shepherd seeks us and restores us,** as He did with David, Jonah, and Peter. When we need to know which way to go, He shows us the right path and then goes before us to prepare the way. Even in the places of danger, we need not be afraid. (Note the change from "He" in verses 1–3 to "You" in verses 4–5.) He is with you! At the end of the dark valley, He has a special blessing for you: you drink of the refreshing water of life, and you receive the Spirit's anointing. **The Shepherd is there to care for every hurt** and heal every bruise.

The words "goodness" (*tov*) and "mercy" (*hesed*) characterize God's dealings with His people. These rich covenantal blessings will never be taken away from His new covenant people. "To length of days" is the special way of expressing this promise (v. 6). The Christian understanding of these words does no violence to them. "Neither death, nor life, … will be able to separate us from the love of God in Christ Jesus our Lord" (Rom. 8:38–39).

One day, you will look back at your life and see that it was only "goodness and mercy," and that includes the valley experiences. If life is difficult today, just keep following the Shepherd like a needy sheep; **He will never lead you where He cannot care for you.**

> *O Sovereign Shepherd, who brought again Your Son Jesus from the valley of death, comfort me with Your protecting presence and with Your angels of goodness and love, that I also may come home and dwell with Him in Your house forever.* AMEN.

The King of Glory

In this majestic psalm we move in procession with the King of Glory from the provinces of His realm to the City and the Temple at its summit. If a ceremonial occasion gave rise to the Psalm, we need look no further than the escorting of the ark by David 'with song and lyres and harps ...' from Kirjath-Jearim to Mount Zion (1 Chron. 13:8), which is also commemorated in Psalm 132.

A Psalm of David.
24:1 The earth is the Lord's and the fullness thereof, the world and those who dwell therein,
2 for he has founded it upon the seas and established it upon the rivers.
3 Who shall ascend the hill of the Lord? And who shall stand in his holy place?
4 He who has clean hands and a pure heart, who does not lift up his soul to what is false and does not swear deceitfully.
5 He will receive blessing from the Lord and righteousness from the God of his salvation.
6 Such is the generation of those who seek him, who seek the face of the God of Jacob.
7 Lift up your heads, O gates! And be lifted up, O ancient doors, that the King of glory may come in.
8 Who is this King of glory? The Lord, strong and mighty, the Lord, mighty in battle!
9 Lift up your heads, O gates! And lift them up, O ancient doors, that the King of glory may come in.
10 Who is this King of glory? The Lord of hosts, he is the King of glory!   Selah
(Psalm 24, ESV)

While "we" the worshippers do appear in this Psalm (vv. 4-6), the attention as always is on the King, who is:

The All-Creating One (vv. 1–2). The Creator and Sustainer (v. 2) is not only the city's founder and establisher, but is the One who oversees the entire earth in all its aspects: a fruitful earth (v. 1a), a peopled earth (v. 1b), a solid earth (v. 2). The *earth* and the *waters* recall the creator of Genesis 1.

Psalm 24

The All-Holy One (vv. 3–6). We have seen similar requirements in Psalm 15:1–5. These qualities are not a test for entering the Temple, as if these things could really be measured, but are a warning to worshipers to come prepared to worship the All-Holy One. Clean hands and hearts cover both the outward and inward spheres of our lives. These are people who genuinely seek God.

The All-Victorious One (vv. 7–10). The ascent completes a march begun in Egypt. Indeed the Psalms that are quoted in 1 Chronicles 16:8–36 as sung on this occasion look back as far as Abraham and on to the coming of the Lord as Judge. If the earth is His (vv. 1, 2) and He is holy (vv. 3–6), the challenge to the 'ancient doors' is not an exercise in pageantry, but (as in 2 Cor. 10:3–5) a battle-cry for the believer.

(I am indebted to Derek Kidner for the above outline).

Final Thought: Heavenly pilgrims are always ascending.

> *Yahweh, in Your hand is all the fullness of the earth. Restore in me true purity of life. As I follow Your Son, may I ascend Your holy mountain and rejoice in the completion of Your good kingdom.*
> *AMEN.*

Psalm 25

The Holy Alphabet

This psalm is an acrostic. The Hebrew alphabet, with an occasional irregularity, supplies its framework, in which the pressure of enemies, the need of guidance and the burden of guilt take turns to be the dominant concerns. The tone is subdued, and the singer's trust is shown in patient waiting rather than the outburst of joy that sometimes marks the climax of such a psalm. The final verse claims for Israel what David has petitioned for himself, so making a personal plea becomes a hymn for the whole congregation (Kidner).

The placement of Psalm 25 after Psalm 24 stresses the role of *King Messiah*, who is often referred to as God (Ps. 45:6; Isa. 9:6). Having come to the Temple to receive the King of Glory (Ps. 24), in Psalm 25 the Psalmist requests guidance from the Divine King ("Guide me in Your truth and teach me, for You are God my savior, and my hope is in You all day long" Ps. 25:5).

Therefore, this Psalm is helpful when you are making decisions and seeking God's will.

Of David.

25:1 To you, O Lord, I lift up my soul.
2 O my God, in you I trust; let me not be put to shame; let not my enemies exult over me.
3 Indeed, none who wait for you shall be put to shame; they shall be ashamed who are wantonly treacherous.
4 Make me to know your ways, O Lord; teach me your paths.
5 Lead me in your truth and teach me, for you are the God of my salvation; for you I wait all the day long.
6 Remember your mercy, O Lord, and your steadfast love, for They have been from of old.
7 Remember not the sins of my youth or my transgressions; according to your steadfast love remember me, for the sake of your goodness, O Lord!
8 Good and upright is the Lord; therefore he instructs sinners in the way.
9 He leads the humble in what is right, and teaches the humble his way.

10 All the paths of the Lord are steadfast love and faithfulness, for those who keep his covenant and his testimonies.
11 For your name's sake, O Lord, pardon my guilt, for it is great.
12 Who is the man who fears the Lord? Him will he instruct in the way that he should choose.
13 His soul shall abide in well-being, and his offspring shall inherit the land.
14 The friendship of the Lord is for those who fear him, and he makes known to them his covenant.
15 My eyes are ever toward the Lord, for he will pluck my feet out of the net.
16 Turn to me and be gracious to me, for I am lonely and afflicted.
17 The troubles of my heart are enlarged; bring me out of my distresses.
18 Consider my affliction and my trouble, and forgive all my sins.
19 Consider how many are my foes, and with what violent hatred they hate me.
20 Oh, guard my soul, and deliver me! Let me not be put to shame, for I take refuge in you.
21 May integrity and uprightness preserve me, for I wait for you.
22 Redeem Israel, O God, out of all his troubles.

(Psalm 25, ESV)

Who are the people God guides?

Those who glorify Him (vv. 1–2). If you want His will for His glory, He will show you the right path. If you have selfish motives, He may let you have your way, and then you may regret getting your way.

Those who wait (v. 3). You are not wasting time when you wait on the Lord in prayer, but sometimes it is SO hard to do. God's promise if you do is that you will eventually soar like an eagle and finish this grueling race (Isa. 40:31).

Those who ask (vv. 4–5). God wants to show you His ways, teach you His paths, and lead you in His truths. Verse 4 is a classic example of the synonymous parallelism that is the chief characteristic of Hebrew poetry. Note the parallels: Make me to know/teach me; Your ways/Your paths. Watch for this literary parallelism as you read. The Word of God and prayer always go together, so spend time in His Word. If you ask Him sincerely, He will answer you clearly.

Those who are clean (vv. 6–7, 16–22). God's *hesed* or His "steadfast love" again is the basis for forgiving those who are in a saving relationship to Him. The terms translated as "steadfast love," "mercy," and "faithfulness" recall Yahweh's self-description in Exodus 34:6. I am convinced that all of the Psalms are efforts to proclaim, defend or even struggle with those attributes of God. More on this as we proceed through the Psalter.

God is not as concerned about our past sins ("youth"), as He is about our present spiritual condition. Believe and accept this and you will finally find victory over the torments of guilt due to past failures.

Those who submit (vv. 8–15). God does not guide rebels, but He joyfully leads those who know Him and submit to His will (Ps. 32:8–10). Keep your eyes on the Lord and let Him have His way. He knows where He is going and what He is doing, so follow Him by faith.

The enemy was slandering David again, and he had no way to vindicate himself before men. Slander has been called "the revenge of a coward" and it is. What should you do when people spread lies about you? First be sure that it is really slander and not an accurate charge they are bringing!

Final Thought: Always place God between you and your troubles and enemies.

> *Father, forgive my sins, which are many. Cause me to know Your ways and to walk in Your truth, that I may be saved from cruel enemies, and daily rejoice in the goodness of Your fellowship.*
> *AMEN.*

Psalm 26

A Claim to Integrity

Integrity means uprightness of purpose and honesty in one's dealings. To lay claim to it is tricky, because such a claim may sound like "boasting," even as the psalmist's pleas here may sound self-serving. But his claims are accompanied with a dread sense of sin and prayer for deliverance. He knows all goodness comes from God and he clings to Him in childlike trust. How can we do the same when our own integrity is assaulted?

Of David.

26:1 Vindicate me, O Lord, for I have walked in my integrity, and I have trusted in the Lord without wavering.
2 Prove me, O Lord, and try me; test my heart and my mind.
3 For your steadfast love is before my eyes, and I walk in your faithfulness.
4 I do not sit with men of falsehood, nor do I consort with hypocrites.
5 I hate the assembly of evildoers, and I will not sit with the wicked.
6 I wash my hands in innocence and go around your altar, O Lord,
7 proclaiming thanksgiving aloud, and telling all your wondrous deeds.
8 O Lord, I love the habitation of your house and the place where your glory dwells.
9 Do not sweep my soul away with sinners, nor my life with bloodthirsty men,
10 in whose hands are evil devices, and whose right hands are full of bribes.
11 But as for me, I shall walk in my integrity; redeem me, and be gracious to me.
12 My foot stands on level ground; in the great assembly I will bless the Lord.

(Psalm 26, ESV)

When your integrity is questioned,

Examine yourself (vv. 1–5). Is your life what it ought to be? Let God test your mind and heart (Ps. 139:23–24). In your walking, standing (Ps. 26:12), and sitting, are you keeping yourself clean (Ps. 1:1)? Sometimes God allows the enemy to attack us just to make us take time for a personal inventory.

Focus on the Lord (vv. 6–10). If you look at others, you will be upset, and if you look at yourself too long, you may get discouraged, so focus your attention on the Lord. Match your defects with His perfections and claim what you need from Him. The integrity of people is measured not only by what they hate ("the congregation of evil-doers," v. 5) but by what they love ("the habitation of your house," v. 8).

Like many of Israel's prophets (Isa. 29:13), the Psalmist stresses the absolute necessity of a sincere heart in worship (Mic. 6:8).

Keep serving the Lord (vv. 11–12). The enemy wants nothing better than to upset you and get you on a detour (Neh. 6:1–14). Continue to walk with the Lord and serve Him, come what may. Bless the Lord and don't complain. **God will vindicate you in His time and in His own way.**

"An absorbed delight in the presence and house of God makes the core of this Psalm (vv. 6–8) a personal confession that shames our 'faint desires.' The surrounding verses point to the source of this joy, in the realm of choice rather than temperament: the costly choice of allegiance which has thrown David back on God's protection and made clear to him where his heart and treasure lie, and in what company he is supremely at home" (Kidner).

"Look at others and be distressed; look at self and be depressed; look at Jesus and be blessed." Anonymous

Final Thought: There cannot be attachment without detachment.

> *Help me, Lord, to follow the way of trusting You and thus becoming "whole." May I stand washed in the innocence of Your Son, and may I love the place of Your glory, and then always abhor everything that is evil. AMEN.*

One Thing

This ardent and eloquent Psalm enlarges on the themes that it shares with its more subdued neighbors, Psalms 26 and 28, namely the Lord's protection, the joy of his house, and the singer's unquestioning loyalty and trust (Kidner).

Most all commentators see two main divisions: verses 1–6 which describes the Psalmist's delight in God while he is faced with many adversaries, and verses 7–14 which describe his confidence that the Lord will not forsake him when he is forsaken by others. Because there is simply so much in these 14 verses, we will study this Psalm in two sections.

> *Of David.*
> 27:1 The LORD is my light and my salvation; whom shall I fear? The LORD is the stronghold of my life; of whom shall I be afraid?
> 2 When evildoers assail me to eat up my flesh, my adversaries and foes, it is they who stumble and fall.
> 3 Though an army encamp against me, my heart shall not fear; though war arise against me, yet I will be confident.
> 4 **One thing** have I asked of the LORD, that will I seek after: that I may dwell in the house of the LORD all the days of my life, to gaze upon the beauty of the LORD and to inquire in his temple.
> 5 For he will hide me in his shelter in the day of trouble; he will conceal me under the cover of his tent; he will lift me high upon a rock.
> 6 And now my head shall be lifted up above my enemies all around me, and I will offer in his tent sacrifices with shouts of joy; I will sing and make melody to the LORD.
>
> (Psalm 27:1–6, ESV)

What makes you afraid? Darkness? The Lord is your light. Danger? He is also your salvation. Deficiency? He is your strength. Then why be afraid? See what He does for you.

God strengthens you (vv. 1–3). We need strength for the battle and strength for the journey, and God abundantly provides. A "stronghold" is the perfect metaphor for the refuge we have in God. Note how often it is used in the OT (Ps. 9:9, 18:2, 94:2, 144:2; Jer.16:19; Nah. 1:7).

God saves you (vv. 4–6). Because he was not a priest, David could not actually go into the tabernacle, but he could still rest in the Lord and trust Him as his refuge. The New Testament equivalent for this is "abide in Me" (John 15:4). In Him is a perfect deliverance.

"**One thing have I asked**..." (v. 4). A solitary focus marked the Psalmist's attitude and this focus must be ours as well. Note that this solitary focus was what Jesus counseled Martha (Luke 10:41–42: "only one thing is necessary," namely, sitting at Jesus' feet and listening to His word). It was also the solitary goal of Paul (Phil. 3:13: "one thing I do, pressing toward ... Jesus").

Psalm 27:7–14 is next!

Inflame my heart with love to You, O Christ my God, that loving You with all my heart, soul, mind and strength, and my neighbor as myself, I may glorify you in all things, through Christ my Lord I pray.
Amen
(Daily Orthodox Prayer).

Psalm 27 (part 2)

Forsaken But Not Abandoned

When I became lost from my parents at the age of four in a huge crowd, it was the scariest moment of my entire life! But my parents had not abandoned me and the joy was inexpressible when they found me.

It is such a scary feeling to find yourself alone. The Psalmist experienced this and shows us his joy in Psalm 27:7–14 when he realized that he was not abandoned forever.

> 27:7 Hear, O Lord, when I cry aloud; be gracious to me and answer me!
> 8 You have said, "Seek my face." My heart says to you, "Your face, Lord, do I seek."
> 9 Hide not your face from me. Turn not your servant away in anger, O you who have been my help. Cast me not off; forsake me not, O God of my salvation!
> 10 For my father and my mother have forsaken me, but the Lord will take me in.
> 11 Teach me your way, O Lord, and lead me on a level path because of my enemies.
> 12 Give me not up to the will of my adversaries; for false witnesses have risen against me, and they breathe out violence.
> 13 I believe that I shall look upon the goodness of the Lord in the land of the living!
> 14 Wait for the Lord; be strong, and let your heart take courage; wait for the Lord!
>
> (Psalm 27:7–14, ESV)

In verses 1–6 faith sings and soars, and in verses 7–14 it sings and sinks. A fear that soars is faith, and a faith that sinks is fear (Scroggie). Continuing from the last post, we see what God does for those who feel alone.

God showers you with goodness (vv. 7–10) You must go beyond merely seeking God's help. Seek His face (Num. 6:24–26). The smile of God is all you need to overcome the scowls of men.

God shows you the way (vv. 11–13). Satan wants to trap you, but the Lord will show you the safe way. Believe His promise and walk by faith. His goodness will be with you.

God strengthens you (v. 14). Be sure to take time to wait on the Lord (Isa. 40:31). If you run ahead of Him or lag behind, you will be a perfect target for the enemy. Relatives in a hospital room can do nothing for their loved one but trust the ones in charge. Trust the skilled hands of the Great Physician if you must spend time in His waiting room!

> "On every level of life from housework to heights of prayer, in all judgment and all efforts to get things done, hurry and impatience are sure marks of the amateur" (Evelyn Underhill).

O Lord, somehow, in some way, help me to wait for You and Your purposes to be accomplished in my life and walk. AMEN

Answered Prayer

In each of Psalms 26–28 the Lord's "house" comes into view. In Psalm 26 the worshiper is searched by God's demand for sincerity (like Psalms 15 and 24) and he rejoices to have found access. In Psalm 27 he sees this house as a sanctuary from his enemies, and as the place of vision, face to face with God. In Psalm 28 he spreads his hands as a suppliant toward the holy of holies, and receives his answer.

Of David.

28:1 To you, O L ORD, I call; my rock, be not deaf to me, lest, if you be silent to me, I become like those who go down to the pit.

2 Hear the voice of my pleas for mercy, when I cry to you for help, when I lift up my hands toward your most holy sanctuary.

3 Do not drag me off with the wicked, with the workers of evil, who speak peace with their neighbors while evil is in their hearts.

4 Give to them according to their work and according to the evil of their deeds; give to them according to the work of their hands; render them their due reward.

5 Because they do not regard the works of the L ORD or the work of his hands, he will tear them down and build them up no more.

6 Blessed be the L ORD! For he has heard the voice of my pleas for mercy.

7 The L ORD is my strength and my shield; in him my heart trusts, and I am helped; my heart exults, and with my song I give thanks to him.

8 The L ORD is the strength of his people; he is the saving refuge of his anointed.

9 Oh, save your people and bless your heritage! Be their shepherd and carry them forever.

(Psalm 28, ESV)

David is doing what we ought to be doing.

David starts by requesting (vv. 1–5). David's enemies were undermining his reputation and his work, so he turned to the Lord with two special requests: that God would speak to him (vv. 1–2) and that God would save him (vv. 3–5). God speaks to us in answered prayer. "If You are silent," said David, "I might just as well be dead! And if You don't deliver me, You are treating me like the enemy!" Pretty powerful arguments!

David finishes by rejoicing (vv. 6–9). God heard him and helped him, and He does the same for you today as you trust Him. You can rejoice in the Lord even when you cannot rejoice in your circumstances (Phil. 4:4, 12). Trust God to be your strength, your song, and your salvation (Isa. 12:2). He is the faithful Shepherd who can carry both you and your burdens.

God's two primary acts by which He insures our well-being are: (1) He rescues us occasionally as circumstances require; and (2) He blesses us daily to make our lives and labors fruitful. The full answer to the prayer in v 9 has come in the ministry of the "good shepherd" (Jn 10:11, 14).

> *Lord and almighty God, You have brought me safely to another day. Work in me today that which is well-pleasing in Your sight, through Jesus my Lord. AMEN (Daily Morning Prayer).*

Psalm 29

Orientation

Walter Brueggemann in *Praying the Psalms* suggests that every psalm is either a **Psalm of Orientation**, a positive description of the Lord and His word; or a **Psalm of Disorientation** where the psalmist struggles with the "why?" and "how long?" of God's ways; or a **Psalm of Reorientation**, where the psalm takes a decided positive turn after an opening disorientation. Psalm 29, like Psalms 1 and 19, is undoubtedly a Psalm of **Orientation**. Here the psalmist celebrates the majestic power of the Lord as He breaks over the land in a dramatic and destructive storm. The vigor of the poetry, with eighteen repetitions of the name *Yahweh* (Lord), wonderfully matches the theme, while the structure of the poem avoids monotony by its movement from heaven to earth, by the path of the storm, and by the final transition from nature in uproar to the people of God in peace. It is a psalm to be read or sung to experience its power.

A Psalm of David.

29:1 Ascribe to the Lord, O heavenly beings, ascribe to the Lord glory and strength.
2 Ascribe to the Lord the glory due his name; worship the Lord in the splendor of holiness.
3 The voice of the Lord is over the waters; the God of glory thunders, the Lord, over many waters.
4 The voice of the Lord is powerful; the voice of the Lord is full of majesty.
5 The voice of the Lord breaks the cedars; the Lord breaks the cedars of Lebanon.
6 He makes Lebanon to skip like a calf, and Sirion like a young wild ox.
7 The voice of the Lord flashes forth flames of fire.
8 The voice of the Lord shakes the wilderness; the Lord shakes the wilderness of Kadesh.
9 The voice of the Lord makes the deer give birth and strips the forests bare, and in his temple all cry, "Glory!"
10 The Lord sits enthroned over the flood; the Lord sits enthroned as King forever.
11 May the Lord give strength to his people! May the Lord bless his people with peace!

(Psalm 29, ESV)

Note the God of the Storm:

God's praise before the storm (vv. 1–2). David calls on the angels in heaven to ascribe praise to God. You never know when a storm is coming, so be sure you are worshiping Him and giving Him all the glory. The greatest beauty of all is the beauty of holiness, and it comes from worshiping the Lord.

God's power in the storm (vv. 3–9). First the thunder rolled over the Mediterranean Sea. Then the storm broke and moved across Mt. Carmel and the land. Seven times the storm is called 'the voice of the LORD." (Rev. 10:3–4). What power there is in a storm! Even the angels shout, "Glory!" as they watch it!

God's peace after the storm (vv. 10–11). David may have seen a rainbow and remembered God's promise given after the Flood (Gen. 9:12–17). If life is stormy right now, worship Him and wait on Him. The storm will pass, and He will give you peace.

The beginning of the Psalm shows us heaven open while its ending shows us His people on earth, blessed with peace in the midst of the terrible utterance of His wrath. "*Gloria in excelsis* is the beginning, and *in terra pax* the close" (Kidner).

> "God moves in a mysterious way, His wonders to perform; He plants His footsteps in the sea, and rides upon the storm. Ye fearful saints, fresh courage take; the clouds ye so much dread Are big with mercy, and shall break with blessing on your head" (William Cowper).

Eternal God, who made and directs all things by Your mighty Word, give me Your peace in all the storms of life. May I come safely to glory and thus sing in Your glory, when You bring all things to perfection, and when I appear forever in the beauty of Your holiness. AMEN.

Joy in the Morning

We just read a Psalm of Orientation. Psalm 30 is a Psalm of Reorientation. David was in a very difficult situation but after crying to the Lord, He healed him and delivered his life (Ps. 30:3–4), transformed his weeping into joy (Ps. 30:5) and turned his morning to dancing (Ps. 30:11). With the open honesty that so marks this literature, the psalmist recounts his move from disorientation to orientation. David has emerged from his early trials into happier days. David's delight at being restored shines through every word, quite undimmed by time.

A Psalm of David. A Song at the Dedication of the Temple.

30:1 I will extol you, O Lord, for you have drawn me up and have not let my foes rejoice over me.

2 O Lord my God, I cried to you for help, and you have healed me.

3 O Lord, you have brought up my soul from Sheol; you restored me to life from among those who go down to the pit.

4 Sing praises to the Lord, O you his saints, and give thanks to his holy name.

5 For his anger is but for a moment, and his favor is for a lifetime. Weeping may tarry for the night, but **joy comes with the morning**.

6 As for me, I said in my prosperity, "I shall never be moved."

7 By your favor, O Lord, you made my mountain stand strong; you hid your face; I was dismayed.

8 To you, O Lord, I cry, and to the Lord I plead for mercy:

9 "What profit is there in my death, if I go down to the pit? Will the dust praise you? Will it tell of your faithfulness?

10 Hear, O Lord, and be merciful to me! O Lord, be my helper!"

11 You have turned for me my mourning into dancing; you have loosed my sackcloth and clothed me with gladness,

12 that my glory may sing your praise and not be silent. O Lord my God, I will give thanks to you forever!

(Psalm 30, ESV)

Notice three transitions in David's experience:

From sickness to health (vv. 1–3). God had healed David and lifted him up from the grave. His sickness had been a discipline from God because of David's pride and self-sufficiency (vv. 6–7). Perhaps this was in connection with the sin of numbering the people (1 Chron. 21:1–8).

From weeping to joy (vv. 4–5). There is a contrast between God's momentary anger and His gift of lasting joy, between weeping and joy, and between the night and the morning. Things may seem dark to you now, but wait for His morning to dawn.

From mourning to singing (vv. 8–12). When God saw that the discipline had done its work, He healed David and forgave his sins. David changed clothes, picked up his harp, and began to sing praises to the Lord. No matter how dark the night, dawn will come. No matter how heavy your heart, one day there will be a song.

> "Joys are always on the way to us. They are always traveling to us through the darkness of the night. There is never a night when they are not coming" (Amy Carmichael).

O Lord my God, deliver me during my times of ease from the false security that hardens my heart toward You. When troubles do come, O Shepherd, help me to cry to You with simple faith, and to be granted joy in the morning, and the new life of thankfulness without end.
AMEN.

Psalm 31

Into Your Hands

We have moved from a psalm of orientation (Ps. 29) to one of reorientation (Ps. 30) and now to one of disorientation (Ps. 31). This paradigm from Walter Brueggemann (*Praying the Psalms*) is helpful as you try to navigate the moods of each psalm.

This Psalm impressed itself on more than one biblical character to come to mind at moments of crisis. Jonah's prayer draws upon verse 6 (Jonah 2:8). Jeremiah was haunted by a phrase from verse 13 (Jer. 20:10). Verse 5 gave words to Jesus for his last utterance on the cross (Luke 23:46). And in old age the author of Psalm 71 opened his prayer with the substance of verses 1–3. This illustrates the role of the Psalms in meeting a great variety of human needs beyond the bounds of formal worship and the particular experiences of the authors.

To the choirmaster. A Psalm of David.

31:1 In you, O Lord, do I take refuge; let me never be put to shame; in your righteousness deliver me!

2 Incline your ear to me; rescue me speedily! Be a rock of refuge for me, a strong fortress to save me!

3 For you are my rock and my fortress; and for your name's sake you lead me and guide me;

4 you take me out of the net they have hidden for me, for you are my refuge.

5 Into your hand I commit my spirit; you have redeemed me, O Lord, faithful God.

6 I hate those who pay regard to worthless idols, but I trust in the Lord.

7 I will rejoice and be glad in your steadfast love, because you have seen my affliction; you have known the distress of my soul,

8 and you have not delivered me into the hand of the enemy; you have set my feet in a broad place.

9 Be gracious to me, O Lord, for I am in distress; my eye is wasted from grief; my soul and my body also.

10 For my life is spent with sorrow, and my years with sighing; my strength fails because of my iniquity, and my bones waste away.

11 Because of all my adversaries I have become a reproach, especially to my neighbors, and an object of dread to my acquaintances; those who see me in the street flee from me.
12 I have been forgotten like one who is dead; I have become like a broken vessel.
13 For I hear the whispering of many— terror on every side!—as they scheme together against me, as they plot to take my life.
14 But I trust in you, O Lord; I say, "You are my God."
15 My times are in your hand; rescue me from the hand of my enemies and from my persecutors!
16 Make your face shine on your servant; save me in your steadfast love!
17 O Lord, let me not be put to shame, for I call upon you; let the wicked be put to shame; let them go silently to Sheol.
18 Let the lying lips be mute, which speak insolently against the righteous in pride and contempt.
19 Oh, how abundant is your goodness, which you have stored up for those who fear you and worked for those who take refuge in you, in the sight of the children of mankind!
20 In the cover of your presence you hide them from the plots of men; you store them in your shelter from the strife of tongues.
21 Blessed be the Lord, for he has wondrously shown his steadfast love to me when I was in a besieged city.
22 I had said in my alarm, "I am cut off from your sight." But you heard the voice of my pleas for mercy when I cried to you for help.
23 Love the Lord, all you his saints! The Lord preserves the faithful but abundantly repays the one who acts in pride.
24 Be strong, and let your heart take courage, all you who wait for the Lord!

(Psalm 31, ESV)

Let's look at three aspects of David's disorientation:

The foes he encounters. David's enemies persecuted him, lied about him, and spread a net to catch him. Where could he turn for help? Only to the Lord! If the hand of the enemy is against you (vv. 8, 15), find safety in the hand of the Lord (vv. 5, 15; John 10:27–29).

The feelings he experiences. David was ill, possibly as the result of his own disobedience (vv. 9–13). God can use enemies and sickness to chasten us and bring us to a place of submission. David's enemies laughed at him and his friends ignored him. All David could do was turn to the Lord for help, and the Lord did not fail him.

The faith he enjoys. The emphasis is on David's faith in the Lord. Because of his faith, David was not ashamed (v. 1) but rejoiced in God (vv. 6–7) and enjoyed the smile of God upon his life (vv. 14–16; Num. 6:22–27). He knew

PSALM 31

that God's goodness would carry him through (v. 19). True faith is never alone, for it leads to love and hope (vv. 23–24; 1 Cor. 13:13), which give you the courage you need to win the battle, whether the foe is within or without.

The words in which the trust of the Psalmist is most evident (v. 5) are recorded in Luke's Gospel (23:46; cf. Acts 7:59) as the last utterance of Jesus on the cross: "Father, into your hand I commit my spirit." It was the Messiah's desire that his people should have no less secure a place of refuge at the hour of their death than he had at his. In the strength of Christ, his people continually give back their life to the God who first gave it. This is a daily dying to self which death only completes.

> *We bless You, Father, that even now, in the days of our trials, we are shown the light of Your face. We pray that we may daily be led by Your Son Jesus to lay our times and our spirit into Your hands.*
> *AMEN.*

Psalm 32

Forgiven

This penitential psalm grew out of David's experiences with the Lord after he had committed adultery and had tried to hide his sins (2 Sam. 11–12). When you refuse to confess your sins, the Lord must deal with you to bring you to repentance (Pr. 28:13). The longer you wait the more miserable you will be, as you can see in David's experience.

A Maskil of David.

32:1 Blessed is the one whose transgression is forgiven, whose sin is covered.
2 Blessed is the man against whom the LORD counts no iniquity, and in whose spirit there is no deceit.
3 For when I kept silent, my bones wasted away through my groaning all day long.
4 For day and night your hand was heavy upon me; my strength was dried up as by the heat of summer. Selah
5 I acknowledged my sin to you, and I did not cover my iniquity; I said, "I will confess my transgressions to the LORD," and you forgave the iniquity of my sin. Selah
6 Therefore let everyone who is godly offer prayer to you at a time when you may be found; surely in the rush of great waters, they shall not reach him.
7 You are a hiding place for me; you preserve me from trouble; you surround me with shouts of deliverance. Selah
8 I will instruct you and teach you in the way you should go; I will counsel you with my eye upon you.
9 Be not like a horse or a mule, without understanding, which must be curbed with bit and bridle, or it will not stay near you.
10 Many are the sorrows of the wicked, but steadfast love surrounds the one who trusts in the LORD.
11 Be glad in the LORD, and rejoice, O righteous, and shout for joy, all you upright in heart!

(Psalm 32, ESV)

You must face the following:

The debt that is against you (vv. 1–2). God sees what you do and keeps His record. David had covered his sins on earth, but he could not cover the record in heaven. When we confess, God wipes the record clean (1 John 1:9).

The pain that is within you (vv. 3–5). Sin sometimes affects the body, and God's disciplines are painful but needful (Heb. 12:4–11). Here we see David "stewing in his juices" during the time he was trying to hide his sin. David also became like an old man carrying a heavy burden.

The flood that is around you (vv. 6–7). God uses difficult circumstances to bring you back to Himself. In fact, because of his sins, David went through many deep waters with his family. David went from silence (v. 3) to singing (v. 7) because he finally was honest with God and confessed his sins (vv. 5–6).

The road that is before you (vv. 8–11). David was like a stubborn animal that needed to be broken. When you are out of the will of God, your decisions will often create problems instead of solve them. The way gets harder. Only God's *hesed*/love (v. 10) will bring you God's *simchah*/joy (v. 11).

To be in close fellowship with God is true happiness. This is the constant theme of the psalm: (a) *positively* in the opening and the close; and (b) *negatively* in the memory of lost fellowship (v. 4), in the gentle mockery of the stubborn mule (v. 9), and in the reminder of the perils (v. 6) and pains (v. 10) which are the lot of those who choose to walk alone.

By trusting in what the Lord has done to overcome the barrier of sin and by trusting in the Lord as your guide and faithful companion, you will find that sheer happiness of which the psalmist sings.

> *"Search me, O God and know my heart. Try me and know my thoughts. See if there is some wicked way in me, and lead me in the everlasting way."* AMEN

Warren Wiersbe's sensitive treatment of this precious psalm has guided my comments.

Psalm 33

Maker and Monarch

If a hymn is praise to God for what He is and does, Psalm 33 is a fine example of an inspired hymn. The Psalm is occupied with the Lord as Creator, Sovereign, Judge and Savior, while the beginning and end express two elements of worship: (1) an offering of praise, doing honor to so great a King, and (2) a declaration of trust in humble expectation (Kidner). That word *hesed* (steadfast love) again dominates the psalm (vv. 5, 18, 22) and recalls Yahweh's self-description in Exodus 34:6–7.

33:1 Shout for joy in the Lord, O you righteous! Praise befits the upright.
2 Give thanks to the Lord with the lyre; make melody to him with the harp of ten strings!
3 Sing to him a new song; play skillfully on the strings, with loud shouts.
4 For the word of the Lord is upright, and all his work is done in faithfulness.
5 He loves righteousness and justice; the earth is full of the steadfast love of the Lord.
6 By the word of the Lord the heavens were made, and by the breath of his mouth all their host.
7 He gathers the waters of the sea as a heap; he puts the deeps in storehouses.
8 Let all the earth fear the Lord; let all the inhabitants of the world stand in awe of him!
9 For he spoke, and it came to be; he commanded, and it stood firm.
10 The Lord brings the counsel of the nations to nothing; he frustrates the plans of the peoples.
11 The counsel of the Lord stands forever, the plans of his heart to all generations.
12 Blessed is the nation whose God is the Lord, the people whom he has chosen as his heritage!
13 The Lord looks down from heaven; he sees all the children of man;
14 from where he sits enthroned he looks out on all the inhabitants of the earth,
15 he who fashions the hearts of them all and observes all their deeds.
16 The king is not saved by his great army; a warrior is not delivered by his great strength.
17 The war horse is a false hope for salvation, and by its great might it cannot rescue.

Psalm 33

> ¹⁸ Behold, the eye of the Lord is on those who fear him, on those who hope in his steadfast love,
> 19 that he may deliver their soul from death and keep them alive in famine.
> ²⁰ Our soul waits for the Lord; he is our help and our shield.
> ²¹ For our heart is glad in him, because we trust in his holy name.
> ²² Let your steadfast love, O Lord, be upon us, even as we hope in you.
>
> (Psalm 33, ESV)

God's Word in worship (vv. 1–5). We dare not separate worship from the word of God, for we must worship "in truth" (John 4:24). The better we know the Scriptures, the better we will be able to praise Him (Col. 3:16–17).

God's Word in creation (vv. 6–9). God spoke the universe into existence: "by the word of the Lord" (Gen. 1:3, 6, 9, 11, 14; John 1:1–3), and His Word controls it: "He commanded and it stayed firm" (Ps. 147:15–18; Col. 1:16–17). The Word of creation is indeed ever the Word of new creation, and for this His creatures wait and at last have cause to rejoice.

God's Word in history (vv. 10–17). The nations may join together and rebel against God, but His Word will prevail (Gen. 11:1–9; Ps. 2:1–4). Military strength is no guarantee of success. God has a plan for the nations, and He will fulfill it (Acts 17:24–28). Never fear the will of God because it comes from the heart of God (v. 11).

God's Word in my life (vv. 18–22). The Word that created and controls the universe can also control your life. When you trust His Word and obey it, all the universe works for you. When you abandon that Word, all the universe works against you (Jonah 1:3–4). The hope of verse 22 is again prompted by God's *hesed*: "Let your *steadfast love*, O Lord, be upon us, even as we *hope* in you." This hope is patient (v. 20a), confident (v. 20b), buoyant (v. 21a), informed (v. 21b). The name of God means his revealed character (see Ex. 34:5–7), and above all, is focused not on the gift but on the Giver. Such hope "will never disappoint us" (Rom. 5:5) (Kidner).

"The perfect church service would be one we were almost unaware of. Our attention would have been on God" (C. S. Lewis).

Eternal Father, Creator of all things by Your Word, may I by that same Word be made new, that I may sing to You the new song in faithfulness and steadfast love. AMEN.

Psalm 34

Thriving in Crisis

The psalm title gives the background: David's strange behavior before Achish, king of Gath. The Biblical text is 1 Sam 21:1–22:2. It is important to note that after this problematic behavior, David hid out in the Cave of Adullam where he was joined by his "mighty men." This background will help us see the significance of some of his statements.

Last year I was so blessed by a message from my seminary intern, Jeff Eckert, that I share below his main points. David's **advice to those in trials** is fivefold:

Of David, when he changed his behavior before Abimelech, so that he drove him out, and he went away.

34:1 I will bless the LORD at all times; his praise shall continually be in my mouth.
2 My soul makes its boast in the LORD; let the humble hear and be glad.
3 Oh, magnify the LORD with me, and let us exalt his name together!
4 I sought the LORD, and he answered me and delivered me from all my fears.
5 Those who look to him are radiant, and their faces shall never be ashamed.
6 This poor man cried, and the LORD heard him and saved him out of all his troubles.
7 The angel of the LORD encamps around those who fear him, and delivers them.
8 Oh, taste and see that the LORD is good! Blessed is the man who takes refuge in him!
9 Oh, fear the LORD, you his saints, for those who fear him have no lack!
10 The young lions suffer want and hunger; but those who seek the LORD lack no good thing.
11 Come, O children, listen to me; I will teach you the fear of the LORD.
12 What man is there who desires life and loves many days, that he may see good?
13 Keep your tongue from evil and your lips from speaking deceit.
14 Turn away from evil and do good; seek peace and pursue it.
15 The eyes of the LORD are toward the righteous and his ears toward their cry.

16 The face of the Lord is against those who do evil, to cut off the memory of them from the earth.
17 When the righteous cry for help, the Lord hears and delivers them out of all their troubles.
18 The Lord is near to the brokenhearted and saves the crushed in spirit.
19 Many are the afflictions of the righteous, but the Lord delivers him out of them all.
20 He keeps all his bones; not one of them is broken.
21 Affliction will slay the wicked, and those who hate the righteous will be condemned.
22 The Lord redeems the life of his servants; none of those who take refuge in him will be condemned.
(Psalm 34, ESV)

1. Praise the Lord (vv. 1–3). The emphasis here is not that we praise the Lord at expected times (Temple, Church, Chapel), but that we praise Him "at all times." Read Hab. 3:17–18 to see the testimony of a prophet who had learned to do this even when the enemy had destroyed every visible thing in which he trusted!

2. Trust the Lord (vv. 4–7). If we have said "trust the Lord" once in these devotionals, we have said it a dozen times. David tells us what trusting really means. It means to "seek" Him (v. 4), to "look to" Him (v. 5), to "cry out" to Him. When you do this, the angel of the Lord encamps around you. This is illustrated by the calm eye in the midst of a powerful hurricane.

3. Taste the Lord (vv. 8–10). To taste is to personally experience. David's knowledge of God was evidenced by his intense personal relationship with him. Are you sometimes afraid that people will think you are "too spiritual" and that "you are so heavenly minded you are no earthly good?" Frankly I have never met such a person. Would that we were cursed with such heavenly minded people!

4. Fear the Lord (vv. 11–14). You fear the Lord by watching your words (v. 13) and by watching your walk (v. 14). This passage is quoted and applied by Peter (1 Pet. 3:10–11). Is this what David taught the mighty men in the Cave of Adullam? "David was at his best when he was running from Saul" (Jeff Eckert).

5. Flee to the Lord (vv. 15–22). It is the troubled and crushed and broken that the Lord hears and delivers and keeps. The high and lofty one comes down to the level of our need (Isa. 57:15).

The psalm is an alphabet acrostic with verse 22 as the final promise added to the acrostic. By doing this, the author focuses our attention on God's deliverance of His servants who "take refuge in Him." This verse links the psalm to a larger Messianic theme in Psalm 2:12 which uses the very same language about the blessedness of those who take refuge in the Son of God who is also the Messianic Son of David.

> *O Lord, Your angels camp around those who fear You. Therefore, hear my cry when I am broken-hearted, so that I may taste of Your goodness and be lightened by the light of Your face, and live to bless Your holy name. AMEN.*

Psalm 35

A Cry for Help

This fervent appeal is a good companion to Psalm 34 not only because of some verbal similarities but because it speaks out of the type of darkness which has just been dispelled in that psalm. Like David, we need God's deliverance from two different enemies: those who attack us and those who accuse us.

35:1 Contend, O Lord, with those who contend with me; fight against those who fight against me!

2 Take hold of shield and buckler and rise for my help!

3 Draw the spear and javelin against my pursuers! Say to my soul, "I am your salvation!"

4 Let them be put to shame and dishonor who seek after my life! Let them be turned back and disappointed who devise evil against me!

5 Let them be like chaff before the wind, with the angel of the Lord driving them away!

6 Let their way be dark and slippery, with the angel of the Lord pursuing them!

7 For without cause they hid their net for me; without cause they dug a pit for my life.

8 Let destruction come upon him when he does not know it! And let the net that he hid ensnare him; let him fall into it—to his destruction!

9 Then my soul will rejoice in the Lord, exulting in his salvation.

10 All my bones shall say, "O Lord, who is like you, delivering the poor from him who is too strong for him, the poor and needy from him who robs him?"

11 Malicious witnesses rise up; they ask me of things that I do not know.

12 They repay me evil for good; my soul is bereft

13 But I, when they were sick—I wore sackcloth; I afflicted myself with fasting; I prayed with head bowed on my chest.

14 I went about as though I grieved for my friend or my brother; as one who laments his mother, I bowed down in mourning.

15 But at my stumbling they rejoiced and gathered; they gathered together against me; wretches whom I did not know tore at me without ceasing;

16 like profane mockers at a feast, they gnash at me with their teeth.

17 How long, O Lord, will you look on?

Rescue me from their destruction, my precious life from the lions!
18 I will thank you in the great congregation; in the mighty throng I will praise you.
19 Let not those rejoice over me who are wrongfully my foes, and let not those wink the eye who hate me without cause.
20 For they do not speak peace, but against those who are quiet in the land they devise words of deceit.
21 They open wide their mouths against me; they say, "Aha, Aha! Our eyes have seen it!"
22 You have seen, O Lord; be not silent! O Lord, be not far from me!
23 Awake and rouse yourself for my vindication, for my cause, my God and my Lord!
24 Vindicate me, O Lord, my God, according to your righteousness, and let them not rejoice over me!
25 Let them not say in their hearts, "Aha, our heart's desire!" Let them not say, "We have swallowed him up."
26 Let them be put to shame and disappointed altogether who rejoice at my calamity! Let them be clothed with shame and dishonor who magnify themselves against me!
27 Let those who delight in my righteousness shout for joy and be glad and say evermore, "Great is the Lord, who delights in the welfare of his servant!"
28 Then my tongue shall tell of your righteousness and of your praise all the day long.

(Psalm 35, ESV)

Do you have anyone who attacks and accuses you?

Those who attack you (vv. 1–10). There are places in this world where it is a dangerous thing to be a Christian, and the number of those places is increasing. Satan is a murderer (John 8:44) and would destroy all of God's people if he could. But the Lord fights for us. He has effective weapons (vv. 2–3) and knows the enemy's plots (v. 4). If you belong to the Lord, He assumes responsibility to care for you (2 Cor 2:11, 10:3–5; Eph 6:10–18).

Those who accuse you (vv. 11–28). Satan is an accuser as well as a murderer (Rev 12:10), so David had to move from the battlefield to the courtroom where his enemies were lying about him. His prayer changed from "Fight for me!" to "Vindicate me!" (vv. 23–24; 1 John 2:1–2). His concern was that God's name, not his own, be magnified (v. 27). When the enemy slanders your name, he attacks the name of the Lord as well.

Note the results: "And my soul shall be joyful" (v. 9) and "And my tongue shall speak of Your righteousness" (v. 28). Complete joy on the inside and a clear witness on the outside!

Psalm 35

"It is not your business to succeed, but to do right. When you have done so, the rest lies with God" (C. S. Lewis).

NOTE: This is one of those "harsh" psalms that includes prayers and wishes that the psalmist's enemies would be punished, and are called *imprecatory* psalms. Modern readers may wince at these expressions, and unbelievers probably will never accept them until they encounter personally the Holy God who hates sin and punishes both sin and sinner. Nevertheless it is good to keep a couple of things in mind. David does not act out his vengeance, which is evidenced by his kind treatment of his greatest enemy, Saul. He leaves the judgment of Saul and his enemies with God. What he prays for is that justice will be displayed in God's world. Scripture writers longed to see God's justice in *this* life, not only in the future one. Furthermore, there is a difference between "then" and "now." Then there was a *theocracy* and now there is a *church*. Such judgment today, for example, might be seen in church discipline, when unrepentant sinners are cut off, not by death but by excommunication. Suffice it to conclude that the "problem" with these psalms is not so much a problem with God, as it is *our own problem*, namely that we have a shallow understanding of all the attributes of God which are clearly revealed in the control text that provides the theological basis for all the Psalms: Exodus 34:6–7.

> *O Lord, in Your own way fight against those who with lies and cruelty assault Your little ones. Do not be not silent when they abuse and destroy Your creatures. Hasten the time of salvation, when all will bless You for the peace You have established through Your Son Jesus. AMEN.*

Hesed Forever!

This is a psalm of powerful contrasts, a glimpse of human wickedness in its most malevolent form, and of divine goodness in its many-sided fullness. Meanwhile the psalmist is menaced by the one (human wickedness) and assured of victory by the other (divine goodness). Few psalms cover such a range in so short a space (Kidner).

The description of David in the title as "the servant of the Lord" is found also in the title of Psalm 18 and in Psalm 89:3. The term recalls the promises to David in 2 Samuel 7. This connection to the Davidic Covenant is also illustrated by the three references in verses 5, 7, and 10 to God's *hesed*, translated by "steadfast love" or "lovingkindness." This heightens the great contrast between the Lord and the wicked who are described in verses 1–4.

To the choirmaster. Of David, the servant of the Lord.

36:1 Transgression speaks to the wicked deep in his heart; there is no fear of God before his eyes.
2 For he flatters himself in his own eyes that his iniquity cannot be found out and hated.
3 The words of his mouth are trouble and deceit; he has ceased to act wisely and do good.
4 He plots trouble while on his bed; he sets himself in a way that is not good; he does not reject evil.
5 Your steadfast love, O Lord, extends to the heavens, your faithfulness to the clouds.
6 Your righteousness is like the mountains of God; your judgments are like the great deep; man and beast you save, O Lord.
7 How precious is your steadfast love, O God! The children of mankind take refuge in the shadow of your wings.
8 They feast on the abundance of your house, and you give them drink from the river of your delights.
9 For with you is the fountain of life; in your light do we see light.
10 Oh, continue your steadfast love to those who know you, and your righteousness to the upright of heart!
11 Let not the foot of arrogance come upon me, nor the hand of the wicked drive me away.
12 There the evildoers lie fallen; they are thrust down, unable to rise.

(Psalm 36, ESV)

The psalm moves from a description of sinful men to the trustworthiness of the faithful God, and ends with the characteristics of blessed men. In this way, it qualifies as a *Psalm of Reorientation*.

The wickedness of man (vv. 1–4). David had seen a good deal of life and knew what human nature was like. He knew his own heart as well! But in this psalm, he shared a special oracle that God gave him. The sinner flatters himself that he "gets away" with sin. He lives on lies as he plots against the godly. His words and his works are evil, but that does not bother him. Paul uses verse 1 to summarize his charge of sinfulness against the human race (Rom. 3:18).

The faithfulness of the Lord (vv. 5–7). What a vivid contrast to the unfaithfulness of the sinner! God can be trusted always to do what is right, and the safest place in the world is under His shadow in the Holy of Holies (v. 7).

The blessedness of the believer (vv. 8–12). God satisfies His people with the water of life and the light of life. He protects from the enemy and provides for every need. The word "delights" in verse 8 is *Eden* in the Hebrew. When you find your delight in God, you dwell in Paradise!

The evil that David portrayed in the first section he was ready to fight. The grace that he praised in the second section he was ready to invoke and to accept as settling the matter in the third section.

"In your light do we see light ..."

Almighty God, give me such an awareness of Your mercies that with a truly thankful heart I may show forth Your praise, not only with my lips, but in my life by giving up myself to Your service, and by walking before You in holiness and righteousness all my days, through Jesus Christ my Lord. Amen.
(Cranmer—one of my favorite petitions).

Psalm 37

Meek Shall Inherit

Derek Kidner states that there is no finer exposition of the third Beatitude (Matt. 5:5: "blessed are the meek") than this psalm, from which the beatitude is drawn (v. 11). It is a wisdom psalm and thus a Psalm of Orientation. Unlike the many praise psalms, it speaks to man, not God, and its tone and style have affinities with Proverbs, whose message of the righteous man's security is its central topic.

Of David.

37:1 Fret not yourself because of evildoers; be not envious of wrongdoers!

2 For they will soon fade like the grass and wither like the green herb.

3 Trust in the LORD, and do good; dwell in the land and befriend faithfulness.

4 Delight yourself in the LORD, and he will give you the desires of your heart.

5 Commit your way to the LORD; trust in him, and he will act.

6 He will bring forth your righteousness as the light, and your justice as the noonday.

7 Be still before the LORD and wait patiently for him; fret not yourself over the one who prospers in his way, over the man who carries out evil devices!

8 Refrain from anger, and forsake wrath! Fret not yourself; it tends only to evil.

9 For the evildoers shall be cut off, but those who wait for the LORD shall inherit the land.

10 In just a little while, the wicked will be no more; though you look carefully at his place, he will not be there.

11 But the meek shall inherit the land and delight themselves in abundant peace.

12 The wicked plots against the righteous and gnashes his teeth at him,

13 but the Lord laughs at the wicked, for he sees that his day is coming.

14 The wicked draw the sword and bend their bows to bring down the poor and needy, to slay those whose way is upright;

15 their sword shall enter their own heart, and their bows shall be broken.

16 Better is the little that the righteous has than the abundance of many wicked.

17 For the arms of the wicked shall be broken, but the LORD upholds the righteous.

18 The LORD knows the days of the blameless, and their heritage will remain forever;

Psalm 37

19 they are not put to shame in evil times; in the days of famine they have abundance.
20 But the wicked will perish; the enemies of the Lord are like the glory of the pastures; they vanish—like smoke they vanish away.
21 The wicked borrows but does not pay back, but the righteous is generous and gives;
22 for those blessed by the Lord shall inherit the land, but those cursed by him shall be cut off.
23 The steps of a man are established by the Lord, when he delights in his way;
24 though he fall, he shall not be cast headlong, for the Lord upholds his hand.
25 I have been young, and now am old, yet I have not seen the righteous forsaken nor his children begging for bread.
26 He is ever lending generously, and his children become a blessing.
27 Turn away from evil and do good; so shall you dwell forever.
28 For the Lord loves justice; he will not forsake his saints. They are preserved forever, but the children of the wicked shall be cut off.
29 The righteous shall inherit the land and dwell upon it forever.
30 The mouth of the righteous utters wisdom, and his tongue speaks justice.
31 The law of his God is in his heart; his steps do not slip.
32 The wicked watches for the righteous and seeks to put him to death.
33 The Lord will not abandon him to his power or let him be condemned when he is brought to trial.
34 Wait for the Lord and keep his way, and he will exalt you to inherit the land; you will look on when the wicked are cut off.
35 I have seen a wicked, ruthless man, spreading himself like a green laurel tree.
36 But he passed away, and behold, he was no more; though I sought him, he could not be found.
37 Mark the blameless and behold the upright, for there is a future for the man of peace.
38 But transgressors shall be altogether destroyed; the future of the wicked shall be cut off.
39 The salvation of the righteous is from the Lord; he is their stronghold in the time of trouble.
40 The Lord helps them and delivers them; he delivers them from the wicked and saves them, because they take refuge in him.

(Psalm 37, ESV)

This psalm shares the wisdom of an old man who had walked with the Lord (v. 25). He had battled with evil men and knew the frustration of seeing the wicked prosper and the righteous suffer. As he reviewed the past, he gave some wise counsel to keep us from fretting against the Lord when things are not going the way we want them to go.

"Trust in the Lord" (v. 3). If you walk by sight and not by faith, you will find it easy to fret. See Psalm 73. The wicked seem to be prospering, but they will not last (Ps. 37:35–36). Believe what God says in His Word because that is where you find reality.

"Delight in the Lord" (v. 4). Find all your joy and pleasure in His will. Make Him your delight, and your desires will be according to His will. Living to please the Lord sets you free from fretting about what men are doing.

"Commit your way to the Lord" (v. 5). When you trust Him and delight in Him, how could you do anything other than commit your way to Him? Let God guide your steps, choose your joys, protect your name, and bless your work.

"Be still before the Lord" (v. 7). Restlessness is an evidence of unbelief. Faith rests in the Lord and enjoys "the peace of God, which surpasses all understanding" (Phil. 4:7). "In the Hebrew this means: 'Be silent to God and let Him mold thee.' Keep still and He will mold thee to the right shape" (Martin Luther). God sometimes waits in answering prayer so that He might strengthen our patience (Jas. 1:2–8).

"Wait on the Lord" (v. 34). For what are you waiting? You are waiting for the inheritance God has for you (vv. 11, 18, 22, 29, 34). It is reserved in heaven just for you (1 Pet. 1:3–5). The wicked have only temporary pleasure on earth, but God's people have eternal treasure in heaven. You will one day receive your inheritance, so be patient.

There is much more in this psalm, so continue to meditate on it (Ps. 1:2). We will look again at more of its wisdom.

O God, grant me the courage to accept the things I cannot change, the courage to change the things I can, and the wisdom to know the difference. AMEN. (attributed to various authors)

Psalm 37 (part 2)

He Shall Not Fall

As I read this psalm again, I am struck by how similar it is to the Proverbs and other Wisdom Psalms. One of the great themes in this literature is the characteristics of the righteous person. Let's examine again verses 23–31 with that in mind:

> 37:23 The steps of a man are established by the LORD, when he delights in his way;
> 24 though he stumble, he shall not fall, for the LORD upholds his hand.
> 25 I have been young, and now am old, yet I have not seen the righteous forsaken or his children begging for bread.
> 26 He is ever lending generously, and his children become a blessing.
> 27 Turn away from evil and do good; so shall you dwell forever.
> 28 For the LORD loves justice; he will not forsake his saints. They are preserved forever, but the children of the wicked shall be cut off.
> 29 The righteous shall inherit the land and dwell upon it forever.
> 30 The mouth of the righteous utters wisdom, and his tongue speaks justice.
> 31 The law of his God is in his heart; his steps do not slip.
> (Psalm 37:23–31, ESV)

This section begins and ends with the **promise that a Godly person may stumble, but a final fall will not take place!** The kind of fall described in verse 24 appears to be a material calamity rather than a moral lapse. There will be ups and downs, but his hand is steady.

The generosity described (vv. 25–26) echoes what was said in verses 21, 22, and 26. This gives an important balance to the catalogue of gains also described—for a righteous man is no longer righteous when he grows selfish; he has joined the "men whose portion ... is of the world" (Ps 17:14; 49:13–20).

The security promised (vv. 27–28) is not unrelated to one's behavior. Old Testament believers were conscious that they were to walk before the Lord and be complete because He is their shield and reward (Gen 15:1, 17:1).

The injunction to "do good" in verse 27 is not as superfluous as it may sound. In the first place, a conflict with evil too often tempts one to fight the enemy with his own weapons. In the second, both the Lord and the structure of life are on the side of justice (vv. 28, 30).

The psalm concludes with **a promise to those who "take refuge in Him"**(v. 40), again echoing the great exhortation/promise in Psalm 2:12 and illustrating how this psalm is actually a commentary on Psalms 1 and 2. Pointing to the only way of peace gives the psalm its lasting value and accounts for its echoes in the New Testament (especially Matt 5:5).

Taking delight in the Lord, having His teaching in our hearts, putting our burdens on Him, being still to Him, having Him know our days and guide our steps, cherishing kindness, humility and purity—this is the way to find peace and to dwell in His land, enjoying the harvest of His faithfulness. These truths are what gives the psalm its lasting value and explain its echo in Matt. 5:5.

> *O merciful and gracious Lord, grant me to know that in You alone I will find true delight and peace. Therefore, may I commit my way to You and come to dwell in Your good land forever. AMEN.*

Psalm 38

A Penitent

This plaintive appeal is an urgent request for relief from a severe and painful illness—God's "rebuke" for a sin David has committed. Neither the specific occasion nor the illness can be identified. David's suffering is aggravated by the withdrawal of his friends (v. 11) and the unwarranted efforts of enemies to seize this opportunity to bring him down (vv. 12, 16, 19–20).

A Psalm of David, for the memorial offering.

38:1 O Lord, rebuke me not in your anger, nor discipline me in your wrath!

2 For your arrows have sunk into me, and your hand has come down on me.

3 There is no soundness in my flesh because of your indignation; there is no health in my bones because of my sin.

4 For my iniquities have gone over my head; like a heavy burden, they are too heavy for me.

5 My wounds stink and fester because of my foolishness,

6 I am utterly bowed down and prostrate; all the day I go about mourning.

7 For my sides are filled with burning, and there is no soundness in my flesh.

8 I am feeble and crushed; I groan because of the tumult of my heart.

9 O Lord, all my longing is before you; my sighing is not hidden from you.

10 My heart throbs; my strength fails me, and the light of my eyes—it also has gone from me.

11 My friends and companions stand aloof from my plague, and my nearest kin stand far off.

12 Those who seek my life lay their snares; those who seek my hurt speak of ruin and meditate treachery all day long.

13 But I am like a deaf man; I do not hear, like a mute man who does not open his mouth.

14 I have become like a man who does not hear, and in whose mouth are no rebukes.

15 But for you, O Lord, do I wait; it is you, O Lord my God, who will answer.

16 For I said, "Only let them not rejoice over me, who boast against me when my foot slips!"

17 For I am ready to fall, and my pain is ever before me.

18 I confess my iniquity; I am sorry for my sin.

19 But my foes are vigorous, they are mighty, and many are those who hate

me wrongfully.
20. Those who render me evil for good accuse me because I follow after good.
21. Do not forsake me, O LORD! O my God, be not far from me!
22. Make haste to help me, O Lord, my salvation!

(Psalm 38, ESV)

In traditional Christian usage, this is one of seven penitential psalms. See also Psalms 6, 32, 51, 102, 130, 143. This psalm reveals what can happen to you when you sin and thus is an example of a psalm of *disorientation*.

What God does (vv. 1–2). God loves you too much to allow you to sin and get away with it. If you disobey, He will first rebuke you and then chasten you. He will shoot His arrows from a distance or come closer and put His hand on you, but He will let you know that He is displeased.

What sin does (vv. 3–10). David suffered from sickness because of his sin (Ps. 32:3–5). He carried a heavy burden and was crushed under it. He sighed and panted and was ready to quit. Sin comes as a friend that entices you and then becomes a master that enslaves you.

What people do (vv. 11–14). Sin can put a wall between you and those who can help you, but it can also build a bridge between you and those who want to exploit you and hurt you.

What the sinner must do (vv. 15–22). The only hope is to confess sin and cry out to God for mercy. He promises to forgive, so claim His promise.

> "What Happens to Your Sins?" When God forgives you, He takes them away (John 1:29); forgets them (Heb. 10:17); washes them away (Isa. 1:18); blots them out (Isa. 43:25); wipes them out like a cloud (Isa. 44:22); pardons them (Isa. 55:7); and buries them in the depths of the sea (Mic. 7:19)" (Wiersbe).

Most merciful God, I confess that I have sinned against You in thought, word, and deed, by what I have done, and by what I have left undone. I have not loved You with my whole heart; I have not loved my neighbor as myself. I am truly sorry and I humbly repent. For the sake of your Son Jesus Christ, have mercy on me and forgive me, that I may delight in Your will, and walk in Your ways, to the glory of Your name. AMEN. (Book of Common Prayer)

Lament

"Protest" would be too strong a title for this ultimate psalm of *disorientation*—if protest implied defiance. Yet David's feelings were running so high that he could be taken for disloyalty. No wonder he was careful about venting these thoughts in the wrong company (v. 1). Rather than reading this psalm in verses, read it as a whole in paragraphs—the way it was written. The word "Selah" ends each paragraph.

> *To the choirmaster to Jeduthun. A Psalm of David.*
>
> 39:1 I said, "I will guard my ways, that I may not sin with my tongue; I will guard my mouth with a muzzle, so long as the wicked are in my presence."
> 2 I was mute and silent; I held my peace to no avail, and my distress grew worse.
> 3 My heart became hot within me. As I mused, the fire burned; then I spoke with my tongue:
> 4 "O Lord, make me know my end and what is the measure of my days; let me know how fleeting I am!
> 5 Behold, you have made my days a few handbreadths, and my lifetime is as nothing before you. Surely all mankind stands as a mere breath! Selah
> 6 Surely a man goes about as a shadow! Surely for nothing they are in turmoil; man heaps up wealth and does not know who will gather!
> 7 "And now, O Lord, for what do I wait? My hope is in you.
> 8 Deliver me from all my transgressions. Do not make me the scorn of the fool!
> 9 I am mute; I do not open my mouth, for it is you who have done it.
> 10 Remove your stroke from me; I am spent by the hostility of your hand.
> 11 When you discipline a man with rebukes for sin, you consume like a moth what is dear to him; surely all mankind is a mere breath! Selah
> 12 "Hear my prayer, O Lord, and give ear to my cry; hold not your peace at my tears! For I am a sojourner with you, a guest, like all my fathers.
> 13 Look away from me, that I may smile again, before I depart and am no more!"
>
> (Psalm 39, ESV)

Years ago I was introduced to the ACTS prayer meeting where participants would pray in Adoration, then in Confession, then with Thanksgiving, and finally with Supplication. The idea was that all types of prayers would be covered by this acronym. Later in life I wondered how the Psalms of Lament fit into this grid. The Psalms are so varied that we can find many examples that fit the ACTS paradigm. But where do the Lament Psalms fit? Furthermore, if psalmists prayed these prayers, like Psalm 39, then they must have an important role in the spiritual life of a believer. I venture to guess, however, that if you started praying publicly in words similar to this psalm, the leader of the prayer meeting would suggest some pastoral counseling for you!

Let's be honest. The Lament Psalms are complaints to God, plain and simple. Even more than the "why" and "how long" psalms which we have read before (Ps. 10:1, e.g.), the Laments express to God the raw feelings that we sometimes experience when what we know about God (His love and mercy) just does not square with what we see happening to us in the real world.

Again, I want to be honest with you. I did not appreciate the Lament Psalms until I went through the awful pain of losing our daughter, Lynda Joy, in a car accident in 2005. It was then that I began to understand the struggle with God that the Psalmist describes. You see, her death at the age of 26 just did not make any sense. But it has been in the days and long nights since that I have begun to read these Laments with some measure of appreciation.

One final word before I comment on the actual contents of Psalm 39. If you respond by saying that it is wrong for a Christian to ever complain, I suggest that it is better to complain directly to God in prayer than to complain to others about Him. I think that the Psalms of Lament provide the proper prayer language for those laments.

Should we then use the acronym LACTS for our prayer meetings? Or maybe SLACT?

> *I bless you, Lord, for life and for the good things that enrich my days. I also bless You as the one who gives and who also takes away. So now, Lord, what else do I wait for? My hope is in You. Give me hope in the midst of my despair. AMEN.*

Psalm 39 (part 2)

O Lord

My favorite stage play is *Fiddler on the Roof*. If you are a Christian, you may at times be shocked by the honest conversations that Tevye has with God. But Tevye's problem with God is much older. It goes back to Jeremiah, Job and the Psalmist. But Tevye did not argue with God from a perspective of unbelief. It was exactly because Tevye was a man of faith that he argued with God. In other words, these laments of Job and Jeremiah and the Psalmist and Tevye are the stops along the journey of a very Jewish train of thought through the ages. Perhaps Christians also need to recognize that these psalms are the record of a struggle that is NOT a mark of unbelief. They rather give voice to a realistic cry of honest belief that still struggles with the ways of the God whom they affirm.

The burning question of this psalm is why God should so severely discipline a creature as frail as man. It is an outburst like that of Job, and especially his cry, "I loathe my life; I would not live forever. Leave me alone, for my days are a breath" (Job 7:16–17; see also Ps. 88:13–18). But the question, like that of Job, is not asked in arrogance but with touching loyalty (v. 1) accompanied by a submissive faith (v. 7) (Kidner). My advice to those who are also perplexed by the struggles expressed in a psalm like this is to *keep reading*. As hard as it is for the writer, he will finally work his way through his thorny problem to the end, and he will do it in faith, although it may be humbly expressed (v. 12).

Like Job and Jeremiah, the psalmist at the present moment can't see much more than death, and request no more than a respite. The prayer of verse 13 makes no more sense than Peter's "depart from me," but God knows when to treat that plea as Jesus does in Luke 5:8–10, and the way He does in

Mark 5:17–19. "The very presence of such prayers in Scripture is a witness to his understanding. He knows how men speak when they are desperate" (Kidner).

These "songs in the night" reveal something of the bewilderment over the human condition that only began to be dispelled when the Word became flesh, and "brought life and immortality to light through the Gospel" (1 Tim. 6:16). "Thus the voice of the psalmist is heard as the voice of the suffering people of God, and of him who entered into their ordeals that he might be their salvation. In this way the psalm can still plead for those in terrible sufferings, expressing also the prayer of the Beloved One who bore the sins of many that he might fulfil all their longing" (Eaton).

A suggested outline of Psalm 39:

1. David's Reticence (vv. 1-3)
2. David's Requests (vv. 4, 12-13)
3. David's Reflections (vv. 5-11)

> *My Almighty Savior and Lord, look with compassion on the wounds of Your people. Do not forsake us, sinful as we are, but for the sake of the passion of Your Beloved One, Jesus, come quickly to our aid. AMEN.*

Psalm 40

Up from the Bog

The theme of waiting, expounded in Psalm 37, has had its painful application in Psalms 38 and 39, but now in Psalm 40 its triumphant outcome. Those two psalms of *disorientation* give way here to a psalm of *reorientation* (Kidner).

To the choirmaster. A Psalm of David.

40:1 I waited patiently for the Lord; he inclined to me and heard my cry.

2 He drew me up from the pit of destruction, out of the miry bog, and set my feet upon a rock, making my steps secure.

3 He put a new song in my mouth, a song of praise to our God. Many will see and fear, and put their trust in the Lord.

4 Blessed is the man who makes the Lord his trust, who does not turn to the proud, to those who go astray after a lie!

5 You have multiplied, O Lord my God, your wondrous deeds and your thoughts toward us; none can compare with you! I will proclaim and tell of them, yet they are more than can be told.

6 In sacrifice and offering you have not delighted, but you have given me an open ear. Burnt offering and sin offering you have not required.

7 Then I said, "Behold, I have come; in the scroll of the book it is written of me:

8 I delight to do your will, O my God; your law is within my heart."

9 I have told the glad news of deliverance in the great congregation; behold, I have not restrained my lips, as you know, O Lord.

10 I have not hidden your deliverance within my heart; I have spoken of your faithfulness and your salvation; I have not concealed your steadfast love and your faithfulness from the great congregation.

11 As for you, O Lord, you will not restrain your mercy from me; your steadfast love and your faithfulness will ever preserve me!

12 For evils have encompassed me beyond number; my iniquities have overtaken me, and I cannot see; they are more than the hairs of my head; my heart fails me.

13 Be pleased, O Lord, to deliver me! O Lord, make haste to help me!

14 Let those be put to shame and disappointed altogether who seek

> to snatch away my life; let those be turned back and brought to dishonor who delight in my hurt!
> 15 Let those be appalled because of their shame who say to me, "Aha, Aha!"
> 16 But may all who seek you rejoice and be glad in you; may those who love your salvation say continually, "Great is the Lord!"
> 17 As for me, I am poor and needy, but the Lord takes thought for me. You are my help and my deliverer; do not delay, O my God!
>
> (Psalm 40, ESV)

Watch David as he progresses through this psalm:

We Watch David waiting (vv. 1–3). While experiencing trials at the hands of his enemies, David asked God for help, but the answer did not come immediately. He waited—and then God worked! What a change took place! David went from a pit to a highway, from dry clay to a rock, and from crying to singing! This is the testimony of a convert—from pit to praise!

We Watch David witnessing (vv. 4–10). When God does a great thing for you, share it with others. God's works and thoughts ought to be a part of your daily conversation. Share the good news by what you say and do. God can use your witness to bring others to Himself (Ps. 40:3). We will explore in the second part of this commentary the Messianic role of Psalm 40:6–8.

We Watch David warring (vv. 11–15). So often David found himself surrounded by danger, and all he could do was turn to the Lord for help. You may not be battling against armies, but you are part of a spiritual warfare that demands diligence and devotion (Eph. 6:10).

We Watch David worshiping (vv. 16–17). When you worship, it helps to put things into perspective, and you see what God is doing for you. The important thing is that God is magnified. You may get impatient with Him, but He truly cares about you and is working everything together for your good (Jer. 29:11).

You are God, we praise You. You are the Lord, we acclaim You. You are the Eternal Father, all creation worships You. To You all angels, all powers of heaven, Cherubim and seraphim, sing endless praise: Holy, Holy, Holy Lord, God of power and might, Heaven and earth are full of Your glory. AMEN. (Te Deum).

Psalm 40 (part 2)

"To Do Your Will"

Much has been written about the Messianic Psalms. Some argue that no psalms are Messianic because they all refer to David or some other psalmist. Others argue that every psalm is Messianic because of Luke 24:44. There certainly are more Messianic Psalms than those directly quoted in the NT. This is because of the pervasive role of the Davidic Covenant in the Psalms (2 Sam. 7:10–14), and because of the numerous references to the ideal King and Anointed One (Ps. 2:2). Perhaps it is best to refer to *explicit* Messianic Psalms like the one here, and *implicit* Messianic Psalms that anticipate that ideal Messianic King that David typifies (Psalm 24, e.g.).

Sailhamer comments on the Messianic nature of this psalm: "Curiously, Psalm 39 concludes on a note of despair, but it is followed in Psalm 40 with an account of God's answer to David's prayer and the assurance of God's promise to send a deliverer. Psalm 40:1–5 points to a deliverance promised for the future (v. 5). That leads David to recall what was written "in the scroll of the book" (the Pentateuch) about God's promised deliverer, the Messiah. It was there that Israel was taught that God did not desire 'sacrifice and offering' but rather service, exemplified by the piercing of the ear (Ex. 21:6). This type of obedience ultimately comes from the heart (Deut. 30:6)" (*NIV Compact Bible Commentary*).

Verses 6–8 are explicitly cited in Hebrews 10:5–7. Consistent with His portrayal throughout Hebrews, Jesus is described there as *The Ultimate Sacrifice*.

Jesus the Messiah came to hear God's will (the "open ear" in Isa. 50:4–6) and to do God's will (the "prepared body"). His body was prepared in Mary's womb by the Holy Spirit (Luke 1:26–38; Isa. 7:14). Jesus delighted to do the Father's will because the Word was in His heart (John 4:34; 8:29). If you delight in God's Word, you will delight in God's will (Ps. 1:1–3). Jesus the Messiah is the sacrifice for sins that God has appointed, and in His death, He fulfilled the Old Testament sacrifices. His one sacrifice has settled the sin question once and for all.

The psalm has illumined the cross as the true sacrifice, the self-offering which by the Father's will brings the salvation of many. In all the sufferings which still beset the people of God, the good news of that royal sacrifice provides the strength to pray and to hope, and in the end to rejoice in the LORD the deliverer.

> *O Messiah Jesus, who took for me the way of sacrifice, deliver me from my innumerable offences. Graft Your teaching within my heart, that I may live to rejoice in You, and ever declare the good news of Your salvation. AMEN.*

Psalm 41

When You're Down

This Psalm of Reorientation describes the change that took place in the psalmist that prompted the beatitude with which it opens. If the greater part of this psalm is somber, the thankfulness at the end shows that the ordeal is already over. The middle verses relive its intensity to bring out the true value of the compassion praised in the prologue and the vindication celebrated in the epilogue. Only the body of the psalm can reveal how heartfelt is the beatitude with which it opens (Kidner).

To the choirmaster. A Psalm of David.

41:1 Blessed is the one who considers the poor! In the day of trouble the Lord delivers him;
2 the Lord protects him and keeps him alive; he is called blessed in the land; you do not give him up to the will of his enemies.
3 The Lord sustains him on his sickbed; in his illness you restore him to full health.
4 As for me, I said, "O Lord, be gracious to me; heal me, for I have sinned against you!"
5 My enemies say of me in malice, "When will he die, and his name perish?"
6 And when one comes to see me, he utters empty words, while his heart gathers iniquity; when he goes out, he tells it abroad.
7 All who hate me whisper together about me; they imagine the worst for me.
8 They say, "A deadly thing is poured out on him; he will not rise again from where he lies."
9 Even my close friend in whom I trusted, who ate my bread, has lifted his heel against me.
10 But you, O Lord, be gracious to me, and raise me up, that I may repay them!
11 By this I know that you delight in me: my enemy will not shout in triumph over me.
12 But you have upheld me because of my integrity, and set me in your presence forever.
13 Blessed be the Lord, the God of Israel, from everlasting to everlasting! Amen and Amen.

(Psalm 41, ESV)

Notice where David "looked" in this psalm:

As he lay sick, he **looked back** (vv. 1–4) and recalled that he had been merciful to others and had helped the poor. This encouraged him, for he knew that God would help him (Deut. 15:7–11). God is merciful to those who show mercy to others (Matt. 5:7). When you are in pain, it is good to have a clear conscience to encourage you.

Then he **looked around** (vv. 5–8) and saw that his enemies were gossiping about him and wishing he were dead. Even his close friend turned against him. Greater than the pain of sickness is the pain of having a treacherous "friend." If you think it is hard for you to experience such treatment, think of Jesus who was betrayed by a companion. How appropriately did the Son of David use the words of verse 9 to describe His own betrayal by Judas (John 13:18).

Finally, **he looked up** (vv. 10–12) and that solved his problems. No matter what others might say, God was well pleased with David, and that was all that mattered. David's enemies can spread their gossip, but his God will raise him up, hold him up, and brighten him up with the light of His presence (v. 12). "Sometimes, how you feel depends on where you look" (Wiersbe).

The fervent doxology of verse 13 not only ends the psalm, but also brings the first of the Five "Books" in the Psalms (1–41) to a stirring conclusion. Each of the five books ends with an outburst of praise, clinched by a double Amen (here and at Ps. 72:19 and 89:52), an Amen and Hallelujah (Ps. 106:48) and a double Hallelujah (Ps. 150:6). Psalm 150 is really a whole psalm of doxology (Kidner).

> *Hallelujah! Baruk HaShem! Praise the Lord! Blessed be the Name. (Yes, that is the prayer for today. Pray it again!)*

Psalms 42 & 43

Drought and Deliverance

The first book I read by Martyn Lloyd-Jones was *Spiritual Depression: Its Causes and Cure*, which was based on Psalms 42 and 43. It was from ML-J and from the psalmist that I learned how to talk to myself when despondent! We will take these two psalms together, since they share so many common expressions. Therefore, read them together.

To the choirmaster. A Maskil of the Sons of Korah.

42:1 As a deer pants for flowing streams, so pants my soul for you, O God.
2 My soul thirsts for God, for the living God. When shall I come and appear before God?
3 My tears have been my food day and night, while they say to me all the day long, "Where is your God?"
4 These things I remember, as I pour out my soul: how I would go with the throng and lead them in procession to the house of God with glad shouts and songs of praise, a multitude keeping festival.
5 Why are you cast down, O my soul, and why are you in turmoil within me? Hope in God; for I shall again praise him, my salvation
6 and my God. My soul is cast down within me; therefore I remember you from the land of Jordan and of Hermon, from Mount Mizar.
7 Deep calls to deep at the roar of your waterfalls; all your breakers and your waves have gone over me.
8 By day the LORD commands his steadfast love, and at night his song is with me, a prayer to the God of my life.
9 I say to God, my rock: "Why have you forgotten me? Why do I go mourning because of the oppression of the enemy?"
10 As with a deadly wound in my bones, my adversaries taunt me, while they say to me all the day long, "Where is your God?"
11 Why are you cast down, O my soul, and why are you in turmoil within me? Hope in God; for I shall again praise him, my salvation and my God.

(Psalm 42, ESV)

> ^{43:1} Vindicate me, O God, and defend my cause against an ungodly people, from the deceitful and unjust man deliver me!
> ² For you are the God in whom I take refuge; why have you rejected me? Why do I go about mourning because of the oppression of the enemy?
> ³ Send out your light and your truth; let them lead me; let them bring me to your holy hill and to your dwelling!
> ⁴ Then I will go to the altar of God, to God my exceeding joy, and I will praise you with the lyre, O God, my God.
> ⁵ Why are you cast down, O my soul, and why are you in turmoil within me? Hope in God; for I shall again praise him, my salvation and my God.
>
> (Psalm 43, ESV)

The refrain "Why are you cast down, O my soul?" ties these two psalms together (Ps. 42:5, 11; 43:5). In what ways did the writer describe his depression? God seemed far from him in his hour of need (Ps. 42:1–3). He felt like a thirsty deer in the desert, searching for water. But the Lord is never far away; He is near even when you do not recognize Him (Isa. 41:10, Heb. 13:5, Ps. 46:7).

The writer's depression was also aggravated because he looked back at "the good old days" (Ps. 42:4–6). He longed to return to Jerusalem and minister in the temple. Remember that this psalm came from the Levite singers, the Sons of Korah. It is the lament of a temple singer sojourning in the north near the sources of the Jordan (Ps. 42:6–7) who longs to be back at God's house. Could 2 Kings 14:14 be the context? This exile, however, turns his longing into resolute faith and hope in God himself. Sometimes retirement or a change of residence will make people depressed. The older we get, the less we enjoy change.

The discouraging talk of others was another contributing factor (Ps. 42:3, 9, 10). "Has God forgotten you? Where is your God?" The answer is in Psalm 115: "Why should the nations say, 'Where is their God?' Our God is in the heavens. He does all that he pleases." Listen to God and not to the foolish talk of others.

What should you do when depression starts to control you? First, *talk to yourself*, but ask the right questions! (Ps. 42:2, 5, 9, 11). Second, *"Hope in God"* (Ps. 42:5, 11; Ps. 43:5). Look at the future and not at the past. If you feel drowned by circumstances, keep in mind that they are His waves and billows (Ps. 42:7), and He knows what is best for you. Stop feeding on your feelings (Ps. 42:3) and start feeding on His Word (Ps. 43:3).

Dr. Martyn Lloyd-Jones wrote an entire book expounding these psalms titled, *Spiritual Depression: Its Causes and Cure.*

> *Inflame my heart with love to You, O Christ my God, that loving You with all my heart, soul, mind and strength, and my neighbor as myself, I may glorify You in all things, through Christ my Lord I pray.*
> *AMEN.*

Psalms 42 & 43 (part 2)

Drought and Deliverance

Yesterday we saw that Psalms 42 and 43 really go together. They share the same expressions and theme—Depression and Its "Cure." Today we add a few technical points and then some practical thoughts on these precious and greatly needed psalms.

These two psalms initiate Book Two of the Psalter Collection which consists of Psalms 42–72. In Book Two, psalms are brought together from various sources: the Sons of Korah, who were temple musicians (Psalms 42–49); Asaph, the founder of another temple group (Psalm 50); David (Psalms 51–65, 68–70); and Solomon (Psalm 72). Like the psalm titles, we are not sure exactly when these divisions were made, but they appear in the oldest manuscripts of psalms so the divisions must be quite ancient. Some equate the five divisions to the Books of the Pentateuch, although it is difficult to see any exact parallels between the contents of the five collections of "books." The number probably reflects an ancient Jewish tendency to gather things into fives because of the Torah's five books (Kidner).

These two psalms were contributed by the Sons of Korah (titles of Psalms 42–49). Their praising the Lord in 2 Chron. 20:19 may be the basis for their mention in the Psalms as a part of Temple psalmody. They were descendants of the Levite Korah who revolted against God's appointed leaders and whose gruesome punishment is vividly described in Numbers 16. How encouraging to know that his descendants learned from the negative example of their ancestor and did not follow in his steps.

With that background, let's look at a simple homiletical outline of the two psalms, with the theme of *despair* binding them together. We could use the term "depression" as well, but since that word has a lot of modern baggage attached to it, let's use the similar word *despair*. Re-read the psalms with these main points in mind:

> **The drought of despair** (Ps. 42:1–5)
> **The depths of despair** (Ps. 42:6–11)
> **The deliverance from despair** (Ps. 43:1–5)

The lament of these psalms is echoed in the words of Jesus in the shadow of death (Mark 14:34; John 12:27). His way to the altar of sacrifice was in the end to be shown as the supreme way of light and truth and gladness. "This prayer for the Lord's light and truth is to direct them to the holy mountain and the music of joy and thanksgiving and to lead them up the way from the waters of death to the beauty of God's face" (Eaton).

And finally, an observation from Oswald Chambers. "When a man gets to despair he knows that all his thinking will never get him out. He will only get out by the sheer creative effort of God. Consequently he is in the right attitude to receive from God that which he cannot gain for himself" (Cited by Wiersbe).

God of my life, my rock and my salvation, when I feel forsaken and rejected and my soul is bowed down, send forth Your light and Your truth to lead me to Your holy dwelling. There may I see the beauty of Your face, and at Your altar may I give thanks for Your salvation.
AMEN.

Psalm 44

A National Lament

With this next psalm attributed to the Sons of Korah, we meet for the first time a **national lament** in a time of unequaled disaster. It was prompted by the fact that the nation was experiencing defeats which they did not understand. This psalm is perhaps the clearest example of a search for some other cause of national disaster than that of guilt and punishment. The Babylonian Captivity would not be so understood by an OT prophet (2 Kings 17:7–14). It comes within sight of an answer at the point of its greatest perplexity: "Yet for your sake we are killed ..." (v. 22), and sees God's people as caught up in a war that is more than local: the struggle of "the kings of the earth ... against the LORD and his Anointed" (Ps. 2:2). Paul will see the suffering church foreshadowed here, and predict not its defeat but its victory (Rom. 8:36–37) (Kidner).

Consider the following approach to its contemporary relevance as you read Psalm 44.

To the choirmaster. A Maskil of the Sons of Korah.

44:1 O God, we have heard with our ears, our fathers have told us, what deeds you performed in their days, in the days of old:

2 you with your own hand drove out the nations, but them you planted; you afflicted the peoples, but them you set free;

3 for not by their own sword did they win the land, nor did their own arm save them, but your right hand and your arm, and the light of your face, for you delighted in them.

4 You are my King, O God; ordain salvation for Jacob!

5 Through you we push down our foes; through your name we tread down those who rise up against us.

6 For not in my bow do I trust, nor can my sword save me.

7 But you have saved us from our foes and have put to shame those who hate us.

8 In God we have boasted continually, and we will give thanks to your name forever. Selah

PSALM 44

9 But you have rejected us and disgraced us and have not gone out with our armies.
10 You have made us turn back from the foe, and those who hate us have gotten spoil.
11 You have made us like sheep for slaughter and have scattered us among the nations.
12 You have sold your people for a trifle, demanding no high price for them.
13 You have made us the taunt of our neighbors, the derision and scorn of those around us.
14 You have made us a byword among the nations, a laughingstock among the peoples.
15 All day long my disgrace is before me, and shame has covered my face
16 at the sound of the taunter and reviler, at the sight of the enemy and the avenger.
17 All this has come upon us, though we have not forgotten you, and we have not been false to your covenant.
18 Our heart has not turned back, nor have our steps departed from your way;
19 yet you have broken us in the place of jackals and covered us with the shadow of death.
20 If we had forgotten the name of our God or spread out our hands to a foreign god,
21 would not God discover this? For he knows the secrets of the heart.
22 Yet for your sake we are killed all the day long; we are regarded as sheep to be slaughtered.
23 Awake! Why are you sleeping, O Lord? Rouse yourself! Do not reject us forever!
24 Why do you hide your face? Why do you forget our affliction and oppression?
25 For our soul is bowed down to the dust; our belly clings to the ground.
26 Rise up; come to our help! Redeem us for the sake of your steadfast love!

(Psalm 44, ESV)

It seemed that God had forsaken His people and was actually helping the enemy (vv. 9–16). **What do you do when it looks like God is on the side of the enemy?**

You must remember what God did in the past (vv. 1–3). This does not mean living in the past but learning from the past. Your situation may be painful, but God has not changed. He can still work wonders and glorify His name.

You should continue to trust Him in the present (vv. 4–8). If you trust your own resources, you will fail. Sometimes God may allow defeat just to remind you that you must trust Him and Him alone.

You then will remain faithful to Him in the future (vv. 17–26), come what may. Remember Satan's lie about Job (Job 1:6–12)? Are you faithful to God only because He does good things for you? God tests your faith to see if it is sincere (1 Pet. 1:6–9). Trust Him even though you may not fully understand what He is doing (Job 13:15).

Cranmer included the first and last verses of this psalm in the *Daily Litany* of the *Book of Common Prayer*. Pray it with me in closing.

> *O God, we have heard with our ears, and our fathers have declared unto us the noble works that You did in their days, and in old time before them. O Lord, arise, help us, and deliver us for Your honor. AMEN.*

Psalm 45

The King in His Beauty

The closing cry of the previous psalm, "Redeem us because of your steadfast love," finds its answer in this glorious Psalm of the Messianic King. As you read it, watch for the change of address to the King in verses 2–9; to the Queen Bride in verses 10–15; and back to the King again in verses 16–17.

Written for a royal wedding, this psalm is truly messianic (vv. 6–7; Heb. 1:8–9) and shows us Jesus in His role as the Royal Bridegroom.

To the choirmaster: according to Lilies. A Maskil of the Sons of Korah; a love song.

45:1 My heart overflows with a pleasing theme; I address my verses to the king; my tongue is like the pen of a ready scribe.

2 You are the most handsome of the sons of men; grace is poured upon your lips; therefore God has blessed you forever.

3 Gird your sword on your thigh, O mighty one, in your splendor and majesty!

4 In your majesty ride out victoriously for the cause of truth and meekness and righteousness; let your right hand teach you awesome deeds!

5 Your arrows are sharp in the heart of the king's enemies; the peoples fall under you.

6 Your throne, O God, is forever and ever. The scepter of your kingdom is a scepter of uprightness;

7 you have loved righteousness and hated wickedness. Therefore God, your God, has anointed you with the oil of gladness beyond your companions;

8 your robes are all fragrant with myrrh and aloes and cassia. From ivory palaces stringed instruments make you glad;

9 daughters of kings are among your ladies of honor; at your right hand stands the queen in gold of Ophir.

10 Hear, O daughter, and consider, and incline your ear: forget your people and your father's house,

11 and the king will desire your beauty. Since he is your lord, bow to him.

12 The people of Tyre will seek your favor with gifts, the richest of the people.

13 All glorious is the princess in her chamber, with robes interwoven with gold.

14 In many-colored robes she is led to

> the king, with her virgin companions following behind her.
> 15 With joy and gladness they are led along as they enter the palace of the king.
> 16 In place of your fathers shall be your sons; you will make them princes in all the earth.
> 17 I will cause your name to be remembered in all generations; therefore nations will praise you forever and ever.
> (Psalm 45, ESV)

The beauty of our King (vv. 1–2). When He was here on earth, Jesus had no special beauty that would attract people (Isa. 53:2). It is the beauty of His character, His words, and His works that makes us love Him even though we have not seen Him with our eyes—yet! (1 Pet. 1:8).

The battles of our King (vv. 3–5). While literally a humble Galilean, He was also spiritually a warrior who defeated Satan (Matt. 12:25–29; Col. 2:15). He conquers today through His people as we yield to Him and practice truth, humility, and righteousness (Rom. 8:37–39). One day He will come to conquer all the kingdoms of the world (Rev. 11:15, 19:11–21).

The bounties of our King (vv. 6–9). He is addressed as Deity and this is not lost on the author to the Hebrews (Heb. 1:8–9). That God had anointed him should remove any doubts that this is the King Messiah ("anointed one"). Who else has an eternal throne, a righteous scepter, gladness, and the fragrance of grace and glory? If you know the King, you share all His bounties.

The bride for our King (vv. 10–15). This is a picture of the church (Eph. 5:25), all those who have been saved through faith in Christ. The Bridegroom is ready (v. 8); the attendants are ready (v. 9); and the bride is brought to the King with rejoicing. What a wedding that will be (Rev. 19:1–10)! Are you eagerly looking forward to being present?

The blessings from our King (vv. 16–17). The name of the Messianic King will be remembered forever and the Gentiles will praise Him forever. This is the devotion that King Jesus will receive from Jews and Gentiles as He is praised forever by His followers. The joyful description is a foretaste of God's bringing "many sons to glory" (Heb. 2:10), who will "reign on the earth" (Rev. 6:10) with their Master, whose praise will be as endless as this benediction makes it. Only the language of the Apocalypse can adequately describe the fulfillment of these promises and blessings to the redeemed (Rev. 5:9–10; 7:13–17; 19:6–8; 21:22–25).

Truly "the testimony of Jesus is the spirit of prophecy" (Rev. 19:10). The warm poetry of this psalm has led the soul of many an individual toward God's eternal throne by way of love for this Savior. Adoring him and forsaking all others, the soul finds in Him the full blessedness of God's eternal kingdom.

> *Eternal Father, lead me into the love of my King Jesus. May my heart be ever stirred by this love and may I live for the cause of faithfulness, humility and righteousness. AMEN*

City of the King

The portrayal of the coming of the ideal Messianic King in Ps. 45 is followed by a description of the King's city, Jerusalem. Luther's battle-hymn of the Reformation, "A Mighty Fortress," took its starting-point from this powerful ode to Zion.

> *To the choirmaster. Of the Sons of Korah. According to Alamoth. A Song.*
>
> 46:1 God is our refuge and strength, a very present help in trouble.
> 2 Therefore we will not fear though the earth gives way, though the mountains be moved into the heart of the sea,
> 3 though its waters roar and foam, though the mountains tremble at its swelling.   Selah
> 4 There is a river whose streams make glad the city of God, the holy habitation of the Most High.
> 5 God is in the midst of her; she shall not be moved; God will help her when morning dawns.
> 6 The nations rage, the kingdoms totter; he utters his voice, the earth melts.
> 7 The LORD of hosts is with us; the God of Jacob is our fortress.   Selah
> 8 Come, behold the works of the LORD, how he has brought desolations on the earth.
> 9 He makes wars cease to the end of the earth; he breaks the bow and shatters the spear; he burns the chariots with fire.
> 10 "Be still, and know that I am God. I will be exalted among the nations, I will be exalted in the earth!"
> 11 The LORD of hosts is with us; the God of Jacob is our fortress.   Selah
>
> (Psalm 46, ESV)

The psalm proclaims the sovereignty of God in one sphere after another: his power over nature (vv. 1–3); over the attackers of his city (vv. 4–7); and over the whole warring world (vv. 8–11). Its tone suggests that it was composed at a time of crisis, but as the crisis is left unidentified, the psalm ranges far beyond any local situation, and there is little to be gained by historical speculation. Not knowing these specific circumstances, as is often the case in the Psalms, makes it all the more applicable to our own personal battles (Kidner).

When things are changing and threatening around you, **focus your attention on God**. He is with you (**His presence**); He is a refuge (**His protection**); He helps you (**His power**). Your world may be shaken with convulsions (vv. 2–3), but He has a river that gives you peace (v. 4). You may be in the midst of battles, but He will end the war victoriously (v. 8–9).

"Be still" (v. 10) means "take your hands off and relax." God knows what He is doing, and His timing is perfect (v. 5). When it is all over, He will be exalted (v. 10), and you will be blessed. The end is stated in terms not of man's hopes but of God's glory. His firm intention that "I will be exalted" is enough to arouse both the resentment of the proud and the resolve and renewed confidence of the humble. The refrain comes back with the added force that such a God is "with us" and one so exalted is "our fortress" (v. 11).

When you are nervous and fidgety, wanting to interfere with God's plans for your life, remember these three admonitions: **"Be still!" (v. 10); "Stand still!" (Exod. 14:13); and "Sit still!" (Ruth 3:18).**

This psalm was such a favorite of Martin Luther's that whenever his colleague Philip Melanchthon told him some sad news, he used to say, "Come, come, let us sing the 46th Psalm." And when he had sung it, his heart was quiet.

> *O God, my refuge and strength, grant that I may not be afraid though storms rage around me. Flood into my heart Your precious gift of peace, and lighten my darkness, so that I may know that You are with me always. AMEN.*

Psalm 47

I'm the King of the World!

In the film, *Titanic*, the Leonardo DiCaprio character shouts, "I'm the king of the world," as he stands on the bow of the soon-to-be-sunk ocean liner. When the director, James Cameron, received his Oscar, he proudly shouted the same words from the stage. There is a great difference between expressing a joyous feeling and proclaiming an arrogant boast! This psalm sets the record straight. *Yahweh* is the true King of the World—and He has no credible rivals.

The psalm continues the theme of the Messianic King—in His beauty (Psalm 45), in His city (Psalm 46) and now in His world.

> *To the choirmaster. A Psalm of the Sons of Korah.*
> 47:1 Clap your hands, all peoples! Shout to God with loud songs of joy!
> 2 For the LORD, the Most High, is to be feared, a great king over all the earth.
> 3 He subdued peoples under us, and nations under our feet.
> 4 He chose our heritage for us, the pride of Jacob whom he loves.   Selah
> 5 God has gone up with a shout, the LORD with the sound of a trumpet.
> 6 Sing praises to God, sing praises! Sing praises to our King, sing praises!
> 7 For God is the King of all the earth; sing praises with a psalm!
> 8 God reigns over the nations; God sits on his holy throne.
> 9 The princes of the peoples gather as the people of the God of Abraham. For the shields of the earth belong to God; he is highly exalted!
>
> (Psalm 47, ESV)

This psalm may challenge your worship style, for it describes a praise celebration that involves clapping, shouting, and loud singing. The cause of this excitement is the greatness of our Messianic King. We should get excited about these three things:

His great victory (vv. 1–4). We do not know what military victory the psalmist was celebrating, but as believers today, we walk in Christ's spiritual victory (2 Cor. 2:14). Like Joshua, we submit to our Captain and trust Him to win the battle (Josh. 5:13–15).

That is something to shout about!

His great throne (vv. 5–7). What a picture of the ascension of our Lord, returning to heaven and sitting at the right hand of God! Satan may be the god of this age, but Jesus is King of all the earth.

That is something to shout about!

His great reign (vv. 8–9). Now the real end in view comes into sight. The innumerable princes and peoples from all over the world are to become one people; and they will no longer be outsiders but within the covenant, which is implied in their being called the people of the God of Abraham. It is the abundant fulfillment of the promise of Genesis 12:3, and it anticipates what Paul expounds about the inclusion of the Gentiles as Abraham's spiritual sons (Rom. 4:11; Gal. 3:7–9). His kingdom is a spiritual kingdom today, but in a future day, the Messianic King will reign on earth, and His people will also reign with Him (Rev. 1:5–6; 5:9–10; 11:15–18).

Now that is something to shout about!

> "In Christian use the psalm is especially appointed for Ascension Day, and there it enriches the understanding of Christ's ascending to the Father" (Eaton).

> *O Lord Most High, in the ascension of Jesus Christ You have given me assurance of the triumph of Your kingdom. I now pray for You to put beneath His feet all that causes strife and cruelty, so that all nations may join together in gladness under Your everlasting reign. AMEN.*

Psalm 48

Zion, City of God

Psalm 48 has much in common with Psalm 46, with their common atmosphere of elation after a great deliverance. Whatever the specific occasion that inspired this psalm, we are conscious of a bigger setting than the hills of Jerusalem. *Zion* is more than a local capital. The struggle here concerns the whole earth and all of time. To Christian believers, Jerusalem and Mount Zion speak of "the Jerusalem above" (Gal. 4:26) and the heavenly Zion (Heb. 12:18–24) where their citizenship is recorded (Phil. 3:20).

A Song. A Psalm of the Sons of Korah.

48:1 Great is the LORD and greatly to be praised in the city of our God! His holy mountain,
2 beautiful in elevation, is the joy of all the earth, Mount Zion, in the far north, the city of the great King.
3 Within her citadels God has made himself known as a fortress.
4 For behold, the kings assembled; they came on together.
5 As soon as they saw it, they were astounded; they were in panic; they took to flight.
6 Trembling took hold of them there, anguish as of a woman in labor.
7 By the east wind you shattered the ships of Tarshish.
8 As we have heard, so have we seen in the city of the LORD of hosts, in the city of our God, which God will establish forever.   *Selah*
9 We have thought on your steadfast love, O God, in the midst of your temple.
10 As your name, O God, so your praise reaches to the ends of the earth. Your right hand is filled with righteousness.
11 Let Mount Zion be glad! Let the daughters of Judah rejoice because of your judgments!
12 Walk about Zion, go around her, number her towers,
13 consider well her ramparts, go through her citadels, that you may tell the next generation
14 that this is God, our God forever and ever. He will guide us forever.

(Psalm 48, ESV)

Behold this City (vv. 1–8). It is the city of God, the Holy City, beautiful and joyful. But to the enemy who does not know the Lord, it is an awesome place that speaks of judgment. Ponder your heavenly destiny so that you may live a happier and holier life.

Rejoice in this City (vv. 9–11). It is a place of God's loving-kindness and righteousness, where His name is praised and His people rejoice. You are not in the heavenly city yet, but you can still enjoy "the powers of the age to come" (Heb. 6:5). "Little faith will take your soul to heaven," said Charles Spurgeon, "but great faith will bring heaven to your soul."

Tell about this City (vv. 12–14). Tell others what God has prepared for His people and invite them to become citizens of Zion by faith in Christ (Luke 10:20). To know the God of glory is to know a faithful Guide who will care for you in life and take you to Mount Zion when you die.

God's love can still be celebrated with joy, and so there can be given the assurance of His defeat of the assaults of evil, and His leading of His world from delusion to truth, from darkness to light, and from death to life.

> "If you read history you will find that the Christians who did most for the present world were precisely those who thought most of the next. It is since Christians have largely ceased to think of the other world that they have become so ineffective in this one" (C. S. Lewis).

Lord God, Your Son my Savior Jesus Christ triumphed over death and prepared for me a place in the new Jerusalem. Grant that I, who have this day given thanks for His resurrection, may praise You in the City of which He is the light, and where He lives and reigns for ever and ever. AMEN. (Compline Prayer for Sunday)

Psalm 49

Ransomed From Sheol

This psalm reads like a passage from Ecclesiastes or Job as it searches and questions the meaning of human existence. In Ecclesiastes, the Preacher leads us through a series of "**goads**" that prod us on to keep reading until he sets one of his "**nails**" that points to the real goal of life: Fear God (Ecc. 12:11–13). In a similar way, one of the sons of Korah goads us with his words until Psalm 49:15 nails the problem—we shall be ransomed from Sheol to see God.

Whether you are rich or poor, this psalm is for you (v. 2) because it deals with two important subjects: death and money. "Do not boast in your wealth or trust in your wealth," wrote the psalmist, and he explained why.

To the choirmaster. A Psalm of the Sons of Korah.

49:1 Hear this, all peoples! Give ear, all inhabitants of the world,
2 both low and high, rich and poor together!
3 My mouth shall speak wisdom; the meditation of my heart shall be understanding.
4 I will incline my ear to a proverb; I will solve my riddle to the music of the lyre.
5 Why should I fear in times of trouble, when the iniquity of those who cheat me surrounds me,
6 those who trust in their wealth and boast of the abundance of their riches?
7 Truly no man can ransom another, or give to God the price of his life,
8 for the ransom of their life is costly and can never suffice,
9 that he should live on forever and never see the pit.
10 For he sees that even the wise die; the fool and the stupid alike must perish and leave their wealth to others.
11 Their graves are their homes forever, their dwelling places to all generations, though they called lands by their own names.
12 Man in his pomp will not remain; he is like the beasts that perish.
13 This is the path of those who have foolish confidence; yet after them people approve of their boasts. Selah
14 Like sheep they are appointed for Sheol; death shall be their shepherd,

and the upright shall rule over them in the morning. Their form shall be consumed in Sheol, with no place to dwell.
15 But God will ransom my soul from the power of Sheol, for he will receive me. Selah
16 Be not afraid when a man becomes rich, when the glory of his house increases.
17 For when he dies he will carry nothing away; his glory will not go down after him.
18 For though, while he lives, he counts himself blessed—and though you get praise when you do well for yourself—
19 his soul will go to the generation of his fathers, who will never again see light
20 Man in his pomp yet without understanding is like the beasts that perish.

(Psalm 49, ESV)

Warrren Wiersbe attempts to outline the message of this sometimes difficult psalm. I have adapted some of his ideas.

Your wealth cannot prevent death (vv. 5–9). When Queen Elizabeth I was dying, she said, "All my possessions for one moment of time." Although money can buy medicine and professional help, it cannot buy God off when the death angel comes to claim you.

Your wealth cannot go with you (vv. 10–15). The dead bodies of both men and beasts turn to dust in the grave, and the rich are not exempt from this end. When a believer dies, the spirit goes to be with the Lord (2 Cor. 5:1–8), but you cannot take your wealth with you (v. 17). However, you can send it ahead as you share it with others in the name of the Lord (Matt. 6:19–34).

Your wealth cannot buy permanent fame (vv. 16–20). Men praise the rich while they live, honor them when they die, and then forget them. The rich man can build himself a monument, but he cannot make people remember him.

Verse 15 is that "nail" that fixes the hope of the psalmist in the midst of his "goading" comments. It reveals the believer's assurance of future resurrection (1 Thess. 4:13–16). That is what conquers death and makes life worth living (1 Cor. 15:58; 1 Pet. 1:3).

The New Testament resumes this warning against trust in riches (Mark 10:23; Luke 12:16ff), and proclaims the gospel of a ransom that is beyond human means (Mark 10:45; 1 Tim. 2:6).

NOTE: It seems unlikely in this context that Ps. 49:15 means only that God will save him from untimely death. Were this the meaning, then the ultimate fate of the psalmist would be no different from that of those who trust in their riches. The psalmist expects that after he dies (goes to *Sheol*) God will take him from there into His presence. Bodily resurrection is consistent also with Ps. 16:9–11 and Ps. 17:15. Kidner calls this verse "one of the mountaintops of Old Testament hope."

> *Richly stir me, Lord, by the music of Your Word, that through all the darkness of death I may recognize that my hope is in You alone, and know that You have ransomed my soul from the grave, to dwell with You forever. AMEN.*

Psalm 50

Here Comes the Judge

This powerful psalm attributed to Asaph (see Psalm 73) is a theophany, God appearing in fire and tempest on mount Zion to summon the entire world to the bar of His judgment. All eyes are on Him, but His eyes are on Israel. The whole psalm is addressed to God's people, speaking first to the unthinking religious, and then to the hardened and the hypocritical, so as to bring them a sharp dose of reality. It is the message which the prophets and Jesus later put to a people who had forgotten they were dealing with the living God (Kidner).

A Psalm of Asaph.

50:1 The Mighty One, God the LORD, speaks and summons the earth from the rising of the sun to its setting.

2 Out of Zion, the perfection of beauty, God shines forth.

3 Our God comes; he does not keep silence; before him is a devouring fire, around him a mighty tempest.

4 He calls to the heavens above and to the earth, that he may judge his people:

5 "Gather to me my faithful ones, who made a covenant with me by sacrifice!"

6 The heavens declare his righteousness, for God himself is judge!   *Selah*

7 "Hear, O my people, and I will speak; O Israel, I will testify against you. I am God, your God.

8 Not for your sacrifices do I rebuke you; your burnt offerings are continually before me.

9 I will not accept a bull from your house or goats from your folds.

10 For every beast of the forest is mine, the cattle on a thousand hills.

11 I know all the birds of the hills, and all that moves in the field is mine.

12 "If I were hungry, I would not tell you, for the world and its fullness are mine.

13 Do I eat the flesh of bulls or drink the blood of goats?

14 Offer to God a sacrifice of thanksgiving, and perform your vows to the Most High,

15 and call upon me in the day of trouble; I will deliver you, and you shall glorify me."

16 But to the wicked God says: "What right have you to recite my statutes or take my covenant on your lips?

17 For you hate discipline, and you cast

my words behind you.
18 If you see a thief, you are pleased with him, and you keep company with adulterers.
19 "You give your mouth free rein for evil, and your tongue frames deceit.
20 You sit and speak against your brother; you slander your own mother's son.
21 These things you have done, and I have been silent; you thought that I was one like yourself. But now I rebuke you and lay the charge before you.
22 "Mark this, then, you who forget God, lest I tear you apart, and there be none to deliver!
23 The one who offers thanksgiving as his sacrifice glorifies me; to one who orders his way rightly I will show the salvation of God!"

(Psalm 50, ESV)

While the psalm is a courtroom scene, all analogies with earth fall short because in this court God is the judge, the witness and the jury. He brings an indictment against two kinds of "religious sinners."

Insincere worshipers (vv. 1–15). He calls the court to order not with the rap of a gavel but with the revelation of His glory (vv. 1–3). He indicts His people who offer sacrifices insincerely—their worship is just empty routine—and hope to "earn" God's blessing. God does not need the things we give Him (Acts 17:24–25), but we need to give Him spiritual sacrifices of thanksgiving, praise, and obedience (vv. 14–15, 23).

Hypocritical worshipers (vv. 16–22). Here the issue is not sacrifices but the covenant they made with God. They profess one thing and practice another (Tit. 1:16) and they are guilty of theft, adultery, deceit, and slander. They thought that God's silence meant escape from punishment, but they were wrong (Ecc. 8:11). Judgment begins with God's people, not with the lost world (1 Pet. 4:17). We must heed the warning of verse 22 ("Mark this, then, you who forget God ... there is none to deliver"), and accept the admonition of verse 23 ("The one who offers thanksgiving glorifies me ... and to him I will show salvation"). The expression, "he who sacrifices a thanksgiving" (lit.), anticipates an offering of pure praise, such as that of Hosea 14:2 and Heb. 13:15. The salvation is from Him and we are to receive it with delighted thanks.

Psalm 50

"To worship is to quicken the conscience by the **holiness** of God, to feed the mind with the **truth** of God, to purge the imagination by the **beauty** of God, to open the heart to the **love** of God, to devote the will to the **purpose** of God." William Temple

> *Most mighty God, grant that in worship I may see the bright light of Your presence and hear the searching words of Your voice. Grant also that I may learn both in worship and in life to truly honor You and to keep the way of Your commandments. This I pray through Him who is Your Light, Your Word and Your Way, my Savior Jesus Christ. AMEN.*

Psalm 51

Have Mercy

We have been sharing the text of each psalm from the English Standard Version. Today we begin to cite a newer version that I like for both its accuracy and readability—the Holman Christian Standard Bible.

Psalm 51 can be read **historically**, against the background in 2 Samuel 11 and 12. It can be read **theologically** to learn its message about true repentance. It can be read **comparatively**, as one of the seven penitential psalms (Psalms 6, 32, 38, 51, 102, 130, 143). But I want us to read it **personally** so as to experience its power. Only if we truly *pray this psalm*, will we internalize its words and David's forgiveness will become ours. **Pray it with me with an open Bible before you or with the following text.**

For the choir director. A Davidic psalm, when Nathan the prophet came to him after he had gone to Bathsheba.

51:1 Be gracious to me, God, according to Your faithful love; according to Your abundant compassion, blot out my rebellion.
2 Wash away my guilt, and cleanse me from my sin.
3 For I am conscious of my rebellion, and my sin is always before me.
4 Against You—You alone—I have sinned and done this evil in Your sight. So You are right when You pass sentence; You are blameless when You judge.
5 Indeed, I was guilty when I was born; I was sinful when my mother conceived me.
6 Surely You desire integrity in the inner self, and You teach me wisdom deep within.
7 Purify me with hyssop, and I will be clean; wash me, and I will be whiter than snow.
8 Let me hear joy and gladness; let the bones You have crushed rejoice.
9 Turn Your face away from my sins and blot out all my guilt.
10 God, create a clean heart for me and renew a steadfast spirit within me.
11 Do not banish me from Your presence or take Your Holy Spirit from me.

12 Restore the joy of Your salvation to me, and give me a willing spirit.
13 Then I will teach the rebellious Your ways, and sinners will return to You.
14 Save me from the guilt of bloodshed, God, the God of my salvation, and my tongue will sing of Your righteousness.
15 Lord, open my lips, and my mouth will declare Your praise.
16 You do not want a sacrifice, or I would give it; You are not pleased with a burnt offering.
17 The sacrifice pleasing to God is a broken spirit. God, You will not despise a broken and humbled heart.
18 In Your good pleasure, cause Zion to prosper; build the walls of Jerusalem.
19 Then You will delight in righteous sacrifices, whole burnt offerings; then bulls will be offered on Your altar.
(Psalm 51, HCSB)

I will personalize this psalm, since it not only refers to David!

My request (vv. 1–2). In desperate need of divine forgiveness, the sinner can do nothing but cast himself on God's mercy. When sin disrupts fellowship with the Lord, the sinner has no right to divine blessings. However, the Lord has promised to forgive, and it is a forgiveness based solely on his "faithful love" and "abundant compassion." That rich word *hesed* appears again! Forgiveness is an act of divine grace whereby sin is blotted out and the sinner is "cleansed" by the washing away of sins (vv. 2, 7, 9; cf. Ex. 32:32; Num. 5:23; Ps. 32:2).

My repentance (vv. 3–5). The variety of words for sin expresses its seriousness (vv. 1–2). He knows himself intimately and sees how rebellious he has been. We should not reject or argue with divine justice (Rom. 3:4), because the Lord's verdict is always "right."

My restoration (vv. 6–9). A series of futures, not imperatives, begins with verse 6b to the end of verse 8. You will teach me, purge me, wash me, let me hear, let me rejoice. Verse 9 concludes with two imperatives: Hide your face and blot out my sins, and these conclude the first part of the psalm which focuses on **sins.** Now he turns his focus toward **salvation** (v. 10ff).

My renewal (vv. 10–12). With the word "create" David asks for a miracle. It is a term for what God alone can do. Forgiveness and cleansing are prerequisites for communion with God. Wisdom maintains that communion. For this reason the psalmist renews his prayer for divine wisdom and sustenance. David prays for a "pure heart," a "steadfast spirit," the "Holy Spirit," and a "willing spirit." Without internal renewal, he fears the possibility of divine rejection, as he had witnessed with Saul (1 Sam. 16:14).

My rejoicing (vv. 13–17). The repentant sinner will become an evangelist, telling others where he has found the bread—of Life! "Praise" is another appropriate response to divine deliverance. A deeper commitment results from a heart of gratitude. The Lord "delights in" truth rather than "sacrifice." God is looking for the heart that knows how little it deserves, and how much it owes.

It appears from **vv. 18–19** that later generations may have made David's penitence their own, adding these verses to make their prayer specific. We can do no better than to make his prayer ours as well.

After you pray the psalm, consider also this prayer:

> *Gracious Lord, as I have prayed this prayer, grant me true penitence, that You may be pleased to wash me from my sins and make my heart anew. May the renewing of Your Holy Spirit cause my tongue to always sing of Your goodness.* AMEN.

Psalm 52

A Really Bad Dude

What a contrast between the humility of Psalm 51 and the boastful arrogance expressed in Psalm 52! The psalm title sets this composition in the story of Doeg the Edomite's treachery during David's fleeing from Saul (1 Sam. 22:17–23).

For the choir director. A Davidic Maskil. When Doeg the Edomite went and reported to Saul, telling him, "David went to Ahimelech's house."

52:1 Why brag about evil, you hero! God's faithful love is constant.
2 Like a sharpened razor, your tongue devises destruction, working treachery.
3 You love evil instead of good, lying instead of speaking truthfully.   Selah
4 You love any words that destroy, you treacherous tongue!
5 This is why God will bring you down forever. He will take you, ripping you out of your tent; He will uproot you from the land of the living.   Selah
6 The righteous will look on with awe and will ridicule him:
7 "Here is the man who would not make God his refuge, but trusted in the abundance of his riches, taking refuge in his destructive behavior."
8 But I am like a flourishing olive tree in the house of God; I trust in God's faithful love forever and ever.
9 I will praise You forever for what You have done. In the presence of Your faithful people, I will put my hope in Your name, for it is good.

(Psalm 52, HCSB)

We have two of David's utterances on this tragic series of events. One is his outcry to Abiathar, Ahimelech's son: 'I have occasioned the death of all…your father's house. Stay with me…; you shall be in safe keeping' (1 Sam. 22:22). The other is this psalm, where he reflects on the kind of man that Doeg is, who carves out his career by slander and intrigue, but whose success is brief (vv. 1–7). Finally he renews his own trust in God, who stands by his own as surely as he, David, has promised to stand by Abiathar (vv. 8–9) (Kidner).

Our recurring word, *hesed*, appears twice in this psalm. In v. 1 it is in contrast to the hatred shown by the wicked. In v. 8 it is the basis of the trust shown by the righteous. Thus while the psalm deals with a very evil man, it is "book-ended" by reminders of the Lord's mercy.

God protected David's name because David trusted God's name (v. 9). Many people call their sons "David" but I personally have never met someone named "Doeg." I think of the same contrast between Lamech and Noah in Genesis 4 and 5. Who is an example to you? Do you know anyone named Lamech?

An outline from the MacArthur Study Bible:

1. The Rashness of the Wicked (vv 1–5)
2. The Reaction of the Righteous (vv 6, 7)
3. The Rejoicing of the Godly (vv 8, 9)

"The green olive tree in the house of the Lord (v. 8) brings the thought of the tree of life, the cross of the Saviour, that gives eternal life to all who trust in the faithful love of God rather than in earthly glory" (Eaton).

"How monotonously alike all the great tyrants and conquerors have been. How gloriously different are the saints" (C. S. Lewis).

> *Faithful Lord, grant that Your people will always be vigilant in prayer against the flaunting of evil and the perversion of words to deceive and destroy. Also defend me with Your mighty Word, and plant me to grow in Your house, that I may enjoy Your truth and Your goodness forever. AMEN.*

Psalm 53

Salvation for Israel

The last two psalms are so very different from the praise and wisdom psalms that all of us love to read. There is dissonance and disappointment because of wicked people who profess to be part of the people of God, but who deny that by their lives. But we cannot bury our heads to avoid this unpleasantness and we must find an outlet for this "Godly frustration" without becoming cynical and pessimistic. In that light, thank God for these psalms of disorientation!

> *For the choir director: on Mahalath. A Davidic Maskil.*
> **53:1** The fool says in his heart, "God does not exist." They are corrupt, and they do vile deeds. There is no one who does good.
> 2 God looks down from heaven on the human race to see if there is one who is wise and who seeks God.
> 3 Everyone has turned aside; they have all become corrupt. There is no one who does good, not even one.
> 4 Will evildoers never understand? They consume My people as they consume bread; they do not call on God.
> 5 Then they will be filled with terror— terror like no other — because God will scatter the bones of those who besiege you. You will put them to shame, for God has rejected them.
> 6 Oh, that Israel's deliverance would come from Zion! When God restores His captive people, Jacob will rejoice; Israel will be glad.
>
> (Psalm 53, HCSB)

In this adaptation of Psalm 14 (check out the commentary there) "God" (Elohim) is used instead of "Lord" (Yahweh), while verse 5 has more words and verse 6 has fewer words. Some psalms were adapted by the musicians for various uses in the temple worship. One of the wonders of Scripture is that it can be applied to many different situations.

What you think about God helps to determine your character and conduct. The fool ignores God and exploits people made in the image of

God. Many people are "practical atheists," who claim to believe in God, but live as though He did not exist.

In my comments on Psalm 14, I referred to Craig Groeschel's book, *The Christian Atheist*. This thought-provoking volume challenges each of us to question how we can live out so many days without consciously acknowledging our belief in and dependence on the God of the Bible. The pessimism and near despair of the psalmist as he ponders a world around him filled with practical atheists causes him to cry out for an intervention of God on behalf of His erring people. "Oh, that salvation for Israel would come out of Zion! When God restores the fortunes of his people, let Jacob rejoice, let Israel be glad."

Have you ever cried out to the Lord for His visible intervention on behalf of His apostate and indifferent church? Then you have shared the frustration of the psalmist who longed to witness God rescuing His people from the mess into which we have gotten ourselves!

> "Who can exercise a worse tyranny over us than the god in our own breast?" K. Barth (Don't worry. I am not a "Barthian.")

> *Grant that I, Lord, may not be anxious about earthly things, but love things heavenly; and even now, while I am placed among things that are passing away, hold fast to those that shall endure; through Jesus Christ our Lord. AMEN (BCP).*

Psalm 54

My Helper

This psalm arose out of trying experiences that followed those of Psalm 52. To be betrayed by Doeg the Edomite had been hardly a surprise, but now David finds himself rejected by men of his own tribe, despite his rescue of one of their border towns from the Philistines (1 Sam. 23). In this disillusioning situation he turns again to God (Kidner).

For the choir director: with stringed instruments. A Davidic Maskil. When the Ziphites went and said to Saul, "Is David not hiding among us?"

54:1 God, save me by Your name, and vindicate me by Your might!
² God, hear my prayer; listen to the words of my mouth.
³ For strangers rise up against me, and violent men seek my life. They have no regard for God. Selah
⁴ God is my helper; the Lord is the sustainer of my life.
⁵ He will repay my adversaries for their evil. Because of Your faithfulness, annihilate them.
⁶ I will sacrifice a freewill offering to You. I will praise Your name, LORD, because it is good.
⁷ For He has delivered me from every trouble, and my eye has looked down on my enemies.

(Psalm 54, HCSB)

What do you do when people you have helped turn against you?

A prayer for deliverance (vv. 1–2). "Save me" and "vindicate me" express the source and the nature of David's deliverance. "God" alone can deliver him from the troubles stated in verse 3. David's confidence lies in his reliance on the Lord's revelation of Himself in the past. He has revealed His "name" and his "might" to Israel. The "name" of the Lord signifies His protection and His blessing.

The occasion of the prayer (v. 3). This verse is nearly identical to Ps. 86:14. David's opponents are called "strangers" and "ruthless men" who have no regard for God. "Strangers" were those who were estranged from God and the covenant community (1 Sam. 23:11–12). They had little regard for God or other people, as they were "ruthless" individuals who insisted on their rights and desires.

The resolution of the prayer (vv. 4–5). The psalm shifts from worry over the arrogant to a confident trust in the Lord. Triumphantly he exclaims, "God is my helper." The resolution of the prayer lies in the conviction that God is just. He will not permit his children to suffer without vindication. Because the Lord is faithful to His people, the psalmist is calm, trusting that his God will protect him from his adversary.

A thanksgiving for deliverance (vv. 6–7). The psalm concludes in a victory hymn of thanksgiving. An offering is presented before the Lord but enjoyed in the fellowship of family and friends. The godly will hear all the Lord has done for His child, and His praise will resound. His "name" will be exalted, because He has brought deliverance and will continue to bring deliverance. His name is "good."

> *O God, You declare Your almighty power chiefly in showing mercy and pity: Grant us the fullness of Your grace, that we, running to obtain Your promises, may become partakers of Your heavenly treasure; through Jesus Christ our Lord. AMEN. (BCP).*

Betrayed!!

This **psalm of disorientation** is a lament by David who is threatened by enemies and has been betrayed by a friend. Although the title does not provide the details, I believe that the historical context is the betrayal by Ahithophel (2 Sam. 15–17), David's brilliant and trusted counselor who joined Absalom's rebellion. David's emotions run high, for he is desperately afraid and cries continuously to God for help. His distress is particularly sharp because of the betrayal by a person who at one time had been his close friend.

As you read it, listen for echoes of another betrayal of the Son of David.

For the choir director: with stringed instruments. A Davidic Maskil.

55:1 God, listen to my prayer and do not ignore my plea for help.
2 Pay attention to me and answer me. I am restless and in turmoil with my complaint,
3 because of the enemy's voice, because of the pressure of the wicked. For they bring down disaster on me and harass me in anger.
4 My heart shudders within me; terrors of death sweep over me.
5 Fear and trembling grip me; horror has overwhelmed me.
6 I said, "If only I had wings like a dove! I would fly away and find rest.
7 How far away I would flee; I would stay in the wilderness. Selah
8 I would hurry to my shelter from the raging wind and the storm."
9 Lord, confuse and confound their speech, for I see violence and strife in the city;
10 day and night they make the rounds on its walls. Crime and trouble are within it;
11 destruction is inside it; oppression and deceit never leave its marketplace.
12 Now it is not an enemy who insults me—otherwise I could bear it; it is not a foe who rises up against me—otherwise I could hide from him.
13 But it is you, a man who is my peer, my companion and good friend!
14 We used to have close fellowship; we walked with the crowd into the house of God.

15 Let death take them by surprise; let them go down to Sheol alive, because evil is in their homes and within them.
16 But I call to God, and the Lord will save me.
17 I complain and groan morning, noon, and night, and He hears my voice.
18 Though many are against me, He will redeem me from my battle unharmed.
19 God, the One enthroned from long ago, will hear and will humiliate them Selah because they do not change and do not fear God.
20 My friend acts violently against those at peace with him; he violates his covenant.
21 His buttery words are smooth, but war is in his heart. His words are softer than oil, but they are drawn swords.
22 Cast your burden on the Lord, and He will sustain you; He will never allow the righteous to be shaken.
23 God, You will bring them down to the Pit of destruction; men of bloodshed and treachery will not live out half their days. But I will trust in You.

(Psalm 55, HCSB)

The psalm begins with a **cry for help (vv. 1–2) and a lengthy description of the psalmist's situation (vv. 2–14)**. This includes personal threats (v. 3), violence and crime in the city (vv. 9b–11), and the treachery of a former friend—Ahithophel? (vv. 12–14). The author prays for his enemy's death (v. 15), which was answered in Ahithophel's suicide (2 Sam. 17:23). He then repeats his cries for help, **confident that God will hear him (vv. 16–19)**. Once again he **denounces his former friend (vv. 20–21) and consoles himself with encouraging words (v. 22), and closes the psalm with a final prophecy of punishment on his enemies (v. 23)**.

As is so often the case in a lament psalm, there is a final positive statement in this **affirmation: "But I will trust in you" (v. 23b)**.

It is easy to condemn the harshness of the sentiments in this imprecatory psalm, but we need to recognize the seriousness of the betrayals and the vicious acts of those in rebellion against God's anointed king. These were not just rivals in a sports contest! Furthermore, the prayers for judgment are best viewed as prophecies, ones that were fulfilled in the deaths of Ahithophel and Absalom. Their demise brought no joy to David (2 Sam. 18:33), although their deaths were necessary because of the heinousness of their crimes. The language also extends to Judas, especially verses 12–14.

"The person who is driven to distraction finds a fellow-sufferer here. Further, the heartrending passages on the betrayal give us added insight into the sufferings of Christ, and at the same time into his self-mastery and redemptive attitude" (Kidner).

> *Satisfy us in the morning with Your hesed, that we may rejoice and be glad all our days (Ps. 90:14). AMEN.*

Psalm 56

When I am Afraid

Trust in God is the presence of danger is the keynote of this and the next psalm. The danger is imminent and fear is inevitable, but faith is victorious over fear. Some teach that such fear is incompatible with being a child of God, but David's experience in Gath and the experience of many mature believers show otherwise. The spirit of the psalm is captured in the twice repeated refrain, **"When I am afraid, I will trust in You" (vv. 3, 11).**

The incident behind this fear is found in 1 Sam. 21:10—David's strange sojourn in Gath that backfired on him (see also Ps. 34). The language there and in this psalm implies that he became a prisoner and escaped. To have someone else determining your future can be scary, whether you are in prison or not.

For the choir director: according to "A Silent Dove Far Away." A Davidic Miktam. When the Philistines seized him in Gath.

56:1 Be gracious to me, God, for man tramples me; he fights and oppresses me all day long.
2 My adversaries trample me all day, for many arrogantly fight against me.
3 When I am afraid, I will trust in You.
4 In God, whose word I praise, in God I trust; I will not fear. What can man do to me?
5 They twist my words all day long; all their thoughts against me are evil.
6 They stir up strife, they lurk; they watch my steps while they wait to take my life.
7 Will they escape in spite of such sin? God, bring down the nations in wrath.
8 You Yourself have recorded my wanderings. Put my tears in Your bottle. Are they not in Your records?
9 Then my enemies will retreat on the day when I call. This I know: God is for me.
10 In God, whose word I praise, in the LORD, whose word I praise,
11 in God I trust; I will not fear. What can man do to me?
12 I am obligated by vows to You, God; I will make my thank offerings to You.
13 For You delivered me from death, even my feet from stumbling, to walk before God in the light of life.

(Psalm 56, HCSB)

PSALM 56

Here are some lessons:

God sees where you are (v. 8a). David should not have been in Gath to begin with, but the Lord was gracious to go with him and help him. God understands your situation far better than you do!

God knows how you feel (v. 8b). He not only knows your tears, but He remembers them and retains them! Why? So that one day He may transform them into gems of joy and glory. No tears are ever wasted when you follow Him. The ancient Jewish tradition of grieving women having a bottle to preserve their tears may have developed from this verse (Luke 7:38).

God hears when you call (v. 9). Terrors and tears must be handled with trust (vv. 3–4, 10–11). But be sure your motive is not just to get out of your jam! He delivers us that we might delight in Him and serve Him (vv. 12–13). The highest purpose of prayer is the glory of God.

When my children were afraid in their beds at night, I taught them to recite the main refrain of this psalm, "When I am afraid, I will trust in You." I remember the trusting sound of their little voices to this day.

> *O LORD, how could those little ones trust You like that but I am still worried and fearful? Have I forgotten that I also am a child? Help me to come to You as they do. AMEN*

Psalm 57

In the Cave with Dave

The psalm title locates its context in "the cave," which could refer to David's hiding from Saul in the cave of Adullam (1 Sam. 22:1, 2 Sam. 23:13) or in the cave at En Gedi (1 Sam. 24:3). Both incidents were during David's fleeing from Saul, a period that is explored in a number of the psalms in this section of the Psalter. This is also one of two "cave psalms" (see the title of Psalm 142). A friend has called the psalm "Survival Skills 101."

A Davidic Miktam. When he fled before Saul into the cave.

57:1 Be gracious to me, God, be gracious to me, for I take refuge in You. I will seek refuge in the shadow of Your wings until danger passes.

2 I call to God Most High, to God who fulfills His purpose for me.

3 He reaches down from heaven and saves me, challenging the one who tramples me.   Selah
God sends His faithful love and truth.

4 I am in the midst of lions; I lie down with those who devour men. Their teeth are spears and arrows; their tongues are sharp swords.

5 God, be exalted above the heavens; let Your glory be above the whole earth.

6 They prepared a net for my steps; I was downcast. They dug a pit ahead of me, but they fell into it!   Selah

7 My heart is confident, God, my heart is confident. I will sing; I will sing praises.

8 Wake up, my soul! Wake up, harp and lyre! I will wake up the dawn.

9 I will praise You, Lord, among the peoples; I will sing praises to You among the nations.

10 For Your faithful love is as high as the heavens; Your faithfulness reaches to the clouds.

11 God, be exalted above the heavens; let Your glory be over the whole earth.

(Psalm 57, HCSB)

Warren Wiersbe counsels us that "your own 'cave' may be a sickroom, a difficult place of ministry, or even a home where there is tension or trouble. If you do what David did, you will experience peace and victory even in the cave." What did he do?

David's faith **transformed his cave into a Holy of Holies** (v. 1)! His confidence was not in the rocks but "under Your wings" (Ruth 2:12). In spite of sharp teeth (v. 4), nets and pits (v. 6), David was sure of God's help. His desire was not just to escape but to exalt the Lord (vv. 5, 11), a truth that places a whole new perspective on his cave and also on our own caves! In fact, when he awakened the next morning, he picked up his harp and sang praises to God! And for all we know—he was still in that cave! Verse 8 provided the title for this book.

Believers may suffer now, but we can know that one day God will vindicate his justice in the world. Our reward is the enjoyment of God and of a renewed world that God promises we will receive (Gal. 6:9).

Trust Him. Exalt Him. Praise Him. This approach worked for Dave in his cave, and it will work for you in your cave, even if you have to remain there for awhile!

"For your hesed (steadfast love) is great to the heavens, your emet (faithfulness) to the clouds." May I rejoice in your hesed and trust in your emet. AMEN.

Psalm 58

Retribution and Reward

In words that may seem unchristian to some, David denounced the unjust rulers of his day—people who promoted evil by condemning the righteous and defending the wicked. In a prayer that would probably not be followed by any "Amens" in churches today, he asked God to judge sinners and establish righteousness on the earth.

> *To the choirmaster: according to Do Not Destroy. A Davidic Miktam.*
> 58:1 Do you really speak righteously, you mighty ones? Do you judge people fairly?
> 2 No, you practice injustice in your hearts; with your hands you weigh out violence in the land.
> 3 The wicked go astray from the womb; liars err from birth.
> 4 They have venom like the venom of a snake, like the deaf cobra that stops up its ears,
> 5 that does not listen to the sound of the charmers who skillfully weave spells.
> 6 God, knock the teeth out of their mouths; Lord, tear out the young lions' fangs.
> 7 They will vanish like water that flows by; they will aim their useless arrows.
> 8 Like a slug that moves along in slime, like a woman's miscarried [child], they will not see the sun.
> 9 Before your pots can feel the heat of the thorns—whether green or burning—He will sweep them away.
> 10 The righteous will rejoice when he sees the retribution; he will wash his feet in the blood of the wicked.
> 11 Then people will say, "Yes, there is a reward for the righteous! There is a God who judges on earth!"
>
> (Psalm 58, HCSB)

You will find similar passages in Psalms 35, 59, 69, 109, and 139. These verses seem to contradict such admonitions as Matthew 5:43–48. How should we respond?

Because he was God's chosen king, David's enemies were God's enemies (Ps. 139:21–22). No doubt his personal feelings were involved in these prayers, but his great concern was the righteousness of God and the good of

God's people. David had the authority to denounce *national* enemies and we have the privilege of forgiving **personal** enemies. The distinction should not be missed.

But you cannot forgive personal enemies until you realize how wicked their words and deeds really are. The person who has no concern to withstand wickedness in this world recognizes neither the sinfulness of sin nor the holiness of God. A believer does need backbone!

One day God will judge the wicked. When you pray the first three petitions of the Lord's Prayer, you are expressing briefly what David wrote in vivid detail. **David left all judgment to the Lord** but did his part to further God's holy will on the earth. If more saints today felt a holy anger against sin (Ps. 4:4; Eph. 4:26), the church might have effective ministry again as the salt of the earth and the light of the world. Such fearsome psalms also convey the word of Christ that in the end will shatter the forces of evil, and which at present serves to warn and to encourage us.

> "If the Jews cursed more bitterly than the pagans this was, I think, at least in part because they took right and wrong more seriously. For if we look at their railings we find that they are usually angry not simply because these things have been done to them but because these things are manifestly wrong, and are hateful to God as well as to the victim" (*Reflections on the Psalms* by C. S. Lewis).

Just and merciful Lord, see how Your children are attacked by the wicked. Hasten the time when the power of evil shall melt away, and all Your creation shall rejoice in Your holy kingdom. AMEN

Night and Morning

As is often the case in this second book of the Psalter (Psalm 42–72), and particularly since Psalm 54, David's life as a fugitive forms the gritty real–life context of this psalm. "These are not the musings of a cloistered poet" (Sailhamer). The psalm is also the vehicle for another affirmation that the Lord is his refuge, not any fortress of stone, which of course was no lasting protection for David's pursuer, Saul. When the psalm bursts out of it local context into a concern about the nations, it has much in common with Psalm 2, just as David the outlaw showed all the promise of David the king.

To the choirmaster: according to Do Not Destroy. A Miktam of David, when Saul sent agents to watch the house and kill him.

59:1 Deliver me from my enemies, my God; protect me from those who rise up against me.

2 Deliver me from those who practice sin, and save me from men of bloodshed.

3 LORD, look! They set an ambush for me. Powerful men attack me, but not because of any sin or rebellion of mine.

4 For no fault of mine, they run and take up a position. Awake to help me, and take notice.

5 You, LORD God of Hosts, God of Israel, rise up to punish all the nations; do not show grace to any wicked traitors. Selah

6 They return at evening, snarling like dogs and prowling around the city.

7 Look, they spew from their mouths— sharp words from their lips. "For who," [they say,] "will hear?"

8 But You laugh at them, LORD; You ridicule all the nations.

9 I will keep watch for You, my strength, because God is my stronghold.

10 My faithful God will come to meet me; God will let me look down on my adversaries.

11 Do not kill them; otherwise, my people will forget. By Your power, make them homeless wanderers and bring them down, Lord, our shield.

12 The sin of their mouths is the word of their lips, so let them be caught in their pride. They utter curses and lies.

13 Consume [them] in rage; consume [them] until they are gone. Then they

will know to the ends of the earth that God rules over Jacob.   Selah
14 And they return at evening, snarling like dogs and prowling around the city.
15 They scavenge for food; they growl if they are not satisfied.
16 But I will sing of Your strength and will joyfully proclaim Your faithful love in the morning. For You have been a stronghold for me, a refuge in my day of trouble.
17 To You, my strength, I sing praises, because God is my stronghold—my faithful God.

(Psalm 59, HCSB)

Despite his circumstances,

David will pray to the Lord (vv. 1–7). David compared his enemies to dogs prowling the city streets and growling over the garbage. Saul was after him again (1 Sam. 19:1–11), and only the Lord could deliver David. David was innocent of what Saul charged (vv. 3–4), so be sure that you are clean before the Lord if you pray these verses (Ps. 66:18).

David will watch for the Lord (vv. 8–15). Three times in the Psalter we read of God's laughter, and each time it is a laugh of derision at the folly of humans (v. 8; Ps. 2:4, 37:13). The text of this psalm *poetically* (vv. 14–15) and the psalm title *historically* recall when David's wife helped him escape from his enemies (1 Sam. 19:11). But David faced several years of danger and exile before he received his rightful throne. Twice he could have killed Saul, but he refused to do so. He knew that God would deal with his enemies in His way and in His time (1 Sam. 26:8–11).

David will sing to the Lord (vv. 16–17). David had a song in the morning because God gave him joy in the morning (Ps. 30:5). Things often look worse at night, so wait for the morning and God will give you your song of praise. As He does over a hundred times in the psalms, God shows to him—and to us—His "steadfast love" (*hesed,* v. 16).

It is good to give thanks to the LORD, to sing praises to Your name, O Most High; to declare Your steadfast love (hesed) in the morning, and Your faithfulness (emunah) by night (Ps. 92:1–2). AMEN.

Trouble Back Home

If it were not for this psalm we would not know about the resilience of David's hostile neighbors at the peak of his power. His very success brought dangers of alliances among his enemies (2 Sam. 8:5) and of battles far from his home. At such a moment, when his main force was with him near the Euphrates (2 Sam. 8:3), Edom evidently fell upon Judah from the south (Kidner).

For the choir director: according to "The Lily of Testimony." A Davidic Miktam for teaching. When he fought with Aram-naharaim and Aram-zobah, and Joab returned and struck Edom in the Valley of Salt, killing 12,000.

60:1 God, You have rejected us; You have broken out against us; You have been angry. Restore us!
2 You have shaken the land and split it open. Heal its fissures, for it shudders.
3 You have made Your people suffer hardship; You have given us a wine to drink that made us stagger.
4 You have given a signal flag to those who fear You, so that they can flee before the archers. Selah
5 Save with Your right hand, and answer me, so that those You love may be rescued.
6 God has spoken in His sanctuary: "I will triumph! I will divide up Shechem. I will apportion the Valley of Succoth.
7 Gilead is Mine, Manasseh is Mine, and Ephraim is My helmet; Judah is My scepter.
8 Moab is My washbasin; on Edom I throw My sandal. Over Philistia I shout in triumph."
9 Who will bring me to the fortified city? Who will lead me to Edom?
10 Is it not You, God, who have rejected us? God, You do not march out with our armies.
11 Give us aid against the foe, for human help is worthless.
12 With God we will perform valiantly; He will trample our foes.

(Psalm 60, HCSB)

Wiersbe effectively applies the circumstances of this psalm to our situation today. I have adapted some of his observations.

David is broken (vv. 1–3). David and Joab were leading the armies of Israel against two enemies in the north when a third enemy invaded in the south. When you get one problem solved, another one comes along! It actually seemed that God had abandoned His people and that the end was near.

David is bold (v. 4). But David did not run away. Instead, he boldly lifted God's banner of truth and listened for God's word of assurance (vv. 4–8). The Lord is our banner (Ex. 17:8–16), and we can trust Him to give the victory.

David is beloved (v. 5). His banner over us is love (Song 2:4; Rom. 8:37). The name David means "beloved." God's people are beloved in Jesus Christ, the Beloved One (Matt. 3:17; Eph. 1:6). In the midst of life's battles, remember that God loves you.

David is a believer (vv. 6–12). God assured David that He was in control of the nations, so David and Joab stepped out by faith and won both battles. The poetic expression, "on Edom I throw My sandal" probably refers to the practice of removing one's shoe to show disdain (Ruth 4:7), or possibly even throwing one at your servant (?).

When you feel **broken**, you are still His **beloved**, but if you **believe**, you can **boldly** advance. Go forward under His victorious banner!

> *O Lord Jesus, conqueror of evil, help me in all my troubles to hear afresh Your gospel words—that my faith may be rekindled, and by Your Spirit I may again do mighty deeds of love. AMEN.*

Messiah and Me

This may have been a cry for help when David was away on campaign (see Psalm 60) or driven out by Absalom. What he may not have foreseen was the abundant answer to the prayer for the king (vv. 6–7), destined to be granted, in the Messiah, above all that he asked or thought. In that regard, notice the shift from being a request for "me" (vv. 1–5) to a request for the occupant of the throne (vv. 6–7). There was no greater occupant than the ultimate Son of David (Luke 1:32–33). "May he be enthroned forever before God; appoint *hesed* and faithfulness to watch over him!" (see Pr. 20:28).

> *For the choir director: on stringed instruments. Davidic.*
> 61:1 God, hear my cry; pay attention to my prayer.
> 2 I call to You from the ends of the earth when my heart is without strength. Lead me to a rock that is high above me,
> 3 for You have been a refuge for me, a strong tower in the face of the enemy.
> 4 I will live in Your tent forever and take refuge under the shelter of Your wings.   Selah
> 5 God, You have heard my vows; You have given a heritage to those who fear Your name.
> 6 Add days to the king's life; may his years span many generations.
> 7 May he sit enthroned before God forever; appoint faithful love and truth to guard him.
> 8 Then I will continually sing of Your name, fulfilling my vows day by day.
> (Psalm 61, HCSB)

My Cry for Help (vv. 1-2)
My Confidence in God (vv. 3–7)
My Commitment to Obey (v. 8)

A question that arises: If this is Messianic, how can *we* pray this psalm? The concept of *corporate solidarity* helps us to see the answer. Israel was the Seed, Messiah was the ultimate Seed, and we are the spiritual Seed. The

PSALM 61

same is true of the promises about the Son and the Servant. We are in the Son/Servant, so we are sons and servants. Now how about the references to him as King? David offered this prayer as king, claiming the promises of 2 Samuel 7:16, and it was to be fulfilled to overflowing in the person of the King Messiah. **Through him also His people share the kingly blessings** (Eph. 2:6; Rev. 22:3–5), so we can pray this magnificent petition on behalf of all His royal priests (Rev. 1:6).

"So will I ever sing praises to your name, as I perform my vows day after day" (v. 8).

Kidner reminds us, "Vows were usually discharged in a single ceremony, but David is conscious of a debt that can never be paid off. As George Herbert expressed it: 'Surely Thy sweet and wondrous love shall measure all my days; And as it never shall remove, so neither shall my praise.'"

> *Father, hear me when I pray from the very limits of my limited endurance, and as You brought up Your Son Jesus, so lead me to Your rock, that I may abide with You forever in praise and thanksgiving. AMEN.*

Theme of the Psalms

Hesed Va'emet

After encountering that rich word *hesed* ("steadfast love" in the ESV) so many times, I am convinced that the Lord's *hesed* is the main theme of the Psalter (the word appears 129 times!). Perhaps that is because the Psalmists are usually expounding on the self-revelation of Yahweh in Exodus 34:6. I just finished a search and analysis of the 13 times in the Old Testament that *hesed* is also coupled with *emet*, as we just saw in Psalm 61:7. I urge you to read the full verses and be blessed as I have been.

Ex. 34:6—Yahweh: "The LORD, the LORD, a God merciful and gracious, slow to anger, and abounding in **steadfast love and faithfulness**."

Gen. 24:49—Eliezer: "So now if you are going to deal **kindly and truly** with my master, tell me."

Gen. 47:29—Jacob: "Please, if I have found favor in your sight, place now your hand under my thigh and deal with me in **kindness and faithfulness**."

Josh. 2:14—Joshua: "When the LORD gives us the land we will deal **kindly and faithfully** with you."

2 Sam. 2:6—David: "Now may the LORD show **steadfast love and faithfulness** to you."

2 Sam. 15:20—David: "Go back and take your brothers with you, and may the LORD show **steadfast love and faithfulness** to you."

Ps. 25:10—"All the paths of the LORD are **steadfast love and faithfulness**."

Ps. 61:7— "Appoint **steadfast love and faithfulness** to watch over him!"

Ps. 85:10—"**Steadfast love and faithfulness** meet."

Ps. 86:15— "But you, O Lord ... abounding in **steadfast love and faithfulness**."

Ps. 89:14— "**Steadfast love and faithfulness** go before you."

Pr. 3:3— "Let not **steadfast love and faithfulness** forsake you."

Pr. 20:28—"**Steadfast love and faithfulness** preserve the king."

As I see it, the psalmists are either (1) proclaiming God's *hesed va'emet* or (2) wrestling with how His *hesed va'emet* squares with what they are experiencing in life!

Now ponder if John is consciously referring to the same couplet of Divine love/grace and faithfulness/truth in his description of the Messiah in John 1:14 as "full of grace and truth."

> *O steadfastly loving LORD of truth, help me when I struggle to see Your will in the difficult affairs of my life, to never doubt Your goodness, faithfulness, and love. AMEN.*

Psalm 62

Absalom, Again!

This psalm probably grew out of David's painful experience during the rebellion led by his son Absalom (2 Sam. 15:13–23). Imagine the king having to leave his comfortable palace and flee to the wilderness to hide! When you find yourself in a "wilderness" situation, take inventory of the things that really are important.

> *For the choir director: according to Jeduthun. A Davidic psalm.*
> 62:1 I am at rest in God alone; my salvation comes from Him.
> 2 He alone is my rock and my salvation, my stronghold; I will never be shaken.
> 3 How long will you threaten a man? Will all of you attack as if he were a leaning wall or a tottering stone fence?
> 4 They only plan to bring him down from his high position. They take pleasure in lying; they bless with their mouths, but they curse inwardly. Selah
> 5 Rest in God alone, my soul, for my hope comes from Him.
> 6 He alone is my rock and my salvation, my stronghold; I will not be shaken.
> 7 My salvation and glory depend on God; my strong rock, my refuge, is in God.
> 8 Trust in Him at all times, you people; pour out your hearts before Him. God is our refuge. Selah
> 9 Men are only a vapor; exalted men, an illusion. On a balance scale, they go up; together they weigh less than a vapor.
> 10 Place no trust in oppression, or false hope in robbery. If wealth increases, pay no attention to it.
> 11 God has spoken once; I have heard this twice: strength belongs to God,
> 12 and faithful love belongs to You, Lord. For You repay each according to his works.
> (Psalm 62, HCSB)

Waiting on the Lord does not mean being idle or indifferent, because sometimes waiting is harder than working. For your waiting to be meaningful and spiritually productive, do what David did.

Wait silently (vv. 1, 5). This means not telling your trials to everybody who will listen or even telling them repeatedly to the Lord. When a child rests in the arms of their mother or father, there is no need to make noise. Much talk is sometimes evidence of little faith.

Wait expectantly (v. 5). God will work as you trust Him and let Him have His way. Your hope is not in human or material resources (vv. 9–10) but in the power of God (v. 11).

Wait continually (v. 8). It is not easy to wait "at all times," especially when you feel that God is not following your schedule. If your times are in His hands (Ps. 31:15), you will have perfect peace as you wait for Him to work (Isa. 26:3). And then you will rise up on wings like an eagle far above the perilous abyss below (Isa. 40:31).

A New Testament application can be found in 1 Cor. 10:13. Just as David found a way out of his trial, Paul exhorts us on the basis of many Old Testament examples (1 Cor. 10:1–12) that our situation or trial is not unique. Many have gone through worse things than you and come out on the other side—better for the experience! Don't keep blaming your supposedly unique trial on your special circumstances, other people, or "bad luck." Take responsibility and live by Truman's motto: "The buck stops here!" Sadly we are so busy blaming others that we forget that both this psalm and 1 Cor. 10:13 declare clearly that "God is faithful." There is a way of escape that He has provided. David found it. Have you?

> *O God, my God, in You alone is my hope and my salvation. Help me through all the blows of life to confess to You my failures and fears. May I pour out my heart before You, until I find that quietness where I am sure that You alone will do all things well. AMEN.*

Psalm 63

General Patton

I will never forget when I first experienced the power of this psalm. It was from an unlikely source—a Hollywood movie! In the film "Patton" the iconic American general slaps a soldier who has lost his nerve. Patton was severely reprimanded and had to ask forgiveness from the young man in the presence of the Third Army. The scene opens with Patton praying in the chapel of an occupied French villa. As he rises and departs, his voiceover prays the words of Psalm 63 about seeking earnestly the face of God. The Psalm concludes as he faces his troops for the apology, and the words about the psalmist's enemies are appropriate since Patton's personal enemies must have been gloating over his humiliation. It is a scene where the raw emotional power of cinema truly reaches its apex.

> *A Davidic psalm. When he was in the Wilderness of Judah.*
>
> 63:1 God, You are my God; I eagerly seek You. I thirst for You; my body faints for You in a land that is dry, desolate, and without water.
> 2 So I gaze on You in the sanctuary to see Your strength and Your glory.
> 3 My lips will glorify You because Your faithful love is better than life.
> 4 So I will praise You as long as I live; at Your name, I will lift up my hands.
> 5 You satisfy me as with rich food; my mouth will praise You with joyful lips.
> 6 When, on my bed, I think of You, I meditate on You during the night watches
> 7 because You are my help; I will rejoice in the shadow of Your wings.
> 8 I follow close to You; Your right hand holds on to me.
> 9 But those who seek to destroy my life will go into the depths of the earth.
> 10 They will be given over to the power of the sword; they will become the jackals' prey.
> 11 But the king will rejoice in God; all who swear by Him will boast, for the mouths of liars will be shut.
>
> (Psalm 63, HCSB)

Whatever was the reality of Patton's personal knowledge of God, as David fled from his pursuers into the wilderness, he could longingly say that:

Psalm 63

"I still have God" (vv. 1–2). Only if you have traveled through the Judean Wilderness or the Biblical Negev can you fully appreciate the ring of truth that sounds from these words. But that physical dryness can also be compared to the spiritual dryness of being absent from the Lord's presence. The God you worship in the sanctuary is with you in your dry periods as well. If you hunger and thirst for Him, He will satisfy you (Matt. 5:6).

"I still have a song" (vv. 3–5). David could not go to the altar and offer sacrifices to God, but he could lift his hands and his voice as "spiritual sacrifices" (Heb. 13:15). When you praise God, your inner person is nourished (v. 5), and you are satisfied. These intensely spiritual longings portray a mystical *communion* that does not slide into mystical *union*, for it never blurs the distinction between the divine and the human. The mysticism of OT piety never transmutes the love of God into pantheism. The world of nature never absorbs the Divine even when the mystic reaches a sublimity that prompts him to sing, "Your love is better than life!" or the apostle Paul to echo and amplify, "For me, to live is Christ and to die is gain" (Phil. 1:21).

"I still have joy in the Lord" (vv. 6–11). If you cannot rejoice in your situation, you can always rejoice in your Savior: His past help (v. 6), His present protection (v. 7), and His future guidance (v. 8). He hides you and holds you, so you have nothing to fear. The sudden mention of "the king" in Psalm 63:11 reminds us of the victorious Messianic King from the tribe of Judah who brings peace and salvation to his people (Gen. 49:8–12; Num. 24:17).

> Personal communion with God forms the center of this profound psalm. "There may be other psalms that equal this outpouring of devotion; few if any that surpass it" (Kidner).

Lord, it is so hard to slow down to think about and consider You and Your works. Teach me the way of meditation and remembrance, that in all the barren places of my life I may be able to find the fountain of Your presence, and so be refreshed for Your service. Amen.

Psalm 64

Bad and Good Fear

While Psalm 63 was focused on God, with the enemy on the edges, here the composition is reversed, although the outcome is the same. This psalm can strike fear in the reader—and it is intended to do so (Kidner). See what I mean.

For the choir director. A Davidic psalm.

64:1 God, hear my voice when I complain. Protect my life from the terror of the enemy.
2 Hide me from the scheming of the wicked, from the mob of evildoers,
3 who sharpen their tongues like swords and aim bitter words like arrows,
4 shooting from concealed places at the innocent. They shoot at him suddenly and are not afraid.
5 They encourage each other in an evil plan; they talk about hiding traps and say, "Who will see them?"
6 They devise crimes and say, "We have perfected a secret plan." The inner man and the heart are mysterious.
7 But God will shoot them with arrows; suddenly, they will be wounded.
8 They will be made to stumble; their own tongues work against them. All who see them will shake their heads.
9 Then everyone will fear and will tell about God's work, for they will understand what He has done.
10 The righteous rejoice in the Lord and take refuge in Him; all the upright in heart offer praise.

(Psalm 64, HCSB)

Fear can be paralyzing but it can also actually be liberating, when it is the Biblical "fear of the Lord." The journey from fear to faith is what this psalm is all about.

David's fear of the enemy. Their plots (vv. 1–2) and their weapons (v. 3) are directed toward the king. Yet he actually asked to be preserved not from the enemy but from the fear (terror) of the enemy. Fear and faith cannot live in the same heart (Mark 4:40). If the enemy can make you afraid, he has almost won the battle. A calm heart makes a confident soldier.

The enemy's fear of nothing. Their methods (v. 4) and their thoughts (v. 5) are portrayed with graphic, in your face, arrogance. They "do not fear" to form secret plans or lead open insurrections (Absalom's?). Their words are like swords and arrows, and they set hidden traps. Can it get any worse for David? It looks like he is defeated! But keep reading!

The believer's fear of the Lord. "But God" is the turning point in the story (v. 7). When the enemy least expects it, God shoots at them, and they fall into their own traps. "All men shall fear" (v. 9), and the righteous shall be glad. The prayer of verse 1, to be preserved from terror, is more than answered. The judgment is still future, but joy can break out already. It is a sober joy, with the facts faced at their bitter worst, but also at their overwhelming best.

The final invitation for the righteous person to "take refuge" in the Lord echoes the refuge found in the Messianic Son in Psalm 2:12. The incarnate Messiah spoke to the fearful, "My peace I leave with you."

Lord Jesus Christ, who for our sakes endured the plotting and poisoned arrows of the evildoers, defend us with Your ever-flowing prayer from dread of the enemy; may we find shelter in You, and ever rejoice in Your faithful love that redeems all creation (Eaton).
AMEN.

Psalm 65

Now Thank We All Our God

After over a dozen lament psalms coming out of David's life as a fugitive, it is refreshing to arrive at a psalm of pure unadulterated praise! This joyous celebration of the God who provides us with nature's bounty makes any harvest hymn (even the one in our title) pale in comparison. Here we almost feel the splash of the rain and sense the springing growth all around us. The whole song has a joyous directness, whether it is speaking of God in His temple courts (vv. 1–4) or in His vast domain (vv. 5–8) or among the hills and valleys which He wakens to life (vv. 9–13) (Kidner).

For the choir director. A Davidic psalm. A song.

65:1 Praise is rightfully Yours, God, in Zion; vows to You will be fulfilled.

2 All humanity will come to You, the One who hears prayer.

3 Iniquities overwhelm me; only You can atone for our rebellions.

4 How happy is the one You choose and bring near to live in Your courts! We will be satisfied with the goodness of Your house, the holiness of Your temple.

5 You answer us in righteousness, with awe-inspiring works, God of our salvation, the hope of all the ends of the earth and of the distant seas;

6 You establish the mountains by Your power, robed with strength;

7 You silence the roar of the seas, the roar of their waves, and the tumult of the nations.

8 Those who live far away are awed by Your signs; You make east and west shout for joy.

9 You visit the earth and water it abundantly, enriching it greatly. God's stream is filled with water, for You prepare the earth in this way, providing people with grain.

10 You soften it with showers and bless its growth, soaking its furrows and leveling its ridges.

11 You crown the year with Your goodness; Your ways overflow with plenty.

12 The wilderness pastures overflow, and the hills are robed with joy.

13 The pastures are clothed with flocks, and the valleys covered with grain. They shout in triumph; indeed, they sing.

(Psalm 65, HCSB)

Scholars debate what festival provided the original context for its writing, but whatever season it first celebrated, David's grateful delight in God as Redeemer, Creator and Provider provides us with a rich experience of praise, not simply a psalm for a harvest festival. While nature is portrayed and "quoted," the focus, as always in the Psalter, is on the God of nature, who is:

The God of grace (vv. 1–4). Did you notice that the doctrines of grace are all here? Depravity, atonement, election, effectual calling, perseverance. Don't believe me? Check out verses 3–4 again!

The God of might (vv. 5–8). This God is not limited to His followers in Israel. We do not have to wait for Acts 1:8 to read that those who live at "the ends of the earth" hope in and are in awe of the God of "awesome deeds" (vv. 5, 8).

The God of plenty (vv. 9–13). The New Testament analogy that "one sows, one waters, but God gives the increase" (1 Cor. 3:6–7) finds its source here. The entire panoply of nature's features has turned out dressed in their finest, as if to sing and make a joyous celebration. While this joy is seasonal and local, we also sense what is described later (Psalms 96 and 98) about a final coming of God, and a welcome from the whole creation.

"You make the going out of the morning and the evening to shout for joy" (v. 8). As great as is the joy at the time of harvest, you can find joy in God's goodness at the beginning and ending of each day, so don't just wait until the "crowning" of the year to praise Him (v. 11).

> *O Elohim, whose work of creation embraces all that exists, grant that I may know what it is to be brought near to dwell in Your courts. Cleanse and replenish my soul, that my prayer about Your creation may be a song that anticipates the final harvest when You will be Lord of all the earth. AMEN.*

Psalm 66

The Many and the One

This is a thanksgiving psalm, in which the focus narrows from corporate praise to which the whole earth is summoned, down to the thanks of one individual, who brings his offerings and summons the faithful to listen to his personal story. Imagine a scene of public worship in which the praise of the multitude gives way to the voice of a single worshipper, who stands with his gifts and speaks of the God whose care is not only world-wide and nation-wide, but also personal: "I will tell what he has done for me" (v. 16). Thus mine is a miniature version of the one testimony proclaimed by the many (Kidner).

For the choir director. A song. A psalm.

66:1 Shout joyfully to God, all the earth!
2 Sing the glory of His name; make His praise glorious.
3 Say to God, "How awe-inspiring are Your works! Your enemies will cringe before You because of Your great strength.
4 All the earth will worship You and sing praise to You. They will sing praise to Your name." Selah
5 Come and see the works of God; His acts toward mankind are awe-inspiring.
6 He turned the sea into dry land, and they crossed the river on foot. There we rejoiced in Him.
7 He rules forever by His might; He keeps His eye on the nations. The rebellious should not exalt themselves. Selah
8 Praise our God, you peoples; let the sound of His praise be heard.
9 He keeps us alive and does not allow our feet to slip.
10 For You, God, tested us; You refined us as silver is refined.
11 You lured us into a trap; You placed burdens on our backs.
12 You let men ride over our heads; we went through fire and water, but You brought us out to abundance.
13 I will enter Your house with burnt offerings; I will pay You my vows
14 that my lips promised and my mouth spoke during my distress.
15 I will offer You fattened sheep as burnt offerings, with the fragrant smoke of rams; I will sacrifice oxen with goats. Selah

16 Come and listen, all who fear God, and I will tell what He has done for me.
17 I cried out to Him with my mouth, and praise was on my tongue.
18 If I had been aware of malice in my heart, the Lord would not have listened.
19 However, God has listened; He has paid attention to the sound of my prayer.
20 May God be praised! He has not turned away my prayer or turned His faithful love from me.

(Psalm 66, HCSB)

Let us heed the psalmist who invites us to:

Come and praise (vv. 1–4). He invites the whole world to praise the Lord because God loves the world and sent His Son to be the Savior of the world. When you know the Savior, you have something to sing about, but don't just do it alone. There is power in communal praise!

Come and see (vv. 5–12). This brief review of Israel's history mentions the Exodus (v. 6), the conquest of Canaan (v. 7), and the nation's times of trial (vv. 10–12). When you go through testing in the will of God, keep in mind that the same God who brings you *in* will see you *through* and make you better for having been in the furnace. "Hitherto hath the Lord helped us" (1 Sam. 7:12, KJV).

Come and sacrifice (vv. 13–15). Have you ever made promises to God when you have been in the furnace of suffering? Did you keep those promises? When the test was over, did you praise God for what you learned?

Come and hear (vv. 16–20). David wanted to tell others that God answers prayer. Worship should lead to a witness for the glory of God. "Let the redeemed of the Lord say so... " (Ps. 107:2).

The Lord and David invite us to "Come!" (vv. 5, 16). The Spirit and the Bride also invite us to "Come!" (Rev. 22:17).

> *Almighty God, whose eyes ever watch over all Your world, help me to view both my troubles and my joys in the light of the suffering and resurrection of Your Son, the Lord Jesus. May I trust You in the time of my affliction, and after my deliverance enable me to give You thanks and to offer up my life to Your service. AMEN.*

Psalm 67

Let the Nations be Glad

This is a devotional commentary on the Psalter, and reading these compositions devotionally is relatively easy because the psalms grew out of life itself. Occasionally, however, I like to introduce a technical or an academic expression, but only when it helps us to see better the psalm's spiritual meaning. Today the word for Psalm 67 is *intertextuality*. That word simply describes the process when the psalmist refers to a previously written scriptural passage and expounds upon it in his psalm. The richness of Psalm 67 lies in the amazing way that the unnamed author reflects back on two key passages in the Pentateuch—Gen. 12:1–3 and Num. 6:24–26. You may recognize those passages as (1) the promise to Abraham that his seed would bless the nations and (2) the Aaronic blessing of the Lord's face to shine upon us. The psalmist develops these two texts and turns them both into prayers for world-wide evangelism—a subject that at first might surprise a Christian reader of the Old Testament.

> *For the choir director: with stringed instruments. A psalm. A song.*
> 67:1 May God be gracious to us and bless us and look on us with favor   Selah
> 2 so that Your way may be known on earth, Your salvation among all nations.
> 3 Let the peoples praise You, God; let all the peoples praise You.
> 4 Let the nations rejoice and shout for joy, for You judge the peoples with fairness and lead the nations on earth.   Selah
> 5 Let the peoples praise You, God, let all the peoples praise You.
> 6 The earth has produced its harvest; God, our God, blesses us.
> 7 God will bless us, and all the ends of the earth will fear Him.
> (Psalm 67, HCSB)

John Piper's book on the worldwide mission of the Church takes its title from this psalm *(Let the Nations Be Glad!)*. Like Psalms 96 and 98 and

Isaiah 40–66, this psalmist recognized that God's plan from the beginning embraced a future blessing, not only for Israel, but for all the Gentiles. They did not have to wait for the Great Commission to learn that!

Wiersbe comments: "This missionary psalm exhorts us to get the message out to all the nations of the world. Why?"

Because they need light (vv. 1–2). The lost walk in darkness and need the light of God's face to shine upon them (2 Cor. 4:3–6). They have lost their way and are headed for eternal darkness. Does that concern you?

Because they need joy (vv. 3–4a). Sin gives pleasure for only a short time, but with the Lord there are "pleasures forevermore" (Ps. 16:11). How can we keep to ourselves the joy that Jesus gives?

Because they need righteousness (v. 4b), which can come only through faith in the Messiah (Rom. 3:21–31). Man's righteousness can never fully satisfy the demands of God's holy law.

Because they need life (vv. 5–7). "The field is the world" (Matt. 13:38), but that field is not producing fruit to the glory of God. Only with God's life and blessing can the harvest of righteousness come.

If every believer did what you do about missions, would all the people of the earth be praising the Lord?

Creator and Savior of the world, grant me to know that I live only by the light of Your face, and flourish only through the pouring out of Your blessing. May the day draw nearer when all the people of the earth will fear Your majesty and sing to You a song of thanksgiving.
AMEN.

Psalm 68

The Most Difficult of All

The genius of twentieth century Biblical scholars, W. F. Albright, wrote that "Psalm 68 has always been considered with justice as the most difficult of all the Psalms." But perhaps the problem lies more with the scholars than with the devoted reader. First we should closely read this the longest psalm we have encountered in our trek through the Psalter. See if you discern the so-called many "problems." My guess is that you won't.

For the choir director. A Davidic psalm. A song.

68:1 God arises. His enemies scatter, and those who hate Him flee from His presence.

2 As smoke is blown away, so You blow them away. As wax melts before the fire, so the wicked are destroyed before God.

3 But the righteous are glad; they rejoice before God and celebrate with joy.

4 Sing to God! Sing praises to His name. Exalt Him who rides on the clouds— His name is Yahweh—and rejoice before Him.

5 A father of the fatherless and a champion of widows is God in His holy dwelling.

6 God provides homes for those who are deserted. He leads out the prisoners to prosperity, but the rebellious live in a scorched land.

7 God, when You went out before Your people, when You marched through the desert, Selah

8 the earth trembled, and the skies poured down [rain] before God, the God of Sinai, before God, the God of Israel.

9 You, God, showered abundant rain; You revived Your inheritance when it languished.

10 Your people settled in it; by Your goodness You provided for the poor, God.

11 The Lord gave the command; a great company of women brought the good news:

12 "The kings of the armies flee—they flee!" She who stays at home divides the spoil.

13 While you lie among the sheepfolds, the wings of a dove are covered with silver, and its feathers with glistening gold.

14 When the Almighty scattered kings in the land, it snowed on Zalmon.

15 Mount Bashan is God's towering

PSALM 68

mountain; Mount Bashan is a mountain of many peaks.
16 Why gaze with envy, you mountain peaks, at the mountain God desired for His dwelling? The Lord will live [there] forever!
17 God's chariots are tens of thousands, thousands and thousands; the Lord is among them in the sanctuary as He was at Sinai.
18 You ascended to the heights, taking away captives; You received gifts from people, even from the rebellious, so that the Lord God might live [there].
19 May the Lord be praised! Day after day He bears our burdens; God is our salvation. Selah
20 Our God is a God of salvation, and escape from death belongs to the Lord GOD.
21 Surely God crushes the heads of His enemies, the hairy head of one who goes on in his guilty acts.
22 The Lord said, "I will bring [them] back from Bashan; I will bring them back from the depths of the sea
23 so that your foot may wade in blood and your dogs' tongues may have their share from the enemies."
24 People have seen Your procession, God, the procession of my God, my King, in the sanctuary.
25 Singers lead the way, with musicians following; among them are young women playing tambourines.
26 Praise God in the assemblies; praise the Lord from the fountain of Israel.
27 There is Benjamin, the youngest, leading them, the rulers of Judah in their assembly, the rulers of Zebulun, the rulers of Naphtali.
28 Your God has decreed your strength. Show Your strength, God, You who have acted on our behalf.
29 Because of Your temple at Jerusalem, kings will bring tribute to You.
30 Rebuke the beast in the reeds, the herd of bulls with the calves of the peoples. Trample underfoot hose with bars of silver. Scatter the peoples who take pleasure in war.
31 Ambassadors will come from Egypt; Cush will stretch out its hands to God.
32 Sing to God, you kingdoms of the earth; sing praise to the Lord, Selah
33 to Him who rides in the ancient, highest heavens. Look, He thunders with His powerful voice!
34 Ascribe power to God. His majesty is over Israel, His power among the clouds.
35 God, You are awe-inspiring in Your sanctuaries. The God of Israel gives power and strength to His people. May God be praised!

(Psalm 68, HCSB)

This is a hymn through which God's people celebrate His care for Israel, remembering how God led them through the wilderness into their inheritance. But the celebration does not stop with Israel for it recognizes that all the Gentiles will come to worship the true God, thus continuing that theme from Psalm 67. It is possible that David composed it to accompany the procession of the ark to the tabernacle (2 Sam. 6:12–15), and Psalm 68:1 also echoes Numbers 10:35. In any event the overall theme is "God's care for Zion and His people." Why is that so hard for the critics to see?

This victory psalm celebrated how God blew the enemy away like smoke and melted them like wax (v. 2). It pictures three triumphal processions.

The victorious nation (vv. 1–16.) Great victories were nothing new to Israel, for God had been with them from the beginning. He had delivered them from Egypt and led them through the wilderness into the Promised Land. He gave them Mount Zion and dwelt with them there. What a history of victory! Have you reviewed lately all that God has done for you?

The victorious Savior (vv. 17–18). Paul quoted verse 18 in Eph. 4:8 and applied it to the ascension of Jesus Christ. Believers today are part of a spiritual army, marching in a triumphal procession (2 Cor. 2:14; Col. 2:15) and claiming their inheritance. They are seated with Christ in the heavenlies (Eph. 2:4–6) using their spiritual gifts to serve Him on earth. What a victory!

The victorious singers (vv. 19–35). The happy procession reached the sanctuary where they lifted their praises to God and asked for His continued strength as new enemies attacked (vv. 34–35). The God of past victories would not forsake them as they trusted Him and obeyed His will (2 Cor. 1:8–11). What a lasting victory!

We are more than conquerors through our King who triumphed over death (Rom. 8:37). Would people mistake your march in a victory procession for that of a mourner in a funeral procession?

> This psalm is "poetry united with song and sacred drama, ancient arts that brought knowledge of God. And still today they can serve the true and the holy, sacraments, no less, of the one who dispels chaos and renews the life of creation" (Eaton).

O Father of the fatherless and consoler of the bereaved, I bless Your name for all Your daily care, and for the glorious position of Your Son Jesus at Your right hand. I beg You to deliver me from the wasteland of my own making to be His captive, and through His bondage to know true freedom. AMEN

Psalm 69

Persecuted But Not Forsaken

This psalm reveals a vulnerable man who cannot simply shrug off slander or betrayal or accusation (v. 5), and yet his sense of justice had not been dulled. His prayers and curses both alike spring from this personal and moral sensitivity, and the New Testament sees the Messiah prefigured in the psalmist's zeal for God's house and in his sufferings (vv. 9, 21). Yet Kidner balances this picture with the following observation: "The very juxtaposition of David cursing his tormentors and Jesus praying for His, brings out the gulf between type and antitype, and indeed between accepted attitudes among saints of the Old Testament and the New."

For the choir director: according to "The Lilies." Davidic.

69:1 Save me, God, for the water has risen to my neck.
2 I have sunk in deep mud, and there is no footing; I have come into deep waters, and a flood sweeps over me.
3 I am weary from my crying; my throat is parched. My eyes fail, looking for my God.
4 Those who hate me without cause are more numerous than the hairs of my head; my deceitful enemies, who would destroy me, are powerful. Though I did not steal, I must repay.
5 God, You know my foolishness, and my guilty acts are not hidden from You.
6 Do not let those who put their hope in You be disgraced because of me, Lord GOD of Hosts; do not let those who seek You be humiliated because of me, God of Israel.
7 For I have endured insults because of You, and shame has covered my face.
8 I have become a stranger to my brothers and a foreigner to my mother's sons
9 because zeal for Your house has consumed me, and the insults of those who insult You have fallen on me.
10 I mourned and fasted, but it brought me insults.
11 I wore sackcloth as my clothing, and I was a joke to them.
12 Those who sit at the city gate talk about me, and drunkards make up songs about me.
13 But as for me, LORD, my prayer to You is for a time of favor. In Your abundant, faithful love, God, answer me with Your sure salvation.

14 Rescue me from the miry mud; don't let me sink. Let me be rescued from those who hate me, and from the deep waters.
15 Don't let the floodwaters sweep over me or the deep swallow me up; don't let the Pit close its mouth over me.
16 Answer me, Lord, for Your faithful love is good; in keeping with Your great compassion, turn to me.
17 Don't hide Your face from Your servant, for I am in distress. Answer me quickly!
18 Draw near to me and redeem me; ransom me because of my enemies.
19 You know the insults I endure—my shame and disgrace. You are aware of all my adversaries.
20 Insults have broken my heart, and I am in despair. I waited for sympathy, but there was none; for comforters, but found no one.
21 Instead, they gave me gall for my food, and for my thirst they gave me vinegar to drink.
22 Let their table set before them be a snare, and let it be a trap for [their] allies.
23 Let their eyes grow too dim to see, and let their loins continually shake.
24 Pour out Your rage on them, and let Your burning anger overtake them.
25 Make their fortification desolate; may no one live in their tents.
26 For they persecute the one You struck and talk about the pain of those You wounded.
27 Add guilt to their guilt; do not let them share in Your righteousness.
28 Let them be erased from the book of life and not be recorded with the righteous.
29 But as for me—poor and in pain—let Your salvation protect me, God.
30 I will praise God's name with song and exalt Him with thanksgiving.
31 That will please the Lord more than an ox, more than a bull with horns and hooves.
32 The humble will see it and rejoice. You who seek God, take heart!
33 For the Lord listens to the needy and does not despise His own who are prisoners.
34 Let heaven and earth praise Him, the seas and everything that moves in them,
35 for God will save Zion and build up the cities of Judah. They will live there and possess it.
36 The descendants of His servants will inherit it, and those who love His name will live in it.

(Psalm 69, HCSB)

The psalm is directly related to its predecessor as both psalms express a desire for the establishment of God's kingdom (vv. 34–36; Ps. 68:32–35). While this psalm is also definitely Messianic, it is another example of how David and his Messianic descendant can voice the painful experiences of those who are in corporate solidarity with them—namely Messiah's followers.

Both psalms look back to the promise to David (2 Sam.7:16; Ps. 2:7) and await its fulfillment in Zion. Here David focuses on the miserable state of God's people as they wait for that salvation. They, like David, have sunk "in the miry depths (vv. 1–3), and have many enemies without cause (v. 4). Like David they are willing to admit their guilt (v. 5) and place their hope in the Lord (vv. 6–12). They call out for deliverance and salvation (vv. 13–18), yet often find no one to comfort them (vv. 19–21). Thus they (should I say "we"?) beseech the Lord in graphic terms for deliverance from their oppressors (vv. 22–28). But in the end, they (we) rest content in the hope that God will cause His name to dwell among us (vv. 29–36). David was the representative of the people of God, and in that role he wrote this as a prayer that is suitable for each of God's people in similar situations, providing our intended response to such trials.

"For the LORD hears the needy and does not despise his own people who are prisoners. Let heaven and earth praise him, the seas and everything that moves in them." The Psalm is yet another reminder that the most desperate of prayers can conclude with a doxology.

Humility is not thinking less of yourself, it is thinking of yourself less!

> *Lord Jesus, You knew the lowest depths of sorrow and the reproach that breaks the heart. Therefore, come to the help of the suffering, and frustrate the forces of cruelty. May the humble see Your work and be glad, and may their hope be renewed, and that they will look forward to the day when all will be healed. AMEN.*

Hurry Up, God!

While this Psalm is almost a repetition of Psalm 40:13–17, there are enough differences to read it on its own, apart from the context of Psalm 40.

> *For the choir director. Davidic. To bring remembrance.*
> 70:1 God, deliver me. Hurry to help me, LORD!
> 2 Let those who seek my life be disgraced and confounded; let those who wish me harm be driven back and humiliated.
> 3 Let those who say, "Aha, aha!" retreat because of their shame.
> 4 Let all who seek You rejoice and be glad in You; let those who love Your salvation continually say, "God is great!"
> 5 I am afflicted and needy; hurry to me, God. You are my help and my deliverer; LORD, do not delay.
>
> (Psalm 70, HCSB)

The Psalm begins and ends with an almost impatient request for God to hurry up! David was in a hurry when he wrote this brief psalm because God was NOT in a hurry. Twice he cries, "Hurry!" and he ends with, "Do not delay!" Like Peter sinking into the water, he did not have time for a long prayer. All he could cry was, "Lord, save me!" (Matt. 14:30). The rapidly repeating petitions in this Psalm emphasize the urgency of the matter. There is not a moment to lose, or so at least it appears on the surface.

Why does God delay answering your prayers? Surely He can see your desperate situation. He promises to give "grace to help in time of need" (Heb. 4:16), which can be translated "grace for well-timed help." Your Father's timing is never wrong. When God waits, He may have a better gift for you than what you are requesting from Him (Isa. 30:18). His delays are neither denials nor defeats, so put your times in His hands and wait on the Lord (Ps. 31:15).

Psalm 70

This little Psalm is notable for its urgency. If the psalmists knew what is was to wait on the Lord, they also knew a suffering which cried out to him to make haste and not delay.

> "*God's Perfect Timing:* Joseph in prison had to wait for God to free him and then to reconcile him to his brothers. Israel had to wait for deliverance from Egypt, and Moses had to wait through ten difficult plagues before Pharaoh would let the people go. Joshua and Caleb had to wait forty years before claiming their inheritance, and the delay was not their fault. David had to wait to receive his throne. Mary and Martha had to wait for Jesus to come to Bethany, and while they waited, their brother died (John 11). God is not in a hurry even when we are, and His schedule is better than ours" (Wiersbe).

O God, our help and deliverer, look with compassion on those who are at the edge of their endurance, and hasten to deliver them. May all who seek You and love Your salvation rejoice in You and bless Your holy name. AMEN

Psalm 71

Growing Old Gracefully

Recently I have been praying a certain prayer and I have shared it with others. "Lord, as I grow older may I not become a grumpy old man." Although there is no title that attributes this psalm to David, from the psalm itself we know that the author is growing old. Along the way he has experienced some serious trouble, which evidently shows no sign of abating (v. 4). And yet, the difficulties and pains have not caused him to become sour. His long years of trusting God have become a source for his assurance that God will now also take care of him.

71:1 LORD, I seek refuge in You; never let me be disgraced.

2 In Your justice, rescue and deliver me; listen closely to me and save me.

3 Be a rock of refuge for me, where I can always go. Give the command to save me, for You are my rock and fortress.

4 Deliver me, my God, from the hand of the wicked, from the grasp of the unjust and oppressive.

5 For You are my hope, Lord GOD, my confidence from my youth.

6 I have leaned on You from birth; You took me from my mother's womb. My praise is always about You.

7 I have become an ominous sign to many, but You are my strong refuge.

8 My mouth is full of praise and honor to You all day long.

9 Don't discard me in my old age: as my strength fails, do not abandon me.

10 For my enemies talk about me, and those who spy on me plot together,

11 saying, "God has abandoned him; chase him and catch him, for there is no one to rescue him.

12 God, do not be far from me; my God, hurry to help me.

13 May my adversaries be disgraced and confounded; may those who seek my harm be covered with disgrace and humiliation.

14 But I will hope continually and will praise You more and more.

15 My mouth will tell about Your righteousness and Your salvation all day long, though I cannot sum them up.

16 I come because of the mighty acts of the Lord GOD; I will proclaim Your righteousness, Yours alone.
17 God, You have taught me from my youth, and I still proclaim Your wonderful works.
18 Even when I am old and gray, God, do not abandon me. Then I will proclaim Your power to [another] generation, Your strength to all who are to come.
19 Your righteousness reaches heaven, God, You who have done great things; God, who is like You?
20 You caused me to experience many troubles and misfortunes, but You will revive me again. You will bring me up again, even from the depths of the earth.
21 You will increase my honor and comfort me once again.
22 Therefore, with a lute I will praise You for Your faithfulness, my God; I will sing to You with a harp, Holy One of Israel.
23 My lips will shout for joy when I sing praise to You, because You have redeemed me.
24 Therefore, my tongue will proclaim Your righteousness all day long, for those who seek my harm will be disgraced and confounded.

(Psalm 71, HCSB)

How can the psalmist's experience help us to **grow old gracefully**?

First of all, like the psalmist, **review your life as a dependence on God**. The Lord cared for him at birth, and he trusted the Lord as a youth (vv. 5–6). God taught him when he was young (v. 16) and was with him during his mature years. Now he is old, and he prays that God will not abandon him (vv. 9, 18).

Second, **discover the ideal way to spend old age as a Christian**. Devote time to prayer and trust the Lord to help you. Instead of complaining about what is wrong, praise God for His righteousness and goodness. Practice continual prayer (v. 3), continual praise (vv. 6, 8), and continual hope (v. 14).

Third, **depend on His strength and use every opportunity to witness for Him** (vv. 15–16), Ask God to make you a walking wonder (v. 7) who will point people to Christ. Keep a song on your lips and in your heart. "I will also praise you with the harp for your faithfulness, O my God; I will sing praises to you with the lyre, O Holy One of Israel. My lips will shout for joy, when I sing praises to you; my soul also, which you have redeemed." This second book of the Psalter (Psalms 42–72) nears its end with this ringing statement of trust.

So with his name cleared and his faith affirmed, this senior saint can set his mind at ease and tune his heart and lips to sing God's praise. After all, the best is yet to come!

> *O Lord, be my rock in time of weakness and when adversities take hold upon me. Remember what You have accomplished in me from the day of my rebirth, and bring me up again from the depths, that I may sing with all my soul the music of Your praise. AMEN.*

The Perfect King

This psalm has a special place in the hearts of Christians through Isaac Watts' hymn, "Jesus Shall Reign." Although the New Testament nowhere quotes it as Messianic, this picture of the king and his realm is so close to Isaiah 11:1–5 that if that passage is Messianic, so is this. Language describing royal extravagance makes sober sense with Messiah as the reference. In speaking of the King's reign as endless, it exalts kingship so far beyond the humanly attainable that its fulfillment is in no less a person than the Messiah. And this is not only seen in Christian thinking but also in Jewish writings! The Targum at verse 1 adds the word "Messiah" to "the king," and there are rabbinic allusions to this psalm which reveal the same opinion (Kidner).

Solomonic.

72:1 God, give Your justice to the king and Your righteousness to the king's son.

2 He will judge Your people with righteousness and Your afflicted ones with justice.

3 May the mountains bring prosperity to the people, and the hills, righteousness.

4 May he vindicate the afflicted among the people, help the poor, and crush the oppressor.

5 May he continue while the sun endures, and as long as the moon, throughout all generations.

6 May he be like rain that falls on the cut grass, like spring showers that water the earth.

7 May the righteous flourish in his days, and prosperity abound until the moon is no more.

8 And may he rule from sea to sea and from the Euphrates to the ends of the earth.

9 May desert tribes kneel before him and his enemies lick the dust.

10 May the kings of Tarshish and the coasts and islands bring tribute, the kings of Sheba and Seba offer gifts.

11 And let all kings bow down to him, all nations serve him.

12 For he will rescue the poor who cry out and the afflicted who have no helper.

¹³ He will have pity on the poor and helpless and save the lives of the poor.
¹⁴ He will redeem them from oppression and violence, for their lives are precious in his sight.
¹⁵ May he live long! May gold from Sheba be given to him. May prayer be offered for him continually, and may he be blessed all day long.
¹⁶ May there be plenty of grain in the land; may it wave on the tops of the mountains. May its crops be like Lebanon. May people flourish in the cities like the grass of the field.
¹⁷ May his name endure forever; as long as the sun shines, may his fame increase. May all nations be blessed by him and call him blessed.
¹⁸ May the Lord God, the God of Israel, be praised, who alone does wonders.
¹⁹ May His glorious name be praised forever; the whole earth is filled with His glory. Amen and amen.
²⁰ The prayers of David son of Jesse are concluded.

(Psalm 72, HCSB)

The psalm affirms a series of prayer requests for the King.

May the King judge Your people justly (vv. 1–4). Righteousness is the soil or climate in which true peace flourishes.

May people fear You because of His reign (vv. 5–7). On the integrity of the righteous king depends the peace and well-being of all the people.

May the kings of earth serve Him (vv. 8–11). "This great Gentile movement was greeted by the Messiah with resolves of self-offering (John 12:20), not with Solomonic self-display" (Kidner).

May He bring justice to the poor (vv. 12–14). Solomon's "heavy yoke" was again the opposite of what his greater Son would be known for (Matt. 11:28).

May all peoples be blessed in Him (vv. 15–17). The terms of verse 17 are virtually those of the promise to Abram in Gen. 12:2–3.

May God be praised who fulfills His promise (vv. 18–19). It is a magnificent prayer for the King and His kingdom, into which "the kings of the earth shall bring their glory and by whose light the Gentiles shall walk" (Rev. 21:24).

Reading a psalm like this will help you to recognize that "glory overcomes gloom." When things around you look dark, know that God will one day fill the earth with his glory (v. 19; Hab. 2:14).

From the last verse (v. 20) it appears that the one word title, *prayers,* is the oldest title for this book of the Bible. The meaning of *psalms* is "praises" so together the two titles sum up the essence of what this collection is all about: our prayers and praises! By prayer and the prophetic word, the king in this psalm becomes a channel of heavenly righteousness, defending the poor and the weak. Then will follow the Divine gifts to the land, and indeed to the whole earth. Hasten that day!

> *O Eternal King, who originally instituted the hope for our Messiah, and answered it in Your Son Jesus, I bless You for the peace and salvation which He brings to those who love Him. I ask that His work may be completed, and that all the earth be filled with Your glory. AMEN AND AMEN.*

Whom Do I Have But You?

This great psalm is the story of a search which was rewarded beyond all expectation. It recalls the kind of troubling questions about life that distracted Job and Jeremiah. At the end those questions no longer seem unanswerable and the psalmist shares one of the clearest confessions in all of Scripture.

Read the whole psalm and look for the moment when the attitude of Asaph begins to change.

A Psalm of Asaph.

73:1 God is indeed good to Israel, to the pure in heart.
2 But as for me, my feet almost slipped; my steps nearly went astray.
3 For I envied the arrogant; I saw the prosperity of the wicked.
4 They have an easy time until they die, and their bodies are well-fed.
5 They are not in trouble like others; they are not afflicted like most people.
6 Therefore, pride is their necklace, and violence covers them like a garment.
7 Their eyes bulge out from fatness; the imaginations of their hearts run wild.
8 They mock, and they speak maliciously; they arrogantly threaten oppression.
9 They set their mouths against heaven, and their tongues strut across the earth.
10 Therefore His people turn to them and drink in their overflowing waters.
11 They say, "How can God know? Does the Most High know everything?"
12 Look at them—the wicked! They are always at ease, and they increase their wealth.
13 Did I purify my heart and wash my hands in innocence for nothing?
14 For I am afflicted all day long, and punished every morning.
15 If I had decided to say these things aloud, I would have betrayed Your people.
16 When I tried to understand all this, it seemed hopeless
17 until I entered God's sanctuary. Then I understood their destiny.
18 Indeed You put them in slippery places; You make them fall into ruin.
19 How suddenly they become a desolation! They come to an end, swept away by terrors.

20 Like one waking from a dream, Lord, when arising, You will despise their image.
21 When I became embittered and my innermost being was wounded,
22 I was a fool and didn't understand; I was an unthinking animal toward You.
23 Yet I am always with You; You hold my right hand.
24 You guide me with Your counsel, and afterwards You will take me up in glory.
25 Whom do I have in heaven but You? And I desire nothing on earth but You.
26 My flesh and my heart may fail, but God is the strength of my heart, my portion forever.
27 Those far from You will certainly perish; You destroy all who are unfaithful to You.
28 But as for me, God's presence is my good. I have made the Lord GOD my refuge, so I can tell about all You do.

(Psalm 73, HCSB)

Asaph provides a clear *inclusio* to this psalm by stressing that God is "good" in verses 1 and 28. Between those statements, things are not so good! The psalm begins with a litany of complaints about the prosperity of the wicked and the suffering of the righteous as he sees this from his human viewpoint (vv. 2–15). His struggle then makes a dramatic turnaround (vv. 16–26) when Asaph begins to see things from the Divine viewpoint. The "conversion" of his attitude is so powerful that when we read the sublime statements about his new God-entranced perspective we wonder how he could have written the earlier part of the psalm. And yet the struggles with his faith in the early part portray accurately the conflicts that believers often have between what they know about God and what they see happening all around them.

If you have ever seen "Fiddler on the Roof," you remember Tevye's voicing of his struggles with God ("Lord, you made many poor people. I know it is no shame to be poor—but it is no great honor either!"). This Jewish argument with God resonates with many Christian believers as well, when we stop to be really honest with ourselves and others. "His ways are not our ways."

The turning point came when he went into the sanctuary and started looking at things from God's perspective (v. 17). The most important thing is not so much what you own or enjoy but where you are going. What good is an easy death (v. 4) if it ushers you into pain? When life seems unfair, take time to worship and get your spiritual vision properly focused.

Asaph realized that because he had God, he really needed nothing more (vv. 24–25). He had more than the wicked, and what he had would last forever. God would hold him, guide him, strengthen him, satisfy his spiritual desires—and one day, take him to glory beyond this life! As it is further unfolded in the New Testament, eternal life is already bestowed on the one who knows the Savior. The failing of flesh and heart only makes clearer the true nature of that life as the enjoyment of God, "my portion forever" (John 6:54; 17:3).

We are not philosophers, living on man's explanations. We are pilgrims, living on God's promises, and His promises never fail!

> *Be my shelter, Lord God, in all the perplexities that assault my faith. Guide me with Your counsel, and bring me so close to You that in this fellowship I may come to know the fulfillment of all my hopes and desires. AMEN.*

Psalm 74

When Heaven Seems Silent

Asaph continues his own group of writings (73–83) in this the third section of the Psalter (Psalms 73–89). This tormented psalm has all the marks of a national disaster that also produced writings like Ps. 137 and the book of Lamentations, namely the Babylonian destruction of Jerusalem and the temple in 587 BC. Perhaps the closest parallel is in Lam. 2:5–9, where the silencing of prophecy, as here (v. 9), was one of the most disorientating blows of all (Kidner).

Read it—and weep!

A Maskil of Asaph.

74:1 Why have You rejected us forever, God? Why does Your anger burn against the sheep of Your pasture?
2 Remember Your congregation, which You purchased long ago and redeemed as the tribe for Your own possession. Remember Mount Zion where You dwell.
3 Make Your way to the everlasting ruins, to all that the enemy has destroyed in the sanctuary.
4 Your adversaries roared in the meeting place where You met with us. They set up their emblems as signs.
5 It was like men in a thicket of trees, wielding axes,
6 then smashing all the carvings with hatchets and picks.
7 They set Your sanctuary on fire; they utterly desecrated the dwelling place of Your name.
8 They said in their hearts, "Let us oppress them relentlessly." They burned down every place throughout the land where God met with us.
9 We don't see any signs for us. There is no longer a prophet. And none of us knows how long this will last.
10 God, how long will the foe mock? Will the enemy insult Your name forever?
11 Why do You hold back Your hand? Stretch out Your right hand and destroy [them]!
12 God my king is from ancient times, performing saving acts on the earth.
13 You divided the sea with Your strength; You smashed the heads of the sea monsters in the waters;
14 You crushed the heads of Leviathan; You fed him to the creatures of the desert.

15 You opened up springs and streams;
You dried up ever-flowing rivers.
16 The day is Yours, also the night; You established the moon and the sun.
17 You set all the boundaries of the earth; You made summer and winter.
18 Remember this: the enemy has mocked the Lord, and a foolish people has insulted Your name.
19 Do not give the life of Your dove to beasts; do not forget the lives of Your poor people forever.
20 Consider the covenant, for the dark places of the land are full of violence.
21 Do not let the oppressed turn away in shame; let the poor and needy praise Your name.
22 Arise, God, defend Your cause! Remember the insults that fools bring against You all day long.
23 Do not forget the clamor of Your adversaries, the tumult of Your opponents that goes up constantly.
(Psalm 74, HCSB)

The questions that begin with "why" and "how long" dominate the first part of the psalm. One can see how why this psalm is often cited during the sad events of Jewish history like the Holocaust. While nothing exactly like this has or ever will happen to most of us, tragedies and severe setbacks can hit any of us with a severe blow. How do we make sense of these experiences?

What we see before us (vv. 1–8). These verses reveal the anguish of one who deeply loved God but could not understand why He permitted the desecration of temple and city. Israel was His flock and His inheritance, and Mount Zion was His dwelling-place! Yet He allowed evil men to destroy His people and His house. Why, O Lord? Asaph shared his perplexity with the prophet Habakkuk, who asked God some very similar questions (Hab. 1:2, 12).

What we don't see around us (vv. 9–17). God is King, but we do not see His hand working as in past centuries. We see no signs, and we have no prophet to interpret the times and give us God's message. One of God's judgments is to leave His people without a word of guidance because they have refused to obey His will (Amos 8:11).

What we desire to see before us (vv. 18–23). Surely Asaph knew that the sins of the nation caused the invasion of the enemy and the destruction of the temple. As a faithful Jew, he wanted to see the city and the people delivered and the enemy defeated. That would happen in due time, when God's discipline of His people is ended and their rebellion is conquered (Heb. 12:9–11).

Some inconspicuous features of the prayer are instructive. Its first request, as in the Lord's prayer, is concerning God's good name (vv. 18, 21). Then the appeal to God's covenant (v. 20) provides a steadying anchor where all else is in turmoil.

We too, like the Biblical authors, can lament, but also like them, we cannot abandon hope (Lam. 3:21–23)!

> *O God, who alone in Your power established the world of life, look with pity upon Your suffering ones and hasten to our help, just as You raised up the Lord Jesus from this world of violence, to the glory of Your name forever. AMEN.*

Psalm 75

The Just Judge

As he faces imminent danger, Asaph trusts in the righteous justice of God, takes courage, and praises! Kidner notes that God's great "reversals", in which he puts down one and lifts up another, is a theme that Asaph here shares with Hannah's Song (1 Sam. 2:1–10) and Mary's Magnificat (Luke 1:46–55). It is well placed after the end of the previous psalm which pleas that God will bring His case to court (v. 22). But He is no plaintiff here, but a Judge. The case will open when He chooses (v. 2) and be settled when He justly decides (Kidner).

For the choir director: "Do Not Destroy." A Psalm of Asaph. A Song.

75:1 We give thanks to You, God; we give thanks to You, for Your name is near. People tell about Your wonderful works.

2 "When I choose a time, I will judge fairly.

3 When the earth and all its inhabitants shake, I am the One who steadies its pillars. Selah

4 I say to the boastful, 'Do not boast,' and to the wicked, 'Do not lift up your horn.

5 Do not lift up your horn against heaven or speak arrogantly.'"

6 Exaltation does not come from the east, the west, or the desert,

7 for God is the judge: He brings down one and exalts another.

8 For there is a cup in the Lord's hand, full of wine blended with spices, and He pours from it. All the wicked of the earth will drink, draining it to the dregs.

9 As for me, I will tell about Him forever; I will sing praise to the God of Jacob.

10 "I will cut off all the horns of the wicked, but the horns of the righteous will be lifted up."

(Psalm 75, HCSB)

God is the Judge: His people are only His witnesses. We can tell others about His great works (v. 1) and His gracious warnings (vv. 4–5), but we cannot tell when His judgment will fall. God will choose the proper time, and His judgment will be just. The proud rulers of the nations think they are secure, but the God who set them up can also pull them down (1 Sam. 2:7–8; Dan. 4:25). The wicked think they are getting away with their evil deeds, but one day they must drink the wine of God's wrath. Meanwhile, God's children continue to sing His praises because they are sure God knows what He is doing. The world needs our witness, and worship is the greatest witness of all.

In verse 10 the worshiper pledges himself to fight God's battles. Thus a resigned patience and suffering are not the end of the story. There will be a time for power without aggression, and glory without pride.

It is so easy to get emotionally down and even pessimistic when you become disturbed by the evil in the world. But pessimism has no place even in the lives of those who understand the real nature of real evil in a really evil world. We must believe what this psalm proclaims: "He will exalt the horns of the righteous." Old Matthew Henry reminds us: "While it is true that God's people must share in drinking the cup of humanity's afflictions, the dregs of that cup are reserved for the wicked."

> *O God, may I follow the wisdom of gentleness (Jas. 3:13) and know that Your name is always nearby. May I not despair when this world seems shattered by the evil acts of the arrogant, but may I know the certainty of Your judgment at Your appointed time, when You will re-erect earth's pillars and cause the beauty of Your kingdom to shine forth forever. AMEN.*

Psalm 76

Resplendent, Majestic, Awe-Inspiring

Now we launch into the second half of the one hundred and fifty psalms. I hope that you have been blessed, but I want to tell you that I have been the one most blessed. Here is the text of Psalm 76:

> *For the choir director: with stringed instruments. A Psalm of Asaph. A song.*
>
> 76:1 God is known in Judah; His name is great in Israel.
> 2 His tent is in Salem, His dwelling place in Zion.
> 3 There He shatters the bow's flaming arrows, the shield, the sword, and the weapons of war.   Selah
> 4 You are resplendent and majestic coming down from the mountains of prey.
> 5 The brave-hearted have been plundered; they have slipped into their [final] sleep. None of the warriors was able to lift a hand.
> 6 At Your rebuke, God of Jacob, both chariot and horse lay still.
> 7 And You—You are to be feared. When You are angry, who can stand before You?
> 8 From heaven You pronounced judgment. The earth feared and grew quiet
> 9 when God rose up to judge and to save all the lowly of the earth.   Selah
> 10 Even human wrath will praise You; You will clothe Yourself with their remaining wrath.
> 11 Make and keep your vows to the LORD your God; let all who are around Him bring tribute to the awe-inspiring One.
> 12 He humbles the spirit of leaders; He is feared by the kings of the earth.
>
> (Psalm 76, HCSB)

This psalm looks back to **a great deliverance (vv. 1–6)**, and then on to **a greater judgment (vv. 7–12)**. The former is local and defensive, with Zion as God's earthly residence under serious attack. The latter half is cosmic, with heaven as God's seat, the world his kingdom, and all who suffer injustice his concern. It is a miniature of the biblical story itself, from the fiercely fought beginnings to the end-time when God's salvation and judgment will have reached their climax and full extent (Kidner). As I have often noticed in this trek through the Psalter, the psalm is not really about us. It is about the resplendent, majestic, and awe-inspiring God (vv. 4, 11).

> "Immortal, Invisible, God Only Wise
> In light inaccessible, hid from our eyes.
> Most Gracious, Most Glorious, The Ancient of Days,
> Almighty, Victorious, Thy Great Name we praise."

The providential rule of the Almighty is celebrated in this psalm, especially in one of its most quoted verses. I like its rendering in the HCSB: "Even human wrath will praise You; You will clothe Yourself with their remaining wrath" (v. 10).

> Some interpreters see a future focus of this psalm while others see a more immediate focus. "The lasting contribution of our psalm, however, is as part of worship that affords a present experience of God in his ultimate majesty. It can still take its part in those present moments of worship where the Lord makes himself known. Here still the psalm shows God as terrible to the mighty impostors, savior to the meek of the earth, and defender of the holy place" (Eaton).

> "Fallen man is not simply an imperfect creature who needs improvement: he is a rebel who must lay down his arms" C. S. Lewis.

O Great and Sovereign Lord, I thank You for this vision of Your appearing, when You will break the flaming arrows and all the weapons of aggression. I also thank You for Your sanctuary where the vision is given, and I pray that You will sustain all who love peace and truth, and hasten the time when the raging of the peoples shall turn to Your praise. AMEN

Psalm 77

Asaph's Autobiography

In the English text of this psalm, I count thirteen occurrences of "I" with a few additional ones in the Hebrew text. Asaph is relating to us his very personal pilgrimage of faith. As you read it, watch the shift from his present attitude to his future resolve and then back to his reflection on God's past redemptive acts.

For the choir director: according to Jeduthun. Of Asaph. A psalm.

77:1 I cry aloud to God, aloud to God, and He will hear me.
2 In my day of trouble I sought the Lord. My hands were lifted up all night long; I refused to be comforted.
3 I think of God; I groan; I meditate; my spirit becomes weak.　　　　Selah
4 You have kept me from closing my eyes; I am troubled and cannot speak.
5 I consider days of old, years long past.
6 At night I remember my music; I meditate in my heart, and my spirit ponders.
7 "Will the Lord reject forever and never again show favor?
8 Has His faithful love ceased forever? Is [His] promise at an end for all generations?
9 Has God forgotten to be gracious? Has He in anger withheld His compassion?"　　　　Selah
10 So I say, "It is my sorrow that the right hand of the Most High has changed."
11 I will remember the Lord's works; yes, I will remember Your ancient wonders.
12 I will reflect on all You have done and meditate on Your actions.
13 God, Your way is holy. What god is great like God?
14 You are the God who works wonders; You revealed Your strength among the peoples.
15 With power You redeemed Your people, the descendants of Jacob and Joseph.　　　　Selah
16 The waters saw You, God. The waters saw You; they trembled. Even the depths shook.
17 The clouds poured down water. The storm clouds thundered; Your arrows flashed back and forth.
18 The sound of Your thunder was in the whirlwind; lightning lit up the world. The earth shook and quaked.
19 Your way went through the sea, and Your path through the great waters, but Your footprints were unseen.
20 You led Your people like a flock by the hand of Moses and Aaron.

(Psalm 77, HCSB)

One of the ways I can identify with Asaph's autobiography is that when this was written (the end of the Old Testament period) the days of miracles evidently were over (v. 5). Today when I look around and see similar troubles I also do not see God throwing down special miracles left and right. Do I become discouraged at that? Asaph's **resolve in the face of current struggles as expressed in verses 1–9** finds its source in **remembering the works of the Lord in verses 10–20**. After his concern with "I," Asaph meditated on Israel's exodus from Egypt and recalled that God kept the people waiting by the Red Sea, that it was night, and that deliverance came just in the nick of time (Ex. 14:10–31). The people were afraid and certain that God had forgotten them, but He showed His power and humiliated the enemy.

By the end of the psalm that pervasive "I" of the early verses has disappeared, and the objective facts of the faith have captured all of Asaph's attention. His autobiography about himself has turned into a biography about God and His deeds (Kidner).

Psalm 77 is an example of the hard labor of intercessors. Taking all the trouble of their people upon themselves and into their own heart, they cry for them to the Lord with outstretched hands and grieving soul. Through many an hour they ponder deeply on the absence of God's help. Their entreaty finds its full force as they address to God the recollection of his ancient salvation, the foundation of present life and hope.

NT believers also should reflect back on God's great acts of redemption in the election of Israel and the miracles accompanying that deliverance. But we should also look back in faith to the Elect One Himself, the Beloved One in whom His Father took delight. Jesus the Messiah became the Passover Lamb and thus brought forth a new Exodus for His people (1 Cor. 5:7–9).

His way is a **holy way** (v. 13) and a **hidden way** (v. 19). You need not understand it all. Just follow as the new Joshua/Jesus leads you into the rest that He has promised (Heb. 4:9–10).

> *You O Lord can enter the deepest waters to rescue Your suffering ones. Strengthen, therefore, those who watch and suffer in prayer for others. Inspire them to grasp with faith the grace which gave birth both to Your world and to Your people, and to rest their pleas upon that sovereign grace.* AMEN.

Psalm 78

Don't Know Much About History

This psalm could be sub-titled, *From Zoan to Zion*, for it reviews the turbulent adolescence of Israel from its time of slavery in Egypt to the reign of David (vv. 12, 68). Like the parting song of Moses (Deut. 32) it is meant to search the conscience because this history must not repeat itself. At the same time, it is meant to warm the heart, for it tells of great miracles, of a grace that persists through all the judgments, and of the promise that displays tokens in the chosen city and king (Kidner). Just like the quotation above from the old popular song, Israel often forgot her history—and suffered because of it. Their history is about great miracles in the past and about a grace that persists through all the judgments, and also about a promise that centers around a chosen city and its chosen king.

A Maskil of Asaph

78:1 My people, hear my instruction; listen to what I say.
2 I will declare wise sayings; I will speak mysteries from the past —
3 things we have heard and known and that our fathers have passed down to us.
4 We must not hide them from their children, but must tell a future generation the praises of the Lord, His might, and the wonderful works He has performed.
5 He established a testimony in Jacob and set up a law in Israel, which He commanded our fathers to teach to their children
6 so that a future generation—children yet to be born—might know. They were to rise and tell their children
7 so that they might put their confidence in God and not forget God's works, but keep His commandments.
8 Then they would not be like their fathers, a stubborn and rebellious generation, a generation whose heart was not loyal and whose spirit was not faithful to God.
9 The Ephraimite archers turned back on the day of battle.
10 They did not keep God's covenant and refused to live by His law.
11 They forgot what He had done, the wonderful works He had shown them.
12 He worked wonders in the sight of their fathers, in the land of Egypt, the

region of Zoan.
13 He split the sea and brought them across; the water stood firm like a wall.
14 He led them with a cloud by day and with a fiery light throughout the night.
15 He split rocks in the wilderness and gave them drink as abundant as the depths.
16 He brought streams out of the stone and made water flow down like rivers.
17 But they continued to sin against Him, rebelling in the desert against the Most High.
18 They deliberately tested God, demanding the food they craved.
19 They spoke against God, saying, "Is God able to provide food in the wilderness?
20 Look! He struck the rock and water gushed out; torrents overflowed. But can He also provide bread or furnish meat for His people?"
21 Therefore, the Lord heard and became furious; then fire broke out against Jacob, and anger flared up against Israel
22 because they did not believe God or rely on His salvation.
23 He gave a command to the clouds above and opened the doors of heaven.
24 He rained manna for them to eat; He gave them grain from heaven.
25 People ate the bread of angels. He sent them an abundant supply of food.
26 He made the east wind blow in the skies and drove the south wind by His might.
27 He rained meat on them like dust, and winged birds like the sand of the seas.
28 He made them fall in His camp, all around His tent.
29 They ate and were completely satisfied, for He gave them what they craved.
30 Before they had satisfied their desire, while the food was still in their mouths,
31 God's anger flared up against them, and He killed some of their best men. He struck down Israel's choice young men.
32 Despite all this, they kept sinning and did not believe His wonderful works.
33 He made their days end in futility, their years in sudden disaster.
34 When He killed some of them, [the rest] began to seek Him; they repented and searched for God.
35 They remembered that God was their rock, the Most High God, their Redeemer.
36 But they deceived Him with their mouths, they lied to Him with their tongues,
37 their hearts were insincere toward Him, and they were unfaithful to His covenant.
38 **Yet** He was compassionate; He atoned for their guilt and did not destroy them. He often turned His anger aside and did not unleash all His wrath.
39 He remembered that they were [only] flesh, a wind that passes and does not return.
40 How often they rebelled against Him in the wilderness and grieved Him in the desert.
41 They constantly tested God and provoked the Holy One of Israel.
42 They did not remember His power [shown] on the day He redeemed them from the foe,
43 when He performed His miraculous signs in Egypt and His marvels in the region of Zoan.

44 He turned their rivers into blood, and they could not drink from their streams.
45 He sent among them swarms of flies, which fed on them, and frogs, which devastated them.
46 He gave their crops to the caterpillar and the fruit of their labor to the locust.
47 He killed their vines with hail and their sycamore-fig trees with a flood.
48 He handed over their livestock to hail and their cattle to lightning bolts.
49 He sent His burning anger against them: fury, indignation, and calamity—a band of deadly messengers.
50 He cleared a path for His anger. He did not spare them from death, but delivered their lives to the plague.
51 He struck all the firstborn in Egypt, the first progeny of the tents of Ham.
52 He led His people out like sheep and guided them like a flock in the wilderness.
53 He led them safely, and they were not afraid; but the sea covered their enemies.
54 He brought them to His holy land, to the mountain His right hand acquired.
55 He drove out nations before them. He apportioned their inheritance by lot and settled the tribes of Israel in their tents.
56 But they rebelliously tested the Most High God, for they did not keep His decrees.
57 They treacherously turned away like their fathers; they became warped like a faulty bow.
58 They enraged Him with their high places and provoked His jealousy with their carved images.
59 God heard and became furious; He completely rejected Israel.
60 He abandoned the tabernacle at Shiloh, the tent where He resided among men.
61 He gave up His strength to captivity and His splendor to the hand of a foe.
62 He surrendered His people to the sword because He was enraged with His heritage.
63 Fire consumed His chosen young men, and His young women had no wedding songs.
64 His priests fell by the sword, but the widows could not lament.
65 Then the Lord awoke as if from sleep, like a warrior from the effects of wine.
66 He beat back His foes; He gave them lasting shame.
67 He rejected the tent of Joseph and did not choose the tribe of Ephraim.
68 He chose instead the tribe of Judah, Mount Zion, which He loved.
69 He built His sanctuary like the heights, like the earth that He established forever.
70 He chose David His servant and took him from the sheepfolds;
71 He brought him from tending ewes to be shepherd over His people Jacob— over Israel, His inheritance.
72 He shepherded them with a pure heart and guided them with his skillful hands.
(Psalm 78, HCSB)

This long psalm reviews the **history of Israel: the Exodus** (vv. 12–16; 42–53); **their wilderness journey** (vv. 17–41); **the conquest of Canaan** (vv. 54–55); **and disciplines God sent them there** (vv. 56–64). A nation's

Psalm 78

true history is a record not only of how the people treated one another but of how they treated God.

But why the long history lesson? For the sake of the generations to follow (vv. 1–8). Jews were commanded to teach their children the works and the ways of the Lord so that each generation would know the Lord and trust Him (Deut. 6.1–9). We have the same obligation today. When Israel stopped doing this, the nation forsook their faithful covenant Lord and God had to chasten them (Judg. 2:7–10).

Israel was a rebellious nation, but God was gracious and gave the people opportunities to start again. And yet notice **the sad refrain appearing four times: "yet they still sinned more"** (vv. 17, 32, 40, 56). This is not an excuse for us to sin and to tempt God, but it is an encouragement to repent when we do sin.

God's answer to Israel's needs was to give them **a Messianic leader: David, the shepherd (v. 70)**. He had both integrity (the heart) and ability (the hands), and he sought to serve the Lord and love the flock of Israel. People have not changed. They still rebel against God. There is still a need for faithful instructors in the home (vv. 1–8) and leaders in the nation (vv. 70–72). Remember, urges this psalm, and hand on that remembrance faithfully, about how the Lord came to save his people, and always be their shepherd. Let your eyes and your heart be fixed upon Him, and so you will be kept in trust and faithfulness. Remember that He split the rock to give you the water of life, and sent down the bread of heaven, that you may eat, and hunger no more. Do all you can to help your next generation to serve the Lord acceptably.

"What are all histories but God manifesting Himself?" (Oliver Cromwell).

> *O LORD my Shepherd, I thank You for the story of faith that has been passed down to me. Help me also to hand it down, having myself been filled with the truth of Your judgment, grace and everlasting love. AMEN*

Psalm 79

The Psalms and Jeremiah

This *psalm of disorientation* refers to the destruction of Jerusalem and the temple and the havoc made of the Jewish people by the Babylonians. I suggest that it is set to the same tune of the Lamentations of Jeremiah, and that the weeping prophet borrows two verses out of it (vv. 6–7) and makes use of them in his prayer (Jer. 10:25). How interesting is it that just as we meditate on this psalm, so did an inspired prophet also meditate on it—and found it useful! So don't conclude as you read it, "Oh, here is still another downer to read." Believe me, if it doesn't express the cry from your heart today, it will do so on some other day!

A Psalm of Asaph

79:1 God, the nations have invaded Your inheritance, desecrated Your holy temple, and turned Jerusalem into ruins.

2 They gave the corpses of Your servants to the birds of the sky for food, the flesh of Your godly ones to the beasts of the earth.

3 They poured out their blood like water all around Jerusalem, and there was no one to bury them.

4 We have become an object of reproach to our neighbors, a source of mockery and ridicule to those around us.

5 How long, Lord? Will You be angry forever? Will Your jealousy keep burning like fire?

6 Pour out Your wrath on the nations that don't acknowledge You, on the kingdoms that don't call on Your name,

7 for they have devoured Jacob and devastated his homeland.

8 Do not hold past sins against us; let Your compassion come to us quickly, for we have become weak.

9 God of our salvation, help us — for the glory of Your name. Deliver us and atone for our sins, because of Your name.

10 Why should the nations ask, "Where is their God?" Before our eyes, let vengeance for the shed blood of Your servants be known among the nations.

11 Let the groans of the prisoners reach You; according to Your great power,

preserve those condemned to die.
12 Pay back sevenfold to our neighbors the reproach they have hurled at You, Lord.
13 Then we, Your people, the sheep of Your pasture, will thank You forever; we will declare Your praise to generation after generation.

(Psalm 79, HCSB)

While his gloom is almost unrelieved until the final verse (v. 13), Asaph never reaches despair. His psalm is largely a description of his bewilderment that God's "great power" (v. 11) should be withheld so long from His people. In other words it is a cry of faith in perplexity, not of skepticism in doubt.

Verse 13: "Then we, Your people, the sheep of Your pasture, will thank You forever; we will declare Your praise to generation after generation." To look back from this final verse to verse 1 is to wonder at the faith which enabled a psalm that shows so much distress to end with such a word as "praise." This is truly a faith tested in the fire, and one that comes forth as gold, despite the pain of the purging (1 Pet. 1:6–7).

The psalm leads worshippers to speak out their indignation and passionate sorrow to God, and acknowledge that salvation is through His will and power alone. Oh how I love the Psalms! Honest, open, and sincere in their struggles, the psalmists (along with Biblical characters like Jeremiah and Job) finally emerge into the bright light of day, even though they have dragged through some seriously dark nights!

> And what else is there for us in this *psalm of disorientation*? Well there is the observation that God does care for His people, but He also chastens us so that we might learn to obey His will. "When you want God to be harder on others than He is on you, it is time to start seeing your sins the way God sees them" (Wiersbe).

Almighty and merciful God, whose name and glory are daily reviled by the wickedness suffered by Your people, let the groaning and the pain of Your servants come before you. Turn the hearts of the destroyers, and through Your mighty Spirit gather all into your flock, to Your everlasting praise. AMEN.

Psalm 80

A Flock and a Vine

Not the fall of Jerusalem but the last days of its northern counterpart, Samaria, about a century-and-a-half earlier, gave rise to this strong cry for help. Asaph prayed for the restoration and illumination of God's people by the shining of God's face (vv. 3, 7, 19) - a clear adaptation of the Aaronic Blessing found in Numbers 6:22–27 (Kidner).

For the choir director: according to "The Lilies." A testimony of Asaph. A psalm.

80:1 Listen, Shepherd of Israel, who guides Joseph like a flock; You who sit enthroned on the cherubim, rise up

2 at the head of Ephraim, Benjamin, and Manasseh. Rally Your power and come to save us.

3 Restore us, God; look on us with favor, and we will be saved.

4 Lord God of Hosts, how long will You be angry with Your people's prayers?

5 You fed them the bread of tears and gave them a full measure of tears to drink.

6 You set us at strife with our neighbors; our enemies make fun of us.

7 Restore us, God of Hosts; look on us with favor, and we will be saved.

8 You uprooted a vine from Egypt; You drove out the nations and planted it.

9 You cleared a place for it; it took root and filled the land.

10 The mountains were covered by its shade, and the mighty cedars with its branches.

11 It sent out sprouts toward the Sea and shoots toward the River.

12 Why have You broken down its walls so that all who pass by pick its fruit?

13 The boar from the forest gnaws at it, and creatures of the field feed on it.

14 Return, God of Hosts. Look down from heaven and see; take care of this vine,

15 the root Your right hand has planted, the shoot that You made strong for Yourself.

16 It was cut down and burned up; they perish at the rebuke of Your countenance.

17 Let Your hand be with the man at Your right hand, with the son of man You have made strong for Yourself.

18 Then we will not turn away from You; revive us, and we will call on Your name.

19 Restore us, Lord God of Hosts; look on us with favor, and we will be saved.

(Psalm 80, HCSB)

The psalm is wrapped around a thrice repeating refrain: "Restore us, Lord God of Hosts; look on us with favor, and we will be saved (vv. 3, 7, 19). Surrounding that request, Asaph employs two metaphors to describe God's people—portrayals also utilized by that One who was greater than either Aaron or Asaph.

God's people as a *flock* (vv. 1–7). Israel was like a flock of sheep led by God (Ps. 77:20; Ps. 78:52): "We are His people and the sheep of His pasture" (Ps. 100:3). But they were wayward sheep who would not follow the Shepherd. So, instead of enjoying green pastures and still waters (Ps. 23:2), they were enduring tears and the reproach of the enemy (v. 5).

God's people as a *vine* (vv. 8–19). This picture parallels Isaiah 5 and our Lord's parables in Matt. 21:28–46. Israel was a fruitful vineyard until she turned from the Lord and began to worship the gods of the nations. God used those very nations to discipline His people and destroy the vineyard. The prayer in verses 17–18 was partially answered when some of the people returned to the land after the captivity, but it is only fully realized in Jesus the Messiah. His people today are sheep in Messiah's Flock (John 10:14–16) and branches in Messiah's Vine (John 15:1–7).

The Jewish Targum found here a prayer for the coming of the Messiah, and the church in turn sees Jesus the Messiah as the bearer of life and salvation. The Messianic themes of Shepherd and Vine are expressed also in the prayer for the man at God's right hand, or "son of man" (v. 17). Ultimately it is through Him that Israel will be "restored" and "saved" (v. 19). That final plea grows from being addressed to "O God" (v. 3) to "God of Hosts" (v. 7) to "Lord God of Hosts" (v. 19), illustrating the increasing earnestness of his prayer for the Messiah. "Through him may be known already the blessing of the face of God (Num. 6:25); the light of the knowledge of the glory of God is given in the face of Jesus Christ (2 Cor. 4:6), and in him shall be made perfect the restoration of the suffering world" (Eaton).

"When we come to God for his grace, his good-will towards us and his good work in us, we should pray earnestly, continue instant in prayer, and pray even more earnestly!" (Matthew Henry).

> *Lord God, You have revealed that Your church is a living flock and a living vine. I pray that You will care for this flock and vine that is so often plundered and harmed. Through Your mighty power come and save us through the Shepherd and Gardener whom You raised in power to Your right hand. AMEN.*

Psalm 81

The Shofar Blows

This powerful psalm commemorates one of the Festivals of Israel. In all probability it was the Festival of Trumpets or *Rosh Hashana*, but more probably the Festival of Tabernacles or *Sukkot* (v. 3). The *shofar*, or ram's horn, was blown for these Fall Festivals. Tabernacles commemorated the wilderness journey, and included a public reading of the law, every seventh year (Deut. 31:10), of which verses 8–10 seem to preserve some echoes (Kidner).

For the choir director: on the Gittith. Of Asaph

^{81:1} Sing for joy to God our strength; shout in triumph to the God of Jacob.
2. Lift up a song play the tambourine, the melodious lyre, and the harp.
3. Blow the horn during the new moon and during the full moon, on the day of our feast.
4. For this is a statute for Israel, a judgment of the God of Jacob.
5. He set it up as an ordinance for Joseph when He went throughout the land of Egypt. I heard an unfamiliar language:
6. "I relieved his shoulder from the burden; his hands were freed from carrying the basket.
7. You called out in distress, and I rescued you; I answered you from the thundercloud. I tested you at the waters of Meribah. *Selah*
8. Listen, My people, and I will admonish you. Israel, if you would only listen to Me!
9. There must not be a strange god among you; you must not bow down to a foreign god.
10. I am Yahweh your God, who brought you up from the land of Egypt. Open your mouth wide, and I will fill it.
11. "But My people did not listen to Me; Israel did not obey Me.
12. So I gave them over to their stubborn hearts to follow their own plans.
13. If only My people would listen to Me and Israel would follow My ways,
14. I would quickly subdue their enemies and turn My hand against their foes."
15. Those who hate the LORD would pretend submission to Him; their doom would last forever.
16. But He would feed Israel with the best wheat. "I would satisfy you with honey from the rock."

(Psalm 81, HCSB)

This psalm is also a mini-sermon on God's mercies shown to His children. Maybe it was actually delivered originally as a sermon on one of the above holidays. If this is a sermon, it appears that the Song of Moses in Deut. 32 could have served as its text, because the psalm echoes many verses in that amazing chapter. We can be thankful that, even if we don't know the historical circumstances of the psalm, it still speaks powerfully to all of us in whatever generation we live. The psalm is also near in spirit to Psalm 95, where a similar joyous opening leads to the reminder that God looks for listeners on whom the sober lessons of the wilderness are not lost.

Like every good sermon (!), it has three points:

The things that were (vv. 1–10). This is an invitation for the people to participate in a joyful celebration like Tabernacles. Asaph exhorts us to gratitude for all that God had done. It is good to set aside special times to meditate on the work of the Lord in your life.

The things that are (vv. 11–12). In spite of all that God did for His people, they would not listen to His Word or do His will. One of God's most painful judgments is to permit you to have your own way. For a time, you enjoy it. Then you will learn how much you have missed.

The things that might have been (vv. 13–16). Had they obeyed, they would have experienced victory instead of defeat, fullness instead of emptiness, and the best instead of the worst. They could have looked back with rejoicing, but instead they had to remember with regret. So the psalm ends with a strong reminder of God's gracious gifts. He gives the best, and brings sweetness out of what is harsh and wholly unpromising.

> "The things that might have been will be if today you let the Master have His way" (Wiersbe).

O God our strength, You have delivered Your people from slavery into the freedom of Your service. Forgive my sins of unfaithfulness, and renew me as part of Your liberated people, who live daily by the gifts from Your hand and by the words from Your mouth. AMEN.

Psalm 82

God and the Gods

This psalm declares that all ruling powers are subject to God and must judge according to His standards. The key question is the exact meaning of "gods." But first, the text of Psalm 82.

> *A psalm of Asaph.*
> **82:1** God has taken His place in the divine assembly; He judges among the gods:
> 2 "How long will you judge unjustly and show partiality to the wicked? *Selah*
> 3 Provide justice for the needy and the fatherless; uphold the rights of the oppressed and the destitute.
> 4 Rescue the poor and needy; save them from the hand of the wicked."
> 5 They do not know or understand; they wander in darkness. All the foundations of the earth are shaken.
> 6 I said, "You are gods; you are all sons of the Most High.
> 7 However, you will die like men and fall like any other ruler."
> 8 Rise up, God, judge the earth, for all the nations belong to You.
>
> (Psalm 82, HCSB)

First of all, the "gods" are not the many gods of the heathen, since this would make no sense at all. An attractive interpretation is that they are the "principalities and powers" (angelic beings)—a way in which the word is sometimes used elsewhere. But this view is unlikely in light of the call to them to judge the poor fairly (vv. 3–4). The best view is that the "gods" are human judges who make decisions in the place of the one true God, and like Him, should judge righteously. The psalm then gives vivid expression to the belief that the crucial duty of the ruler is to prevent the exploitation of the weak by the strong. This helps us to make sense of the way our Lord referred to human judges as "gods" in John 10:34–36. There He argues from the lesser to the greater—if it is true of human judges, how much more is it true of me!

But what is the message of the psalm for all of us? The answer is in the final verse: "Rise up, God, judge the earth, for all the nations belong to

You!" The psalm ends very much like the Apocalypse with its "Come, Lord Jesus." The psalm then shows no further interest in the "gods"—only in God himself and His salvation. Finally, the psalmist declares that the whole world is God's possession, an echo of the promise to Abraham (Gen. 12:3). Our Lord's prayer ("Your kingdom come") is our most appropriate response to this psalm. So much for the devil's claim (Luke 4:6) that is still urged on us, "I give it to whom I will."

> *O Lord of justice, You have told us to care for Your little ones. Grant us both the faith that sees the certainty of Your kingdom, and also the perseverance that ever prays for Your will to be done on earth.*
> *AMEN.*

Let's Wipe Them Out!

Israel is surrounded by an unholy alliance dedicated to her destruction. It is so difficult to find an exact situation like this in Biblical history that many of us have found Israel's situation in the *Yom Kippur* War of 1973 as at least an illustration of this peril. Surrounded by enemies pledged to her destruction, Israel was attacked on its holiest day—and was the nearest to defeat that it has ever been! Many Israelis and some sympathetic Christians have pointed out the amazing parallels in this psalm with the events of 1973.

Read the psalm with that background and see if you agree:

A song. A psalm of Asaph.

83:1 God, do not keep silent. Do not be deaf, God; do not be idle.

2 See how Your enemies make an uproar; those who hate You have acted arrogantly.

3 They devise clever schemes against Your people; they conspire against Your treasured ones.

4 They say, "Come, let us wipe them out as a nation so that Israel's name will no longer be remembered."

5 For they have conspired with one mind; they form an alliance against You

6 the tents of Edom and the Ishmaelites, Moab and the Hagrites,

7 Gebal, Ammon, and Amalek, Philistia with the inhabitants of Tyre.

8 Even Assyria has joined them; they lend support to the sons of Lot. *Selah*

9 Deal with them as You did with Midian, as You did with Sisera and Jabin at the Kishon River.

10 They were destroyed at En-dor; they became manure for the ground.

11 Make their nobles like Oreb and Zeeb, and all their tribal leaders like Zebah and Zalmunna,

12 who said, "Let us seize God's pastures for ourselves."

13 Make them like tumbleweed, my God, like straw before the wind.

14 As fire burns a forest, as a flame blazes through mountains,

15 so pursue them with Your tempest and terrify them with Your storm.

16 Cover their faces with shame so that they will seek Your name, LORD.

17 Let them be put to shame and terrified forever; let them perish in disgrace.

18 May they know that You alone whose name is Yahweh are the Most High over all the earth.

(Psalm 83, HCSB)

Asaph was perplexed (vv. 1–8). Israel was in danger, and God was silent and inactive. The nations were noisily forming a military confederacy against the Jewish people, but God was speechless and seemingly doing nothing. The enemy wanted to destroy the nation (v. 4) and take the land (v. 12), and apparently God was going to let them do it.

So, **Asaph prayed (vv. 9–18)** and reminded God of what He did to Israel's enemies during the days of the judges (vv. 9–12). Then he shifted from history to nature and asked God to send a storm to wipe them out (vv. 13–15).

Asaph had a purpose: not just the safety of Israel but the glory of the Lord (vv. 16–18). Some of the enemy soldiers might even come to trust in the God of Israel! It was not as important that Israel's name be preserved (v. 4), as it was important that God's name be glorified. But if God fails in His promise to preserve His people, His name *will* be dishonored! This is one attempt among many by the kingdom of darkness to wipe out the bearers of salvation (Pharaoh, Sennacherib, Haman, Antiochus, Herod, Hitler) but they all ultimately failed.

When it seems that God is saying and doing nothing, rest assured that He is working on your behalf. He is not as noisy as the enemy, but He is more powerful. And those who curse His people will end up being cursed themselves (Gen. 12:3; Num. 24:9).

> *O God, when Your working seems to be a silence of indifference, inspire me to pray all the more for the wonders of Your salvation. I request that those who are in league against Your people may be overcome by the wind and fire of your Spirit, until they turn to seek You, and with me worship You as Lord of all.* AMEN

Psalm 84

Longing For God

"Longing is written all over this Psalm" (Kidner). The mood of the psalm is like Psalms 42 and 43, which are a product of the same group of Korahite singers. If that is the case, the singer has now come out of his gloom from which he was beginning to break free in the earlier songs. We have mentioned some psalms of *disorientation*. Without a doubt this is a psalm of *orientation*. Three times he employs the word "Blessed" or "Happy." Once it is used wistfully (v. 4), once resolutely (v. 5), and once in deep contentment (v. 12). These can guide us in exploring the development within the psalm.

Pray these words, don't just read them:

> *For the choir director: on the Gittith, A psalm of the sons of Korah.*
> 84:1 How lovely is Your dwelling place, LORD of Hosts.
> 2 I long and yearn for the courts of the LORD; my heart and flesh cry out for the living God.
> 3 Even a sparrow finds a home, and a swallow, a nest for herself where she places her young near Your altars, LORD of Hosts, my King and my God.
> 4 How happy are those who reside in Your house, who praise You continually. Selah
> 5 Happy are the people whose strength is in You, whose hearts are set on pilgrimage.
> 6 As they pass through the Valley of Baca, they make it a source of springwater; even the autumn rain will cover it with blessings.
> 7 They go from strength to strength; each appears before God in Zion.
> 8 LORD God of Hosts, hear my prayer; listen, God of Jacob. Selah
> 9 Consider our shield, God; look on the face of Your anointed one.
> 10 Better a day in Your courts than a thousand anywhere else. I would rather be at the door of the house of my God than to live in the tents of the wicked.
> 11 For the LORD God is a sun and shield. The LORD gives grace and glory; He does not withhold the good from those who live with integrity.
> 12 LORD of Hosts, happy is the person who trusts in You!
>
> (Psalm 84, HCSB)

As was mentioned, if we take the word "happy" as a marker, we see:

The happiness of dwelling (v. 4). Perhaps the priests and Levites took for granted their privilege of dwelling in the courts of the Lord, but the psalmist did not. The altars were to him what a nest was to a bird, a place of safety and satisfaction. This dwelling, however, is not a matter of geography, for you can worship Him and love Him wherever you are (Heb. 13:10).

The happiness of desiring (v. 5). What is in your heart is what counts. He would rather serve in the temple than be served anywhere else. When your desires are godly, the Lord will give you all you need. When life disappoints you, be sure your heart's desires are pleasing to God.

The happiness of depending (vv. 12). God's pilgrims go "from strength to strength" and "from faith to faith" (Rom. 1:17). As you trust the Lord, He gives "grace and glory," for He is your sun (provision) and shield (protection). He gives you all you need on the pilgrimage of life.

"Better is a day in Your courts… " (v. 10). This is far more than the church usher's verse! It is a spiritual longing comparable to Paul's "all things but loss" (Phil. 3:8), or to Asaph's "Whom have I in heaven but You?" (Ps. 73:25).

The psalmist has found the blessing of "those who have not seen and yet believe" (John 20:29). His is the experience of Peter's readers, "Although you have never seen Him, you love Him" (1 Pet. 1:8). May it be so in all our hearts!

> *O Lord of Hosts, I long to dwell more closely with You. As I move toward You bless my steps through the dry places, that fruit may also be gathered there for You. Then may my soul at last take flight to Your holy dwelling, where I will behold You face to face. AMEN.*

Revival!! 85

Yahweh's righteousness, His steadfast love, His salvation, His glory, His peace—these are the Divine attributes that dominate this prayer for revival and renewal. This is not just a pining for "the good old days." It is a fervent prayer that God's people will continue to experience His presence and blessing rather than settle for "life as it is." Jesus blessed those who hunger and thirst for righteousness and this is a prayer that evidences that hunger and thirst.

Pray it with me:

For the choir director: A psalm of the sons of Korah.

85:1 LORD, You showed favor to Your land; You restored Jacob's prosperity
2 You took away Your people's guilt; You covered all their sin. *Selah*
3 You withdrew all Your fury; You turned from Your burning anger.
4 Return to us, God of our salvation, and abandon Your displeasure with us.
5 Will You be angry with us forever? Will You prolong Your anger for all generations?
6 Will You not revive us again so that Your people may rejoice in You?
7 Show us Your faithful love, LORD, and give us Your salvation.
8 I will listen to what God will say; surely the LORD will declare peace to His people, His godly ones, and not let them go back to foolish ways.
9 His salvation is very near those who fear Him, so that glory may dwell in our land.
10 Faithful love and truth will join together; righteousness and peace will embrace.
11 Truth will spring up from the earth, and righteousness will look down from heaven.
12 Also, the LORD will provide what is good, and our land will yield its crops.
13 Righteousness will go before Him to prepare the way for His steps.

(Psalm 85, HCSB)

Nourished by a holy recollection (vv. 1–3), the first half of the psalm is primarily a chastened prayer (vv. 4–7). The second half is a resolve to

listen (vv. 8–9), resulting in a climax (vv. 10–13) that is one of the most satisfying descriptions to be found anywhere in Scripture of a true harmony between God and His creation.

According to verse 10 heaven and earth reach out towards each other in perfect partnership. The Hebrew can mean "kiss each other" or "embrace each other." Here is that meeting of reconciliation between the righteous justice of the Almighty with His loving and compassionate mercy. New Testament believers can rejoice that this is most clearly accomplished in the atoning work of our Messiah (Rom. 3:21–26; 1 Cor. 1:30). Both God's justice was satisfied and His mercy displayed when Jesus in love bore the wrath our sins deserved. "Through His faithfulness God displayed Jesus as the 'mercy seat' by means of His blood" (Rom. 3:25a, paraphrased).

The practical application of these sublime truths is summed up in the following quotation from Oswald Chambers: "It is no use to pray for the old days. Stand square where you are and make the present better than any past has been. Base all on your relationship to God and go forward, and presently you will find that what is emerging is infinitely better than the past ever was."

> *O God, through Your Living Word You sent pardon and peace to restore Your creation. Now may I experience afresh Your love and be revived by Your salvation. May I rejoice in the knowledge that You are redeeming all things through Your faithfulness. AMEN.*

Psalm 86

In The Day of My Trouble

This is the only song attributed to David in the third book of the Psalms. Its form is simple, with an opening and closing supplication punctuated by a deliberate act of praise—deliberate, because the final verses reveal no lessening of the pressure and no sign of an answer (Kidner). Psalm 86 in the HCSB:

A Davidic prayer.

86:1 Listen, LORD, and answer me, for I am poor and needy.
2 Protect my life, for I am faithful. You are my God; save Your servant who trusts in You.
3 Be gracious to me, Lord, for I call to You all day long.
4 Bring joy to Your servant's life, since I set my hope on You, Lord.
5 For You, Lord, are kind and ready to forgive, abundant in faithful love to all who call on You.
6 LORD, hear my prayer; listen to my plea for mercy.
7 I call on You in the day of my distress, for You will answer me.
8 Lord, there is no one like You among the gods, and there are no works like Yours.
9 All the nations You have made will come and bow down before You, Lord, and will honor Your name.
10 For You are great and perform wonders; You alone are God.
11 Teach me Your way, LORD, and I will live by Your truth. Give me an undivided mind to fear Your name.
12 I will praise You with all my heart, Lord my God, and will honor Your name forever.
13 For Your faithful love for me is great, and You deliver my life from the depths of Sheol.
14 God, arrogant people have attacked me; a gang of ruthless men seeks my life. They have no regard for You.
15 But You, Lord, are a compassionate and gracious God, slow to anger and abundant in faithful love and truth.
16 Turn to me and be gracious to me. Give Your strength to Your servant; save the son of Your female servant.
17 Show me a sign of Your goodness; my enemies will see and be put to shame because You, LORD, have helped and comforted me.

(Psalm 86, HCSB)

David's prayer revolves around three requests:

"Preserve my life" (vv. 1–10). David was in trouble again. As he always did, he turned to the Lord for help, and he presented some reasons why God should answer him. God was his God, and he was God's servant. God was merciful, and he needed mercy. He wanted God alone to be glorified in the victory.

"Unite my heart" (vv. 11–13). A divided heart leads only to instability (Jas. 1:8), because you cannot serve two masters (Matt. 6:24). With a single heart, fear the Lord, learn from the Lord, obey the Lord, and praise His name.

"Strengthen my hands" (vv. 14–17). David's strength and experience were inadequate to face the foe. He needed the strength of the Lord. David knew his theology (v. 15) and that helped him in his praying. The better you know God, the better you can approach Him with your needs.

Psalm 85:15 is the most concise yet profound confession of the Divine attributes in all of the Bible. "But You, Lord, are a compassionate and gracious God, slow to anger and abundant in faithful love and truth." It is also an example of my proposal, suggested many psalms ago, that the divine self-revelation in Exodus 34:6–7 forms the theological framework of the Psalms. It seems to me that the Psalms are a celebration of this great confession and also a further reflection on it. This is true even when the Psalmist, as he does in this song, wrestles with exactly how those truths apply to his own difficult circumstances.

The psalm still speaks for those exposed to horrible hatred. It leads them to rest in the recollection of the sovereign Adonai, the Lord, who guards those bound by His love, and is able to deliver them from the lowest pit. It prompts them with many cries of prayer, most notably that the Lord should make the heart single in devotion, with all our faculties united.

> *Unite my heart, good Lord, to fear You alone, and guard me with the sign of Your favor, whatever You choose that to be. May I fear no foes, nor the deepest darkness, but may I ever walk gladly in Your way, giving thanks for Your forgiveness and the abundance of Your faithful love. AMEN.*

Glorious Things of Thee Are Spoken

We take the title from John Newton's great hymn, which itself is based on verse 3. The psalm is essentially prophetic and views Zion as the metropolis of a world-wide kingdom of God viewed spiritually (Heb. 11:10). In that city there will be a glad acceptance of God as Lord and King, while all sources of international friction are removed (Heb. 12:22, 28; Rev. 7:9).

> *A Psalm of the sons of Korah. A Song.*
> 87:1 His foundation is on the holy mountains.
> 2 The LORD loves the gates of Zion more than all the dwellings of Jacob.
> 3 Glorious things are said about you, city of God. Selah
> 4 "I will mention those who know Me: Rahab, Babylon, Philistia, Tyre, and Cush each one was born there.
> 5 And it will be said of Zion, "This one and that one were born in her." The Most High Himself will establish her.
> 6 When He registers the peoples, the LORD will record, "This one was born there." Selah
> 7 Singers and dancers alike will say, "All my springs are in you."
> (Psalm 87, HCSB)

Zion is exalted by the choice of God (vv. 1–3) Of all the great cities of the world only one is the city where God chose to put His name (Deut. 12:11). God speaks gloriously of this city here and elsewhere (Isa. 2:2–4).

Zion is exalted by the ingathering of Gentiles (vv. 4–6). A number of Gentile peoples are mentioned, some of whom at one time had serious conflicts with Israel. But when God draws up His eschatological role of the peoples in this city, there will be no aliens there (Ps. 47:9; Eph. 3:6; Rev. 7:9, 10).

Zion is exalted by the testimony of the redeemed (v. 7). "All my springs are in you." These words summarize the thought that the new life of the redeemed finds perpetual inspiration and vigor in the experience of dwelling in the "city of our God."

"Who can faint while such a river
Ever flows their thirst to assuage—
Grace which, like the Lord the Giver,
Never fails from age to age?" (John Newton).

The little poem prefigures a spiritual city where all nations will be born again as fellow citizens, a temple where they will meet with God in his love, a heavenly garden where together they will drink of the fountain of life. The New Testament teaches that something of this wonder is already to be experienced—the citizenship that is in heaven (Phil. 3:20), belonging to a Jerusalem that is above, the mother of many children (Gal. 4:26).

> *O Lord Most High, in love You have founded a place where heaven and earth meet, and by Your Word You have prepared a new birth for all who belong to that place. I beseech You to strengthen me by this vision and prepare my spirit through forgiveness and reconciliation. Hasten the time when all will rejoice together at the wells of Your salvation. AMEN*

"Song Sung Blue"

There is no sadder song in the Psalter. Here there is a companion in prayer for depressed people whose state of mind the psalm puts into words. If there is hardly a spark of hope in the psalm itself, the title does supply it, for this struggling author seems to have been one of the pioneers of the singing guilds set up by David, to which we owe the Korahite psalms (42–49, 84–85, 87–88), one of the richest sections of the Psalter. "Burdened and despondent as he was, his existence was far from pointless. If it was a living death, in God's hands it was to bear much fruit" (Kidner).

Read it and weep:

A song. A psalm of the sons of Korah. For the choir director: according to Mahalath. A Maskil of Heman the Ezrahite.

88:1 LORD, God of my salvation, I cry out before You day and night.
2 May my prayer reach Your presence; listen to my cry.
3 For I have had enough troubles, and my life is near Sheol.
4 I am counted among those going down to the Pit. I am like a man without strength,
5 abandoned among the dead. I am like the slain lying in the grave, whom You no longer remember, and who are cut off from Your care.
6 You have put me in the lowest part of the Pit, in the darkest places, in the depths.
7 Your wrath weighs heavily on me; You have overwhelmed me with all Your waves. *Selah*
8 You have distanced my friends from me; You have made me repulsive to them. I am shut in and cannot go out.
9 My eyes are worn out from crying. LORD, I cry out to You all day long; I spread out my hands to You.
10 Do You work wonders for the dead? Do departed spirits rise up to praise You? *Selah*
11 Will Your faithful love be declared in the grave, Your faithfulness in Abaddon?
12 Will Your wonders be known in the

> darkness, or Your righteousness in the land of oblivion?
> 13 But I call to You for help, Lord; in the morning my prayer meets You.
> 14 Lord, why do You reject me? Why do You hide Your face from me?
> 15 From my youth, I have been afflicted and near death. I suffer Your horrors; I am desperate.
> 16 Your wrath sweeps over me; Your terrors destroy me.
> 17 They surround me like water all day long; they close in on me from every side.
> 18 You have distanced loved one and neighbor from me; darkness is my only friend.
>
> (Psalm 88, HCSB)

Call it a *lament psalm* or a *psalm of disorientation*, the result is still the same. If "glorious things" were sung in the last psalm, the minor key is the only sound in this one. You should pray it when that song departs from your soul.

> "Song sung blue, Everybody knows one
> Song sung blue, Every garden grows one
> Me and you are subject to the blues now and then
> But when you take the blues and make a song
> You sing them out again."

Neil Diamond recommended that you sing a song, even if it is a blue one! When we lament through a song like Psalm 88, at least we are lamenting to God, not just complaining to others!

The next time you want to say, "Nobody knows how I feel," take time to read this psalm. With a host of metaphors, Heman described himself as a doomed man whom God had forsaken—but he did not give up (vv. 10–12). It is among the living that his miracles are performed, his praises sung, and his acts of deliverance exhibited. Death, however, is the last word in inactivity, silence, gloom, and oblivion. Even the New Testament calls it the last enemy. Not death but resurrection is the goal. The psalmist's questions allow no satisfying answer short of this.

The psalm recalls the fact that although sometimes godly people live lives of trouble (Ps. 73:14), they can still hold on to the hope that God is Savior. Many church fathers interpreted this psalm as a prayer of the suffering Christ (as Ps. 22), and for this reason it became part of Good Friday observances.

Your feelings may change, but God never changes. You can trust Him even in the dark, even when you seem to be drowning. God knows how you feel (Heb. 4:14–16) and is working out His purposes for you. The final verses of your "psalm" have not been written yet, but God knows what they are, so wait for Him. They are worth waiting for!

> *Lord God of my salvation, hear my cry and also those who are full of torments and terrors. Have mercy on those of us who have fallen without memory and are cut off from friends. By the intercession of Your Son and through the mystery of Your eternal purpose, raise us up to see the light of Your face where all is made well. AMEN.*

Psalm 89

Sure Mercies of David

In stark contrast to the despair of Psalm 88, Psalm 89 opens with the praise of "the Lord's faithul love" (v. 1). One of the most theological psalms in the Psalter, Psalm 89 is a commentary on the great prophecy of 2 Sam. 7:4–17. There is the promise of a throne for David's dynasty forever, and of unique honors for that king: 'I will establish the throne of his kingdom forever. I will be his father, and he shall be my son' (2 Sam.7:13–14). Other scriptures explore the Father-Son relationship more fully (Ps. 2:7–9). This psalm seizes chiefly on the phrase "forever," which promise seemed to be frustrated by the demise of that kingdom and the exile of its people.

It is a long one, but read it first:

A Maskil of Ethan the Ezrahite.

89:1 I will sing about the LORD's faithful love forever; with my mouth I will proclaim Your faithfulness to all generations.
2 For I will declare, "Faithful love is built up forever; You establish Your faithfulness in the heavens."
3 The LORD said, "I have made a covenant with My chosen one; I have sworn an oath to David My servant:
4 'I will establish your offspring forever and build up your throne for all generations.'" *Selah*
5 LORD, the heavens praise Your wonders Your faithfulness also in the assembly of the holy ones.
6 For who in the skies can compare with the LORD? Who among the heavenly beings is like the LORD?
7 God is greatly feared in the council of the holy ones, more awe-inspiring than all who surround Him.
8 LORD God of Hosts, who is strong like You, LORD? Your faithfulness surrounds You.
9 You rule the raging sea; when its waves surge, You still them.
10 You crushed Rahab like one who is slain; You scattered Your enemies with Your powerful arm.
11 The heavens are Yours; the earth also is Yours. The world and everything in it You founded them.
12 North and south You created them. Tabor and Hermon shout for joy at Your name.
13 You have a mighty arm; Your hand is powerful; Your right hand is lifted high.
14 Righteousness and justice are the

PSALM 89

foundation of Your throne; faithful love and truth go before You.

15 Happy are the people who know the joyful shout; LORD, they walk in the light of Your presence.

16 They rejoice in Your name all day long, and they are exalted by Your righteousness.

17 For You are their magnificent strength; by Your favor our horn is exalted.

18 Surely our shield belongs to the LORD, our king to the Holy One of Israel.

19 You once spoke in a vision to Your loyal ones and said: "I have granted help to a warrior; I have exalted one chosen from the people.

20 I have found David My servant; I have anointed him with My sacred oil.

21 My hand will always be with him, and My arm will strengthen him.

22 The enemy will not afflict him; no wicked man will oppress him.

23 I will crush his foes before him and strike those who hate him.

24 My faithfulness and love will be with him, and through My name his horn will be exalted.

25 I will extend his power to the sea and his right hand to the rivers.

26 He will call to Me, 'You are my Father, my God, the rock of my salvation.'

27 I will also make him My firstborn, greatest of the kings of the earth.

28 I will always preserve My faithful love for him, and My covenant with him will endure.

29 I will establish his line forever, his throne as long as heaven lasts.

30 If his sons forsake My instruction and do not live by My ordinances,

31 if they dishonor My statutes and do not keep My commandments,

32 then I will call their rebellion to account with the rod, their sin with blows.

33 But I will not withdraw My faithful love from him or betray My faithfulness.

34 I will not violate My covenant or change what My lips have said.

35 Once and for all I have sworn an oath by My holiness; I will not lie to David.

36 His offspring will continue forever, his throne like the sun before Me,

37 like the moon, established forever, a faithful witness in the sky." *Selah*

38 But You have spurned and rejected him; You have become enraged with Your anointed.

39 You have repudiated the covenant with Your servant; You have completely dishonored his crown.

40 You have broken down all his walls; You have reduced his fortified cities to ruins.

41 All who pass by plunder him; he has become a joke to his neighbors.

42 You have lifted high the right hand of his foes; You have made all his enemies rejoice.

43 You have also turned back his sharp sword and have not let him stand in battle.

44 You have made his splendor cease and have overturned his throne.

45 You have shortened the days of his youth; You have covered him with shame. *Selah*

46 How long, LORD? Will You hide Yourself forever? Will Your anger keep burning like fire?

47 Remember how short my life is. Have You created everyone for nothing?

48 What man can live and never see death? Who can save himself from the power of Sheol? *Selah*

49 Lord, where are the former acts of Your faithful love that You swore to David in

>   Your faithfulness?
> 50 Remember, Lord, the ridicule against Your servants—in my heart I carry abuse from all the peoples—
> 51 how Your enemies have ridiculed, Lord, how they have ridiculed every step of Your anointed.
> 52 May the Lord be praised forever. Amen and amen.
>
> (Psalm 89, HCSB)

Ethan the Ezrahite had a problem. One of the Davidic kings had been defeated in war and had lost his throne (vv. 38–45). It seemed to Ethan that God had broken His covenant (vv. 3, 28, 34, 39) and that God was not faithful to His people.

Faithfulness is a key word in this psalm (vv. 1, 2, 5, 8, 24, 33). **God's faithfulness is seen from generation to generation** (vv. 1–4), **among His people** (vv. 5–10), **in creation** (vv. 11–13), **among the nations** (vv. 14–18), **and toward David and his family** (vv. 19–37). **Ethan knew all of this because he knew the Scriptures, but recent events seemed to cast doubt on the truth of the covenant and the faithfulness of the Lord** (vv. 38–48).

Ethan's problem was caused by looking at the immediate and forgetting the ultimate. He prayed for the fulfillment of these great Davidic promises (vv. 49–51), and the answer came in Messiah Jesus, the Son of David (Matt. 1:1), who will reign forever (Luke 1:26–33). God's faithfulness does not fail!

Jeremiah felt as Ethan did when he wept over the demise of Judah's king and kingdom. Instead of questioning God's faithfulness, Jeremiah reaffirmed it: "Great is Your faithfulness" (Lam. 3:23). Never judge God's faithfulness on the basis of what you see or how you feel. His promises do not fail (2 Cor. 1:18–20).

The Doxology of the last verse (v. 52) is a blessing and double Amen, like Psalm 41:13 and Psalm 72:19. Thus the Third Book of the Psalter, in which national suffering has played a large part, ends on a firm note of praise.

O Ruler of heaven and earth, by the coming of Your Son You were faithful. Make out of His sufferings the rock of my salvation. Help me and all those afflicted to praise and bless Your holy name, that I also may be gladdened by the light of Your face through all the shadows of this world, until with Him I come to Your eternal glory. AMEN.

Psalm 90

O God Our Help in Ages Past

For a description of God's eternal grandeur over against our human frailty, only Isaiah 40 can be compared to this Psalm attributed to Moses. But while Isaiah is comforting, this Psalm is sobering, with the clouds dispersing in the final prayer. Often read at funerals, it is powerfully recalled in Isaac Watts' immortal hymn mentioned in today's title. It is a prayer supremely appropriate to any time of crisis.

Read about the contrast between God the Eternal and Man the Ephemeral in Psalm 90:

A prayer of Moses the man of God.

90:1 Lord, You have been our refuge in every generation.

2 Before the mountains were born, before You gave birth to the earth and the world, from eternity to eternity, You are God.

3 You return mankind to the dust, saying, "Return, descendants of Adam."

4 For in Your sight a thousand years are like yesterday that passes by, like a few hours of the night.

5 You end their life; they sleep. They are like grass that grows in the morning

6 in the morning it sprouts and grows; by evening it withers and dries up.

7 For we are consumed by Your anger; we are terrified by Your wrath.

8 You have set our unjust ways before You, our secret sins in the light of Your presence.

9 For all our days ebb away under Your wrath; we end our years like a sigh.

10 Our lives last seventy years or, if we are strong, eighty years. Even the best of them are struggle and sorrow; indeed, they pass quickly and we fly away.

11 Who understands the power of Your anger? Your wrath matches the fear that is due You.

12 Teach us to number our days carefully so that we may develop wisdom in our hearts.

13 Lord how long? Turn and have compassion on Your servants.

14 Satisfy us in the morning with Your faithful love so that we may shout with joy and be glad all our days.

> 15 Make us rejoice for as many days as You have humbled us, for as many years as we have seen adversity.
> 16 Let Your work be seen by Your servants, and Your splendor by their children.
> 17 Let the favor of the Lord our God be on us; establish for us the work of our hands establish the work of our hands!
> (Psalm 90, HCSB)

Wiersbe suggests that Moses may have written this psalm after the nation rebelled in unbelief at Kadesh Barnea (Num. 13–14). God announced that everybody twenty years and older would die within the next forty years. No wonder Moses prayed, "So teach us to number our days" (v. 12).

Although we measure our age by *years*, it is wiser to number our *days*, for we live a day at a time. Life is brief, like changing the guard, taking a nap, or mowing the lawn (vv. 3–6). In the camp of Israel, a twenty-year-old would not live beyond sixty. It was a funeral march for forty long years!

In the light of eternity (vv. 1–4), life is brief, no matter how long you live. We need God's help to use our days wisely (v. 12) and joyfully (vv. 14–15). There is real satisfaction in doing God's will (v. 14), revealing God's glory (v. 16) and growing in God's beauty (v. 17).

A regular prayer of mine since I reached three-score years is that God would not allow me to become a grumpy old man! In this psalm I think that I just discovered His answer to my prayer!!!

> *O Lord my God, may your beauty be upon me! When that happens, may I never think of being grumpy or dissatisfied.*
> *Amen.*

Psalm 91

Under His Wings

This is the preeminent psalm of refuge. That word appears three times (vv. 2, 4, 9), and other figures for safety abound, such as the title of today's comments (v. 4). This psalm of orientation is a promise of protection and safety for those on a journey. Isn't the metaphor of a *pilgrim* one of the most picturesque descriptions of a believer, both in Scripture and also in John Bunyan's immortal classic? Some of God's most beloved promises are found here, and yet these promises have been perverted to serve an evil purpose (Satan in Matt. 4:6).

Watch the change of pronouns and speakers as you read Psalm 91:

91:1 The one who lives under the protection of the Most High dwells in the shadow of the Almighty.
2 I will say to the LORD, "My refuge and my fortress, my God, in whom I trust."
3 He Himself will deliver you from the hunter's net, from the destructive plague.
4 He will cover you with His feathers; you will take refuge under His wings. His faithfulness will be a protective shield.
5 You will not fear the terror of the night, the arrow that flies by day,
6 the plague that stalks in darkness, or the pestilence that ravages at noon.
7 Though a thousand fall at your side and ten thousand at your right hand, the pestilence will not reach you.
8 You will only see it with your eyes and witness the punishment of the wicked.
9 Because you have made the LORD my refuge, the Most High your dwelling place,
10 no harm will come to you; no plague will come near your tent.
11 For He will give His angels orders concerning you, to protect you in all your ways.
12 They will support you with their hands so that you will not strike your foot against a stone.
13 You will tread on the lion and the cobra; you will trample the young lion and the serpent.

> ¹⁴ Because he is lovingly devoted to Me, I will deliver him; I will exalt him because he knows My name.
> ¹⁵ When he calls out to Me, I will answer him; I will be with him in trouble. I will rescue him and give him honor.
> ¹⁶ I will satisfy him with a long life and show him My salvation.
>
> (Psalm 91, HCSB)

These promises of security are not for people who run to the Lord only in times of danger but for those who dwell in His presence (v. 1) and make the Holy of Holies their habitation (v. 9).

What are the dangers we face? **Snares and pestilences (v. 3), arrows (v. 5), plagues (v. 10), stones (vv. 11–12), and lions and snakes (v. 13—perhaps referring to Satan)**. You can easily find the modern equivalents for these perils that ancient Jewish pilgrims encountered.

The **abiding life (vv. 1–4)** produces an **assuring life (vv. 5–13)**, the life without fear, which leads to **the abounding life (vv. 14–16)**, the life of victory and peace. The safest place in the world is in the center of the will of the Almighty under His protective shadow.

In this psalm *angels* play an important role (v. 11). God commands them to guard His people and the NT adds that they serve those who will inherit salvation (Heb. 1:14). Then why do believers sometimes experience accidents that end their lives? I like the observation that "we are immortal until our work is finished."

In the final verses of the psalm there is progress from the thought of God's initial deliverance to that of His abiding companionship and crowning gifts of glory, length of days, and a salvation no longer waited for but seen. These gifts (Rom. 8:18, 11, 23–25) reveal experiences only occasionally evident to the saints of the Old Testament.

> *Grant to me, LORD, the faith to believe in Your unfailing love and protection during the time of suffering. May I always hold on to Christ, so that I may know with Him at last the glory and salvation of Your eternal life. AMEN.*

How to Thrive

We have moved from the despair of Psalm 88 to a mood shift in Psalms 89–91 where the psalmists extol the greatness and grace of God. Psalm 92 continues that theme and brings it to a new height as it prepares the way for the "theocratic hymns" that follow in Psalms 93–99.

Read Psalm 92 in the HCSB:

> *A psalm. A song for the Sabbath day.*
> 92:1 It is good to praise the Lord, to sing praise to Your name, Most High,
> 2 to declare Your faithful love in the morning and Your faithfulness at night,
> 3 with a ten-stringed harp and the music of a lyre.
> 4 For You have made me rejoice, Lord, by what You have done; I will shout for joy because of the works of Your hands.
> 5 How magnificent are Your works, Lord, how profound Your thoughts!
> 6 A stupid person does not know, a fool does not understand this:
> 7 though the wicked sprout like grass and all evildoers flourish, they will be eternally destroyed.
> 8 But You, Lord, are exalted forever.
> 9 For indeed, Lord, Your enemies—indeed, Your enemies will perish; all evildoers will be scattered.
> 10 You have lifted up my horn like that of a wild ox; I have been anointed with oil.
> 11 My eyes look down on my enemies; my ears hear evildoers when they attack me.
> 12 The righteous thrive like a palm tree and grow like a cedar tree in Lebanon.
> 13 Planted in the house of the Lord, they thrive in the courtyards of our God.
> 14 They will still bear fruit in old age, healthy and green,
> 15 to declare: "The Lord is just; He is my rock, and there is no unrighteousness in Him."
>
> (Psalm 92, HCSB)

This "Song for the Sabbath" is proof that the Old Testament Sabbath was a day not only for rest but for corporate worship and intended to be a delight rather than a burden. The psalm's contrast of transient worldlings with the godly who ever renew their strength is vivid and compelling.

The psalmist looks at **God's love and faithfulness (vv. 1–3), His power in the creation around him (v. 4) and the depth of God's thoughts in His word (v. 5). The foolish do not understand His natural and supernatural revelation (vv. 6–7).**

In light of these certainties of God's provision, the **Godly do not need to fret over the actions of the wicked (vv. 9–11). Instead they will thrive because God is their Rock (vv. 12–15).**

A local hospital advertises that their purpose is to help you "thrive." To "thrive" or to "flourish" is a Biblical way of expressing the same idea.

The final verses, while applying to everyone, have particular relevance for those of us entering our mature years (note my euphemism for "getting old"). May our maturity be accompanied by the fully ripened fruit of the Spirit in our lives. The last verse (v. 15) returns us to the keynote of the psalm, which is the **praise of God**. The opening verses challenge us to declare this with our lips. The concluding verses encourage us to do so with our lives.

> *O Lord, Most High, when false teachings seem to abound, enable me to make music to Your name night and day. Grant that as I am nourished by Your grace, I may ever declare the greatness of Your deeds and Your truth. AMEN.*

The Lord Reigns!

A group of psalms directed to God as King begins here and continues to Psalms 99 or 100 (with the exception of Psalm 94). The cry "The Lord reigns" (Ps. 93:1, 96:10, 97:1, 99:1) links them together. Kidner observes, "There is a decisiveness in the Hebrew for 'the Lord reigns' which at least calls for an exclamation mark like 'The Lord is King'!" But this affirmation is far more than a timeless truth—it is an announcement that demands an obedient response from the subjects of that King!

When I wrote this, the NIV 2011 had just been published. Here is how it renders Psalm 93:

> 93:1 The LORD reigns, he is robed in majesty; the LORD is robed in majesty and armed with strength, indeed, the world is established, firm and secure.
> 2 Your throne was established long ago; you are from all eternity.
> 3 The seas have lifted up, LORD, the seas have lifted up their voice; the seas have lifted up their pounding waves.
> 4 Mightier than the thunder of the great waters, mightier than the breakers of the sea—the LORD on high is mighty.
> 5 Your statutes, LORD, stand firm; holiness adorns your house for endless days.
>
> (Psalm 93, NIV)

Wiersbe reminds us that when the seas are rising (v. 3), we should lay hold of three anchors that will steady us.

God's throne (v. 1–4). No matter what may happen to you today, "the LORD reigns!" God is sovereign and everything is under control. His majestic throne is strong, established, and everlasting. His throne is above the waters, but He is with you in your fiery trials and will see you through both the fire and the flood (Isa. 43:1–2).

God's testimonies (v. 5). You can trust the Word of God because it never fails (Josh. 21:45; 23:14). Cling to His testimonies (Ps. 119:31) and withstand those floods by faith. We have not yet reached that Golden Psalm 119, but it is always a steady guide in the midst of change all around us.

God's temple (v. 5). God's throne was the mercy seat in the Holy of Holies (Ps. 99:1), and there His *shekinah* glory rested. Satan himself cannot dethrone our Lord, and the men who attempt it are trying in vain to do so (Ps. 2:1–3).

When the storms arrive and the floods arise, you can experience peace and safety, because "the LORD is in His holy temple. Let all the earth keep silence before Him" (Hab. 2:20).

> "This and related psalms accordingly have something of peculiar value to offer in the way of spirituality. Let other texts exhort and promise. In these psalms the gates are open to a celebration already begun. Even now they invite us to a time-transcending experience of the great intervention, the world's transformation" (Eaton).

Open, O Lord, the eyes of my heart, that I may already see You as the victor over all evil, the eternal King of peace. May I always love Your commands, and adore You in the beauty of Your house forever.
AMEN

Psalm 94

How Do They Get Away With It?

I have heard concerned Christians say in despair, "If God does not judge America for its sins, He will have to apologize to Sodom and Gomorrah!" My purpose is not to evaluate that opinion, but to point out that the author of Psalm 94 may have felt the same way. Although the opening is almost belligerent, there emerges an underlying reflective tone and a confident spirit. The psalm is driven by the conviction of God's self-consistency which is similar to that of Psalm 37 and the Proverbs, plus an ardent personal faith which knows God's faithfulness first hand.

94:1 LORD, God of vengeance—God of vengeance, appear.
2 Rise up, Judge of the earth; repay the proud what they deserve.
3 LORD, how long will the wicked—how long will the wicked gloat?
4 They pour out arrogant words; all the evildoers boast.
5 LORD, they crush Your people; they afflict Your heritage.
6 They kill the widow and the foreigner and murder the fatherless.
7 They say, "The LORD doesn't see it. The God of Jacob doesn't pay attention."
8 Pay attention, you stupid people! Fools, when will you be wise?
9 Can the One who shaped the ear not hear, the One who formed the eye not see?
10 The One who instructs nations, the One who teaches man knowledge—does He not discipline?
11 The LORD knows man's thoughts, they are meaningless.
12 LORD, happy is the man You discipline and teach from Your law
13 to give him relief from troubled times until a pit is dug for the wicked.
14 The LORD will not forsake His people or abandon His heritage,
15 for justice will again be righteous, and all the upright in heart will follow it.
16 Who stands up for me against the wicked? Who takes a stand for me against evildoers?
17 If the LORD had not been my help, I would soon rest in the silence of death.
18 If I say, "My foot is slipping," Your faithful love will support me, LORD.

¹⁹ When I am filled with cares, Your comfort brings me joy.
²⁰ Can a corrupt throne—one that creates trouble by law—become Your ally?
²¹ They band together against the life of the righteous and condemn the innocent to death.
²² But the Lord is my refuge; my God is the rock of my protection.
²³ He will pay them back for their sins and destroy them for their evil. The Lord our God will destroy them.

(Psalm 94, HCSB)

What about our enemy in battle? The best preparation for battle is knowing your enemy. Paul wrote that he was not ignorant of Satan's methods (2 Cor. 2:11).

God knows all about our enemy (vv. 1–11). He hears their insolent speech, He sees their wicked deeds, and He will eventually bring them to judgment. The Captain of your salvation will not be caught off guard!

God will teach us what to do about our enemy (vv. 12–15). The basic "Handbook for War" is the Word of God, and God will teach you in it what you need to know. Gideon was an ordinary farmer when God called him, and yet he became a mighty warrior because he learned from God (Judg. 6–7). Although he may not have felt like it, God called him a "mighty man of valor" (Judg. 6:11–12).

God will help us to defeat our enemy (vv. 16–23). God is for you if you are against what He is against. When you fight, He will help you. If you slip, He will hold you. If you worry, He will comfort you, and if you are attacked, He will defend you.

Who is on the Lord's side? Are you? And what does that mean if you are? VICTORY! And don't you forget it!! "We are more than conquerors" (Rom. 8:37).

Lord of Lords, I thank You that You are at the right hand of the Father, interceding for me and for all the rest of your sheep. I thank You that we are more than conquerors through You who loved us. O Lord, when I feel defeated, help me to realize afresh that I am on the victor's side in this battle. May I put on the armor of God that You have provided for me and stand strong against the enemy. Through Jesus the Victor. AMEN.

Psalm 95

The Way to Worship

Ministers have often used this psalm as a call and guide to worship. Its serious conclusion balances the exuberant opening with the same realism as that of the prophets with their call to match noble words with noble deeds. In the middle, the voice of God breaks in to challenge Israel with the claims of the covenant. But Heb. 3:7–4:13, in expounding this psalm, forbids us to confine its thrust to Israel. The "Today" of which it speaks is this very moment, while the "you" is none other than ourselves, and the promised "rest" is not Canaan but salvation in the Messiah (Kidner). Read the psalm and notice the shift in the middle (v. 7) from exalting God to an exhortation to obey Him.

95:1 Come, let us shout joyfully to the Lord, shout triumphantly to the rock of our salvation!
2 Let us enter His presence with thanksgiving; let us shout triumphantly to Him in song.
3 For the Lord is a great God, a great King above all gods.
4 The depths of the earth are in His hand, and the mountain peaks are His.
5 The sea is His; He made it. His hands formed the dry land.
6 Come, let us worship and bow down; let us kneel before the Lord our Maker.
7 For He is our God, and we are the people of His pasture, the sheep under His care. Today, if you hear His voice:
8 "Do not harden your hearts as at Meribah, as on that day at Massah in the wilderness
9 where your fathers tested Me; they tried Me, though they had seen what I did.
10 For 40 years I was disgusted with that generation; I said, 'They are a people whose hearts go astray; they do not know My ways.
11 So I swore in My anger, 'They will not enter My rest.'"

(Psalm 95, HCSB)

In this psalm think of God's existence and His exhortation in two brief ways:

God is great in His faithfulness (vv. 1–7). This is a call to jubilant worship, not just participation in services as usual. He invites us to "shout joyfully" and to "kneel before the LORD our Maker."

God is grieved by our faithlessness (vv. 8–11). The opposite of a worshiping heart that pleases the Lord is a hard heart that grieves the Lord. Unbelieving Israel's failure to enter the land is a lesson to us! (Heb. 3–4).

"If this is a psalm about worship, it could give no blunter indication that the heart of the matter is severely practical—nothing less than a bending of wills and a renewal of pilgrimage" (Kidner).

I am reading a book by a theology professor who bemoans the fact that God-centered worship has all but disappeared in evangelical worship services, replaced by performers and entertainment rather than God-focused praise and adoration. Has our Protestant desire to avoid *transubstantiation* in the Eucharist impoverished the "real presence" of the Lord in our services? Israel did not gather to be entertained. This psalm focuses on the centrality of the Lord in Israel's worship, but that does not mean that the effect on the behavior of its readers and singers is neglected. The latter part of this psalm (vv. 7–11) is a strong exhortation to us and is the "therefore" that is based on the very real truth that God should be the center of both our affections and our service!

> *Come, Thou Almighty King, help us thy name to sing. Help us to praise. Father, All Glorious, o'er all victorious, come and reign over us, Ancient of Days! AMEN.*

Psalm 96

Tell His Glory Among the Gentiles

While describing the triumphal entry of the ark into Jerusalem, the Chronicler (Ezra?) includes nearly the whole of this psalm, with parts of two others (Psalms 105 and 106), as the centerpiece of his chapter (1 Chron. 16:8–36). The repeated words and phrases rising in intensity ("sing," "ascribe," "he comes") provides the psalm with an increasing vigor (see Ps. 93:1) and contributes to the excitement at the prospect of God's coming. "The creation's 'eager longing,' of which Paul speaks in Romans 8:19, breaks out here into singing at the moment of its fulfillment" (Kidner).

In this intensely Jewish scene there is a clear emphasis on the Gentiles bringing glory to the God of Israel. This is another evidence, not only for the inclusion of Gentiles in the promise to Abram (Gen. 12:3), but also that the parochialism associated with later Judaism was foreign to these Biblical authors. Along with Isaiah (Isa. 11:9–10; 49:6), theirs was a world vision.

As this psalm exhorts, sing this "new song" to Yahweh.

96:1 Sing a new song to the LORD; sing to the LORD, all the earth.
2 Sing to the LORD, praise His name; proclaim His salvation from day to day.
3 Declare His glory among the nations, His wonderful works among all peoples.
4 For the LORD is great and is highly praised; He is feared above all gods.
5 For all the gods of the peoples are idols, but the LORD made the heavens.
6 Splendor and majesty are before Him; strength and beauty are in His sanctuary.
7 Ascribe to the LORD, you families of the peoples, ascribe to the LORD glory and strength.
8 Ascribe to the LORD the glory of His name; bring an offering and enter His courts.
9 Worship the LORD in the splendor of His holiness; tremble before Him, all the earth.
10 Say among the nations: "The LORD reigns. The world is firmly established; it cannot be shaken. He judges the peoples fairly."
11 Let the heavens be glad and the earth

rejoice; let the sea and all that fills it resound.
12 Let the fields and everything in them exult. Then all the trees of the forest will shout for joy
13 before the Lord, for He is coming—for He is coming to judge the earth. He will judge the world with righteousness and the peoples with His faithfulness.
(Psalm 96, HCSB)

In Psalm 96 we are told to:

Sing to the Lord (vv. 1–6). Sing a new song because you have had a new experience with Him. Sing a worship hymn because God is glorious (v. 3) and great (vv. 4–5). Sing a gospel song because the nations need to hear the good news of salvation.

Give to the Lord (vv. 7–10). Give Him glory with your lips and heart, and give Him offerings with your hands. God does not need your gifts, but you need to bring your gifts to God. He deserves the best (Mal. 1:6–14).

Look to the Lord (vv. 11–13). All nature is eagerly anticipating the Lord's return, for then creation will be set free (Rom. 8:18–25). The oppressed people will be vindicated, and sinners will be judged when Jesus Christ comes to reign. God's people shall reign with Christ and then worship Him perfectly.

This ecstatic welcome for the Lord has its NT counterpart on Palm Sunday when given the opportunity "the very stones would cry out." How much more the teeming seas, fields and forests. At creation "the morning stars sang together." At his coming, the earth will join in again.

Lord, I thank You for those precious moments of vision where I see for myself that Yours is the kingdom, the power and the glory, and Yours is the victory of salvation and the dominion over a redeemed creation. I pray with all my heart that Your kingdom will come, and Your will be done on earth as it is in heaven, when the fellowship of all the redeemed shall join in the thunder of Your praise. AMEN.

Psalm 97

Reigning and Ruling

This psalm begins like the other theocratic psalms in this section, with a celebration of God's kingly rule: "The Lord reigns, let the many coasts and islands be glad" (v. 1). It turns quickly to the theme of judgment: "Clouds and darkness surround Him. Righteousness and justice are the foundation of His throne" (v. 2). These two themes are worked out in the two main sections:

The Lord Reigns with Power and Cannot Be Resisted (vv. 1–7).
Therefore, the Wicked Should Tremble at His Coming
The Lord Rules His People and Causes Rejoicing (vv. 8–12).
Therefore, the Righteous Should Rejoice at His Coming

With these two emphases in mind, let's read the psalm:

97:1 The LORD reigns! Let the earth rejoice; let the many coasts and islands be glad.
2 Clouds and thick darkness surround Him; righteousness and justice are the foundation of His throne.
3 Fire goes before Him and burns up His foes on every side.
4 His lightning lights up the world; the earth sees and trembles.
5 The mountains melt like wax at the presence of the LORD—at the presence of the LORD of all the earth.
6 The heavens proclaim His righteousness; all the peoples see His glory.
7 All who serve carved images, those who boast in idols, will be put to shame. All the gods must worship Him.
8 Zion hears and is glad, and the towns of Judah rejoice because of Your judgments, LORD.
9 For You, LORD, are the Most High over all the earth; You are exalted above all the gods.
10 You who love the LORD, hate evil! He protects the lives of His godly ones; He rescues them from the hand of the wicked.
11 Light dawns for the righteous, gladness for the upright in heart.
12 Be glad in the LORD, you righteous ones, and praise His holy name.
(Psalm 97, HCSB)

God's righteousness is revealed in the booming thunderstorm of verses 2–5, which brings shame to the idol-worshipers. God's people, however, hear His voice in the storm and they rejoice (v. 8). The psalmist builds a world-view out of vivid contrasts—the idolaters with the pious, the good with the evil, and the faithful with the faithless. There are no shades of gray here, and it appears that Psalm 1 has set the agenda for these bi-polar contrasts of life and death, of false gods and the True God, and of the righteous and the wicked.

The psalmist envisions the glorious coming of the Lord in all His splendor. In light of His coming to reign and to judge His adversaries in righteousness, the psalmist exhorts the saints to hate evil and rejoice in the Lord (cf. 2 Peter 3:10-11, 14).

> Moderns are drowning in a cesspool of ambiguities. The Biblical authors saw things starkly and simply. May we affirm anew their view of an ultimate reality that is painted in black and white colors, "without our hesitating retinue of finer shades" (T.E. Lawrence).

O God Most High, whose conquering glory is now often veiled in thick darkness, create in me a clean and obedient heart, that I may ever rejoice in the salvation You have accomplished through the sacrificial death and reigning life of Your Son, our Lord Jesus Christ. AMEN.

Psalm 98

King and Savior

Evangelical Anglican scholar, Derek Kidner, introduces this psalm with these words, which I quote because I can't improve on them! "Known as the *Cantate Domino* ('O sing to the Lord'), this psalm was interposed in the *Book of Common Prayer* between the evening Old Testament reading and its New Testament fulfillment. It is a close companion to Psalm 96, but is wholly given up to praise. Here there are no comparisons with the heathen, no instructions in right worship: all is joy and exhilaration."

Read it and rejoice:

> *A Psalm.*
> 98:1 Sing a new song to the LORD, for He has performed wonders; His right hand and holy arm have won Him victory.
> 2 The LORD has made His victory known; He has revealed His righteousness in the sight of the nations.
> 3 He has remembered His love and faithfulness to the house of Israel; all the ends of the earth have seen our God's victory.
> (Psalm 98:1–3, HCSB)

The word victory that dominates this section (vv. 1–3) is a richer word in Scripture than in our English language. Its chief aspect is "salvation" as in the name "Jesus." This salvation/victory is wholly supernatural, a monergistic exploit of the Lord.

> 4 Shout to the LORD, all the earth; be jubilant, shout for joy, and sing.
> 5 Sing to the LORD with the lyre, with the lyre and melodious song.
> 6 With trumpets and the blast of the ram's horn shout triumphantly in the presence of the LORD, our King.
> (Psalm 98:4–6, HCSB)

The joyful shout of verses 4 and 6 is the spontaneous acclamation that might greet a king or a moment of victory. It is the word translated "shout aloud" in Zech. 9:9, the prophecy that was fulfilled on Palm Sunday.

> 7 Let the sea and all that fills it, the world and those who live in it, resound.
> 8 Let the rivers clap their hands; let the mountains shout together for joy
> 9 before the LORD, for He is coming to judge the earth. He will judge the world righteously and the peoples fairly.
> (Psalm 98:7–9, HCSB)

This praise from nature is inarticulate, unlike the praise of man. But it too can be heard already, since the whole earth even now is full of God's glory (see Ps. 19:1–3). With its companions in this section of the Psalter, Psalm 98 makes the point which Rom. 8:19–21 expounds: that nature will not come into its own until man himself is ruled in righteousness and equity. That truth is the source of this psalm's jubilation and is expressed succinctly in the statement which sums up the Christian hope: for He is coming (v. 9).

> "The scene in this psalm is as ultimate as it can be, involving a drastic revolution in our ways; but it is nothing if not a present reality, more real than what passes for reality, and the true worshippers of God, those who know his salvation, must enter it now" (Eaton).

I thank You, LORD, for the Psalms which reveal the fulfillment of Your love in Your kingdom. Help me to respond and enter that circle of praise, that along with the multitude of Your creation, I may give thanks for Your marvelous salvation, through Christ the Word by whom all things were made. AMEN

Holy Is He!

Three times in this psalm comes the refrain: **"He is Holy"** (vv. 3, 5, 9). The last appearance is exactly **"the Lord our God is Holy."** There are some who think that the acclamation should be translated "Holy Is It" referring to the Lord's name in verse 3 and His footstool in verse 5, but the clear application of "Holy" to the Lord Himself in verse nine indicates that it is the Lord Himself who is "the Holy One." The expression "Holy One of Israel" is also a favorite Divine title in Isaiah (Isa. 1:4, plus 29 more times).

Because many Bible readers think of words like *good* and *righteous* and *pure* when they hear the word "Holy," they are surprised when they are told that it basically means "set apart" or "unique." Actually it implies more than that, because in the Biblical context it means "set apart from normal uses." God is pure and good and righteous BECAUSE He is wholly unique and different from anything or anyone common. After the exuberant praise of the preceding psalms, the reader has to be struck by the exhortation to recollect how exalted and holy He is, and how profound should be the reverence we owe him.

Read the psalm and pause at the three statements about God's holiness and reflect on the truth in your own mind and heart. Some translations place "He" first, but the Hebrew order is clear—"Holy" is the first word in each sentence.

99:1 The Lord reigns! Let the peoples tremble. He is enthroned above the cherubim. Let the earth quake.
2 The Lord is great in Zion; He is exalted above all the peoples.
3 Let them praise Your great and awe-inspiring name. **He is holy**.
4 The mighty King loves justice. You have established fairness; You have administered justice and righteousness in Jacob.
5 Exalt the Lord our God; bow in worship at His footstool. **He is holy.**
6 Moses and Aaron were among His

> priests; Samuel also was among those calling on His name. They called to the Lord, and He answered them.
> 7 He spoke to them in a pillar of cloud; they kept His decrees and the statutes He gave them.
> 8 Lord our God, You answered them. You were a God who forgave them, but punished their misdeeds.
> 9 Exalt the Lord our God. Bow in worship at His holy mountain, for **the Lord our God is holy**.
>
> (Psalm 99, HCSB)

The central focus of these theocratic psalms (93–99) has been on the universal rule of God over the nations. Now the focus shifts to His special care for Israel (vv. 2, 4, 6).

The final verse admonishes us in summary: "Exalt the Lord our God. Bow in worship at His holy mountain, for **the Lord our God is Holy**." Holiness returns in a refrain which is a partner to verses 3 and 5. "He is Holy" is now expanded and given warmth, to read "For the Lord our God is Holy!" His majesty is undiminished, but the last word is now given to intimacy. He is holy but He is also not ashamed to be called ours.

Well may we worship. "Holy, Holy, Holy is the Lord of Hosts; the whole earth is full of His glory" (Isa. 6:3).

> *Holy, holy, holy! Lord God Almighty! All Thy works shall praise Thy Name, in earth, and sky, and sea. Holy, holy, holy; merciful and mighty! God in three Persons, blessed Trinity!*
> *AMEN*

Is It Thanksgiving Yet?

This greatly beloved psalm of orientation is a favorite at Thanksgiving, but is suitable for anytime of the year. In my fourth grade class in public school we memorized some Bible passages—and Psalm 100 was one of them. I am sure that dear old Mrs. Frey would be happy to know that I never forgot those passages (also the Beatitudes and Psalm 23!). Because I memorized them from the King James Version, I include the words of Psalm 100 from that venerable version which celebrated its 400th anniversary in 2011.

The hymn, "All People That On Earth Do Dwell," is based on Psalm 100.

A Psalm of Praise.
100:1 Make a joyful noise unto the LORD, all ye lands.
2 Serve the LORD with gladness: Come before his presence with singing.
3 Know ye that the LORD he is God: It is he that hath made us, and not we ourselves; We are his people, and the sheep of his pasture.
4 Enter into his gates with thanksgiving, And into his courts with praise: Be thankful unto him, and bless his name.
5 For the LORD is good; his mercy is everlasting; And his truth endureth to all generations.

(Psalm 100, KJV)

The mention of the Lord's eternal goodness and mercy (steadfast love) in verse five recalls the confident affirmation that ends another famous psalm: "surely *goodness* and *mercy* shall follow me all the days of my life" (Ps. 23:6). These themes of the Lord's goodness, mercy and truth again remind us that the Psalms are basically an exposition of that amazing Divine self-revelation to Moses in Exo. 34:6.

Amid the familiarity of these words, we can forget the amazing symmetry of its message:

A^1 (vs 1–2) Threefold invitation; make a noise, serve, come
   B^1 (v 3) Threefold affirmation: God ... made us ... his
A^2 (v 4) Threefold invitation: enter ... give thanks ... praise
   B^2 (v 5) Threefold affirmation of God's nature: Good ... mercy ... truth

"When gratitude dies on the altar of a man's heart, he is well nigh hopeless" (Bob Jones, Sr.).

> *O God, my maker and shepherd, lift up in me the joy that is a sincere response to Your work of salvation. Grant that with a thankful heart I may ever serve before Your face, You who have drawn near to me in the name of the Lord Jesus. AMEN.*

Psalm 100 (part 2)

"The Old Hundredth"

Are you aware that from ancient times the Psalter was the hymn book for Israel? Are you aware that for the last two thousand years, Christians privately and publicly sang the psalms? There is even a Presbyterian denomination that still holds to "exclusive psalmody" in their congregational singing! We need not go to the extreme of neglecting hymns other than Psalter since the saints in Revelation sing other hymns to our great God and Savior (Rev. 5:9–13). But singing the Psalms as one aspect of our private devotions and public worship is still a wonderful practice.

Below is what was once a well-known hymn based on a paraphrase of Psalm 100. It is now usually referred to by its first line, "All People That on Earth Do Dwell." Its tune is called "The Old Hundredth."

> All people that on earth do dwell,
> Sing to the Lord with cheerful voice.
> Him serve with mirth, His praise forth tell;
> Come ye before Him and rejoice.
>
> Know that the Lord is God indeed;
> Without our aid He did us make;
> We are His folk, He does us feed;
> And for His sheep He doth us take.
>
> O enter then His gates with praise,
> Approach with joy His courts unto;
> Praise, laud and bless His name always,
> For it is seemly so to do.

> For why? The Lord our God is good,
> His mercy is forever sure;
> His truth at all times firmly stood,
> And shall from age to age endure." William Kethe (1561)

The goodness of the Lord is demonstrated in the formation and care of his people, which is affirmed in v 3. According to Deuteronomy, he sets before His people "life and good" versus "death and evil" (30:15) and urges them to choose life, which is found in obedience to the ways of the Lord (Deut 30:19–20; "For He is your life and the length of your days").

Another psalm expresses it this way:

> Good and upright is the LORD,
>   therefore he instructs sinners in his ways.
> He guides the humble in what is right
>   and teaches them his way.
> All the ways of the LORD are loving and faithful
>   for those who keep the demands of his covenant
>
> (Ps 25:8–10).

Sing it and pray this psalm of Yahweh's goodness with thanksgiving in your heart. Now ask someone to join with you!

The Ruler and the Ruled

In this Wisdom Psalm David reappears after a long absence to speak first about himself and then about his subjects. Both should meet the theocratic requirements for the **ruler** and the **ruled**. The psalm, therefore, may be outlined simply:

Truth in the Ruler (vv. 1–4)
Truth in the Ranks (vv. 5–8)

Read it in that light:

A Psalm of David.
101:1 I will sing of lovingkindness and justice, To You, O LORD, I will sing praises.
2 I will give heed to the blameless way. When will You come to me? I will walk within my house in the integrity of my heart.
3 I will set no worthless thing before my eyes; I hate the work of those who fall away; It shall not fasten its grip on me.
4 A perverse heart shall depart from me; I will know no evil.
5 Whoever secretly slanders his neighbor, him I will destroy; No one who has a haughty look and an arrogant heart will I endure.
6 My eyes shall be upon the faithful of the land, that they may dwell with me; He who walks In a blameless way is the one who will minister to me.
7 He who practices deceit shall not dwell within my house; He who speaks falsehood shall not maintain his position before me.
8 Every morning I will destroy all the wicked of the land, So as to cut off from the city of the LORD all those who do iniquity.

(Psalm 101, NASB)

Determination and dedication characterize this psalm as David says "I will" nine times. He wanted a perfect heart (v. 2), not a perverse heart (v. 4) nor a proud heart (v. 5). To be "perfect" before the Lord does not mean to be sinless. It means to be sincere and without pretense. John called it "walking in the light" (1 John 1:5–10).

David wanted justice in the land and the city (v. 8), just as we do today. But civic righteousness must begin in the heart and in the home (vv. 2, 7). Yes, we need honest people enforcing just laws, but we also need godly people living righteous lives, starting at home.

Whether king or subject, we must be careful what we look at (v. 3) and listen to (v. 5), and with whom we fellowship (v. 6). In a world full of deceit, we must avoid lies and walk in God's wisdom (vv. 2, 7).

On the king and his people this psalm impressed the Lord's requirement of faithful love, truth and sincerity. Only to a king so minded would the Lord come as a partner to rule. In his private and his public life the king should follow the Lord's way with a whole heart and exert himself to employ only those true to this way. How far David was to fall short of this pattern in his own reign is sadly recounted in 2 Samuel. But the psalm was still an inspired model, set forth to challenge him and his successors, among whom are all of us who run any organization and choose its leaders.

> "For its perfect fulfilment we are forced to look beyond our approximations, to the Messiah himself" (Kidner).

Help me, Lord, to sing about Your faithful love as I make my way through work, home, and leisure. May humility and kindness resound in my heart, that I may be acceptable for the service of my king, Your Son, Jesus Messiah. AMEN.

Psalm 102

"But You..."

This psalm has been called a Penitential, a Lament, and a Messianic Psalm because it shares characteristics of all three types. This reminds us that the Psalms don't always fit into our neat categories. Aren't our lives that way too? Sometimes our problems just defy any counselor's stereotypes! Maybe that is another reason why we love these psalms!

The troubles of the psalmist are initially private griefs, but later they broaden to a concern for Zion, whose destiny is slow in being fulfilled. The closing passage portrays the contrast between human time and the Lord's eternity, bringing it to a majestic conclusion (Kidner). The psalm is also quoted in praise of the Son in Heb. 1:10–12. So the psalm *is* Messianic, and the sufferings of the speaker recall those of the Sufferer in Psalm 22.

Read this psalm of re-orientation:

A prayer of the Afflicted when he is faint and pours out his complaint before the LORD.

102:1 Hear my prayer, O LORD! And let my cry for help come to You.
2 Do not hide Your face from me in the day of my distress; Incline Your ear to me; In the day when I call answer me quickly.
3 For my days have been consumed in smoke, And my bones have been scorched like a hearth.
4 My heart has been smitten like grass and has withered away, Indeed, I forget to eat my bread.
5 Because of the loudness of my groaning My bones cling to my flesh.
6 I resemble a pelican of the wilderness; I have become like an owl of the waste places.
7 I lie awake, I have become like a lonely bird on a housetop.
8 My enemies have reproached me all day long; Those who deride me have used my name as a curse.
9 For I have eaten ashes like bread And mingled my drink with weeping
10 Because of Your indignation and Your wrath, For You have lifted me up and cast me away.
11 My days are like a lengthened shadow, And I wither away like grass.

12 But You, O LORD, abide forever, And Your name to all generations.
13 You will arise and have compassion on Zion; For it is time to be gracious to her, For the appointed time has come.
14 Surely Your servants find pleasure in her stones And feel pity for her dust.
15 So the nations will fear the name of the LORD And all the kings of the earth Your glory.
16 For the LORD has built up Zion; He has appeared in His glory.
17 He has regarded the prayer of the destitute And has not despised their prayer.
18 This will be written for the generation to come, That a people yet to be created may praise the LORD.
19 For He looked down from His holy height; From heaven the LORD gazed upon the earth,
20 To hear the groaning of the prisoner, To set free those who were doomed to death,
21 That men may tell of the name of the LORD in Zion And His praise in Jerusalem,
22 When the peoples are gathered together, And the kingdoms, to serve the LORD.
23 He has weakened my strength in the way; He has shortened my days
24 I say, "O my God, do not take me away in the midst of my days, Your years are throughout all generations.
25 "Of old You founded the earth, And the heavens are the work of Your hands.
26 " Even they will perish, but You endure; And all of them will wear out like a garment; Like clothing You will change them and they will be changed.
27 "But You are the same, And Your years will not come to an end.
28 "The children of Your servants will continue, And their descendants will be established before You."

(Psalm 102, NASB)

The personal time of my distress (vv. 1–11)
The appointed time of Zion's deliverance (vv. 12–22)
The eternal time of Yahweh's duration (vv. 23–28)

God enjoys endless years, but we endure shortened days (vv. 23–24), troubled days (vv. 2), and days that vanish like smoke, grass, and a shadow (vv. 3, 4, 11). We sit alone like birds in a desert and dying patients in a hospital (vv. 5–9). Looking at yourself and your feelings will only make things worse. Things will be different when you look away from yourself to God and say, "But You" (v. 12).

"But You shall endure" (vv. 12–22). If you know Jesus Christ by faith, you possess eternal life (1 John 5:11–13). So, living in a world of death and decay need not be a threat to you because you will live forever with the Lord (1 Thess. 4:13–18).

"But You are the same" (vv. 25–28). Everything around us is changing. People die and my own body weakens, and it is easy to become either afraid or sour—or both! But God does not change (Heb. 13:5–8), and He is your guide to the end (Ps. 73:24).

Oh, didn't you hear? It's not all about you!

> *"Swift to its close ebbs out life's little day; Earth's joys grow dim, its glories pass away; Change and decay in all around I see; O Thou who changest not, abide with me."* AMEN.

Psalm 103

"Don't You Forget It!"

There are no requests directed toward God in this psalm. It is all praise and a huge reminder to not forget His blessings, or as verse two calls them: "His benefits." He focuses on three of those benefits in verses three to five and structures the psalm around them. They are forgiveness, redemption, and satisfaction. But first, let's read the psalm and look for those three benefits.

A Psalm of David

103:1 Bless the LORD, O my soul, And all that is within me, bless His holy name.
2 Bless the LORD, O my soul, And forget none of His benefits;
3 Who pardons all your iniquities, Who heals all your diseases;
4 Who redeems your life from the pit, Who crowns you with lovingkindness and compassion;
5 Who satisfies your years with good things, So that your youth is renewed like the eagle.
6 The LORD performs righteous deeds And judgments for all who are oppressed.
7 He made known His ways to Moses, His acts to the sons of Israel.
8 The LORD is compassionate and gracious, Slow to anger and abounding in lovingkindness.
9 He will not always strive with us, Nor will He keep His anger forever.
10 He has not dealt with us according to our sins, Nor rewarded us according to our iniquities.
11 For as high as the heavens are above the earth, So great is His lovingkindness toward those who fear Him.
12 As far as the east is from the west, So far has He removed our transgressions from us.
13 Just as a father has compassion on his children, So the LORD has compassion on those who fear Him.
14 For He Himself knows our frame; He is mindful that we are but dust.
15 As for man, his days are like grass; As a flower of the field, so he flourishes.
16 When the wind has passed over it, it is no more, And its place acknowledges it no longer.
17 But the lovingkindness of the LORD is from everlasting to everlasting on those who fear Him, And His righteousness to children's children,
18 To those who keep His covenant And remember His precepts to do them.

PSALM 103

¹⁹ The LORD has established His throne in the heavens, And His sovereignty rules over all.
²⁰ Bless the LORD, you His angels, Mighty in strength, who perform His word, Obeying the voice of His word!
²¹ Bless the LORD, all you His hosts, You who serve Him, doing His will.
²² Bless the LORD, all you works of His, In all places of His dominion; Bless the LORD, O my soul!

(Psalm 103, NASB)

Bless the Lord for forgiveness (vv. 3, 10–14). Notice how David mentions the blessing (v. 3) and then elaborates on it later (vv. 10–14). Forgiveness is like relief when you are burdened (vv. 11–12), and reconciliation when you have hurt someone (vv. 13–14).

Bless the Lord for redemption (vv. 4, 6–9). God redeemed the nation from bondage and from the difficulties they faced on their journey to Canaan. He frees us that He might be our Master and care for us forever. When He crowns us, He transforms slaves into princes (Rom. 5:17).

Bless the Lord for satisfaction (vv. 5, 15–18). Man is frail and temporary, but believers can enjoy "eternal youth" and spiritual renewal. David likens us to an old eagle who still soars upward with new strength because of the thermals that lift him (Isa. 40:31).

You belong to the King who rules over everything (v. 19)! The angels praise Him (vv. 20–22), so how much more should we praise who have experienced His benefits!

Oh, didn't you hear? It's not all about you! Now don't you forget it!!

Wiersbe adds: "Just as God renews the face of the earth and brings it new life and beauty (Ps. 104:30), so He can renew your life. It begins with a renewed mind (Rom. 12:1–2) as the Spirit teaches you God's Word (Eph. 4:23). Wait before the Lord in worship, and He will renew your strength (Isa. 40:31). When you walk by faith, you have constant renewal in spite of the changes of life (2 Cor. 4:16–18)."

> *Father, grant me a heart that blesses You with such sincerity that I am drawn ever deeper into Your forgiving love and Your renewing grace. May I rejoice to obey Your will and do Your commandments, as You have removed my sins far away by Your mercy in Jesus Christ. AMEN.*

Psalm 104

Creator – Sustainer

Psalm 104 was written as a companion to Psalm 103, in light of their identical openings and closings. Together the two psalms praise God as Savior and Creator, Father and Sustainer. "In the galaxy of the Psalter these are twin stars of the first magnitude" (Kidner). Like its twin sister it is long, but reading it as a whole yields the benefits it intends to convey.

104:1 Bless the Lord, O my soul! O Lord my God, You are very great; You are clothed with splendor and majesty,
2 Covering Yourself with light as with a cloak, Stretching out heaven like a tent curtain.
3 He lays the beams of His upper chambers in the waters; He makes the clouds His chariot; He walks upon the wings of the wind;
4 He makes the winds His messengers, Flaming fire His ministers.
5 He established the earth upon its foundations, So that it will not totter forever and ever.
6 You covered it with the deep as with a garment; The waters were standing above the mountains.
7 At Your rebuke they fled, At the sound of Your thunder they hurried away.
8 The mountains rose; the valleys sank down To the place which You established for them.
9 You set a boundary that they may not pass over, So that they will not return to cover the earth.
10 He sends forth springs in the valleys; They flow between the mountains;
11 They give drink to every beast of the field; The wild donkeys quench their thirst.
12 Beside them the birds of the heavens dwell; They lift up their voices among the branches.
13 He waters the mountains from His upper chambers; The earth is satisfied with the fruit of His works.
14 He causes the grass to grow for the cattle, And vegetation for the labor of man, So that he may bring forth food from the earth,
15 And wine which makes man's heart glad, So that he may make his face glisten with oil, And food which sustains man's heart.
16 The trees of the Lord drink their fill, The cedars of Lebanon which He planted,
17 Where the birds build their nests, And the stork, whose home is the fir trees.
18 The high mountains are for the wild

goats; The cliffs are a refuge for the shephanim.
19 He made the moon for the seasons; The sun knows the place of its setting.
20 You appoint darkness and it becomes night, In which all the beasts of the forest prowl about.
21 The young lions roar after their prey And seek their food from God.
22 When the sun rises they withdraw And lie down in their dens.
23 Man goes forth to his work And to his labor until evening.
24 O Lord, how many are Your works! In wisdom You have made them all; The earth is full of Your possessions.
25 There is the sea, great and broad, In which are swarms without number, Animals both small and great
26 There the ships move along, And Leviathan, which You have formed to sport in it.
27 They all wait for You To give them their food in due season.
28 You give to them, they gather it up; You open Your hand, they are satisfied with good.
29 You hide Your face, they are dismayed; You take away their spirit, they expire And return to their dust.
30 You send forth Your Spirit, they are created; And You renew the face of the ground.
31 Let the glory of the Lord endure forever; Let the Lord be glad in His works;
32 He looks at the earth, and it trembles; He touches the mountains, and they smoke.
33 I will sing to the Lord as long as I live; I will sing praise to my God while I have my being.
34 Let my meditation be pleasing to Him; As for me, I shall be glad in the Lord.
35 Let sinners be consumed from the earth And let the wicked be no more. Bless the Lord, O my soul. Praise the Lord!

(Psalm 104, NASB)

This wisdom psalm celebrates the Lord as Creator. It structure is parallel with Genesis 1, alongside which it should be read. Notice the shared themes as the days described in Genesis overlap and mingle.

Day 1 (Gen. 1:3–5) light—v. 2

Day 2 (Gen. 1:6–8) firmament divides the waters—vv. 2–4

Day 3 (Gen. 1:9–10) land and water distinct—vv. 5–9

Day 3 (Gen. 1:11–13) vegetation and trees—vv. 14–17

Day 4 (Gen. 1:14–19) luminaries as timekeepers—vv. 19–23

Day 5 (Gen. 1:20–23) creatures of sea and air—vv. 25–26

Day 6 (Gen. 1:24–28) animals and man—anticipated in vv. 21–24

Day 6 (Gen. 1:29–31) food appointed for all creatures—vv. 27–28

This is the poet's version of Genesis One. The spirit of fervent praise runs through the whole. No human author is attached to the psalm, but Spurgeon's observation is so appropriate: "Whoever the human penman may have been, the exceeding glory and perfection of the Holy Spirit's own divine authorship are plain to every spiritual mind." Christopher Wordsworth, the nephew of the great English poet, called the psalm "An Oratorio of Creation."

The psalm ends with a mighty "Hallelujah" (v. 35), the first time that this familiar word appears in the Psalter—but not the last! It is *retrospective* of the old creation which appeared "good" from the Creator's hand (Gen. 1:31). It is also *prospective* of the future new creation when the veil of evil that corrupted the good creation will be removed. Notice how the last book of the Bible celebrates a fourfold "Hallelujah" at the judgment which eventually leads to the new creation (Rev. 19:1, 3, 4, 6; 21:1).

And all God's people said, "Hallelujah!"

> *O glorious God, creating and caring for all that has being, help me to sing to You through all my life with joyful adoration. Deepen my tenderness for all Your creation and creatures and remove from the hearts of people the callousness and greed which harm Your world. Hasten that day when this creation will be removed from the bondage under which it groans. AMEN.*

Psalm 105

Faithful!

This is often called a "Hallelujah Psalm," since it ends with that word, which really conveys an entire sentence: "Praise the LORD!" It is a song of praise to God for his dealings with his people, resembling Psalm 78. The opening is nearly identical with 1 Chron. 16:8–22, and was probably the original from which that passage was taken. The first six verses are an exhortation to praise. The remainder is an account of God's mercies to Israel as a nation, traced from the promise to Abraham to the occupation of Canaan. Israel should say "Praise the Lord" (*Halleluja*h) for the fulfillment of His promises to father Abraham—through them!

Read it in that light. Yes, I know it's long, but it is worth it!

105:1 Oh give thanks to the LORD, call upon His name; Make known His deeds among the peoples.
2 Sing to Him, sing praises to Him; Speak of all His wonders.
3 Glory in His holy name; Let the heart of those who seek the LORD be glad.
4 Seek the LORD and His strength; Seek His face continually.
5 Remember His wonders which He has done, His marvels and the judgments uttered by His mouth,
6 O seed of Abraham, His servant, O sons of Jacob, His chosen ones!
7 He is the LORD our God; His judgments are in all the earth.
8 He has remembered His covenant forever, The word which He commanded to a thousand generations,
9 The covenant which He made with Abraham, And His oath to Isaac.
10 Then He confirmed it to Jacob for a statute, To Israel as an everlasting covenant,
11 Saying, "To you I will give the land of Canaan As the portion of your inheritance,"
12 When they were only a few men in number, Very few, and strangers in it.
13 And they wandered about from nation to nation, From one kingdom to another people.
14 He permitted no man to oppress them, And He reproved kings for their sakes:

15 "Do not touch My anointed ones, And do My prophets no harm."
16 And He called for a famine upon the land; He broke the whole staff of bread.
17 He sent a man before them, Joseph, who was sold as a slave.
18 They afflicted his feet with fetters, He himself was laid in irons;
19 Until the time that his word came to pass, The word of the Lord tested him.
20 The king sent and released him, The ruler of peoples, and set him free.
21 He made him lord of his house And ruler over all his possessions,
22 To imprison his princes at will, That he might teach his elders wisdom.
23 Israel also came into Egypt; Thus Jacob sojourned in the land of Ham.
24 And He caused His people to be very fruitful, And made them stronger than their adversaries.
25 He turned their heart to hate His people, To deal craftily with His servants.
26 He sent Moses His servant, And Aaron, whom He had chosen.
27 They performed His wondrous acts among them, And miracles in the land of Ham.
28 He sent darkness and made it dark; And they did not rebel against His words.
29 He turned their waters into blood And caused their fish to die.
30 Their land swarmed with frogs Even in the chambers of their kings.
31 He spoke, and there came a swarm of flies And gnats in all their territory.
32 He gave them hail for rain, And flaming fire in their land.
33 He struck down their vines also and their fig trees, And shattered the trees of their territory.
34 He spoke, and locusts came, And young locusts, even without number,
35 And ate up all vegetation in their land, And ate up the fruit of their ground.
36 He also struck down all the firstborn in their land, The first fruits of all their vigor.
37 Then He brought them out with silver and gold, And among His tribes there was not one who stumbled.
38 Egypt was glad when they departed, For the dread of them had fallen upon them.
39 He spread a cloud for a covering, And fire to illumine by night.
40 They asked, and He brought quail, And satisfied them with the bread of heaven.
41 He opened the rock and water flowed out; It ran in the dry places like a river.
42 For He remembered His holy word With Abraham His servant;
43 And He brought forth His people with joy, His chosen ones with a joyful shout.
44 He gave them also the lands of the nations, That they might take possession of the fruit of the peoples' labor,
45 So that they might keep His statutes And observe His laws, Praise the Lord!
(Psalm 105, NASB)

God's faithfulness in His covenant (vv. 8–11, 42–44). In the midst of oppression and misery in Egypt, it seemed that He had forgotten His covenant, but He didn't forget (see Ex. 2:24). So it often seems to us when we ask, "Why have you forgotten me?" (Ps. 42:9). But when we see the purpose of the Lord, then we will realize our own faithlessness and adore His faithfulness.

God's goodness in adversity (vv. 12–15). As God sheltered his people, and held back the threatening hand of the strong so that in their days of pilgrimage they were preserved, so has He guarded his people in all ages, not suffering the great world-powers to crush them.

God's love in redemption (vv. 20–22, 26, 27). God's redeeming kindness shown to Joseph in his bondage and then to the whole nation in its suffering is an anticipation and a type (1) of delivering grace shown to us His children and (2) of our redemption in the gospel. One greater than Moses was "sent"—that "Servant of the Lord" (Isa. 53), who would work out a salvation compared with which the deliverance from Egyptian bondage was small indeed.

Psalm 105 is LONG, so we'll take more time with it.

> *O Lord, gladden the hearts of those who seek you in the far reaches of this earth. From the powers of evil, O God, deliver us but also preserve us in times of success and favor. AMEN.*

Psalm 105 (part 2)

Faithful 105

To refresh your mind about this *Hallelujah Psalm*, try reading Psalm 105 again! We will pick up its content at v. 16.

His mysterious ways (vv. 16–19). The famines which afflicted Canaan (see Gen. 12:10; 26:1), which ultimately brought Israel into Egypt, and the disgrace and hard experience of Joseph, were "trying" to the faith of those who passed through them. "The trial of our faith" is intended to draw us nearer to Himself, and to deepen the roots of our trust in Him.

His mastery of impossibilities (vv. 40, 41). He who gave "bread from heaven" and "water from the rock" can interpose and save in the darkest hour from the direst necessity. Nothing is too hard for the Lord, and certainly not our own particular situation.

His leading by the glory cloud (v. 39). God led Israel in a way as well as by a way which they knew not—a way his people could not possibly have imagined. God led them out of Egypt, not by the shortest way nor by the easiest way, but by the best way (see Exo. 13:17–18). We cannot predict the means nor the manner of the way He chooses to lead us.

His Purpose in our Prosperity (vv. 43–45). Yahweh brought his people into the land of promise in order to become a holy nation. The same God enriches us and redeems us, in order that we may attain His own likeness and be "partakers of His own holiness." Not comfort for us but conformity to Him is the true goal toward which all blessings lead.

> "Put first things first and we get second things thrown in. Put second things first and we lose both first and second things" (C. S. Lewis).

Psalm 105

God of Abraham, Isaac, and Jacob, grant that when I hear the story of Your work in ancient times, I may recognize You now as the Lord my God, ever marvelous in power and love. May I be strengthened by the examples of those whom You tested, refined and found faithful in Your service. AMEN.

Psalm 106

Nevertheless!

Psalms 105 and 106 are a matching pair that round off the Fourth Book of the Psalter. They represent two contrasting strands of sacred history: the acts of God the unfailing (Psalm 105), and the acts of man the unfaithful (Psalm 106). The first fifteen verses of Psalm 105, the last two verses of 106, and the greater part of Psalm 96 are quoted in the account of David's procession with the ark to Jerusalem in 1 Chron. 16. Even if you can't remember all that, you can be challenged by the way this psalm keeps reminding us that, despite all that God does for us, we still like to turn to our own way (Isa. 53:6). And although we are faithless, He still remains faithful (2 Tim. 2:13).

106:1 Praise the LORD! Oh give thanks to the LORD, for He is good; For His lovingkindness is everlasting.
2 Who can speak of the mighty deeds of the LORD, Or can show forth all His praise?
3 How blessed are those who keep justice, Who practice righteousness at all times!
4 Remember me, O LORD, in Your favor toward Your people; Visit me with Your salvation,
5 That I may see the prosperity of Your chosen ones, That I may rejoice in the gladness of Your nation, That I may glory with Your inheritance.
6 We have sinned like our fathers, We have committed iniquity, we have behaved wickedly.
7 Our fathers in Egypt did not understand Your wonders; They did not remember Your abundant kindnesses, But rebelled by the sea, at the Red Sea.
8 **Nevertheless** He saved them for the sake of His name, That He might make His power known.
9 Thus He rebuked the Red Sea and it dried up, And He led them through the deeps, as through the wilderness.
10 So He saved them from the hand of the one who hated them, And redeemed them from the hand of the enemy.
11 The waters covered their adversaries; Not one of them was left.
12 Then they believed His words; They sang His praise.
13 They quickly forgot His works; They

Psalm 106

did not wait for His counsel,
14 But craved intensely in the wilderness, And tempted God in the desert.
15 So He gave them their request, But sent a wasting disease among them.
16 When they became envious of Moses in the camp, And of Aaron, the holy one of the Lord,
17 The earth opened and swallowed up Dathan, And engulfed the company of Abiram.
18 And a fire blazed up in their company; The flame consumed the wicked.
19 They made a calf in Horeb And worshiped a molten image.
20 Thus they exchanged their glory For the image of an ox that eats grass.
21 They forgot God their Savior, Who had done great things in Egypt,
22 Wonders in the land of Ham And awesome things by the Red Sea.
23 Therefore He said that He would destroy them, Had not Moses His chosen one stood in the breach before Him, To turn away His wrath from destroying them.
24 Then they despised the pleasant land; They did not believe in His word,
25 But grumbled in their tents; They did not listen to the voice of the Lord.
26 Therefore He swore to them That He would cast them down in the wilderness,
27 And that He would cast their seed among the nations And scatter them in the lands.
28 They joined themselves also to Baal-peor, And ate sacrifices offered to the dead.
29 Thus they provoked Him to anger with their deeds, And the plague broke out among them.
30 Then Phinehas stood up and interposed, And so the plague was stayed.
31 And it was reckoned to him for righteousness, To all generations forever.
32 They also provoked Him to wrath at the waters of Meribah, So that it went hard with Moses on their account;
33 Because they were rebellious against His Spirit, He spoke rashly with his lips.
34 They did not destroy the peoples, As the Lord commanded them,
35 But they mingled with the nations And learned their practices,
36 And served their idols, Which became a snare to them.
37 They even sacrificed their sons and their daughters to the demons,
38 And shed innocent blood, The blood of their sons and their daughters, Whom they sacrificed to the idols of Canaan; And the land was polluted with the blood.
39 Thus they became unclean in their practices, And played the harlot in their deeds.
40 Therefore the anger of the Lord was kindled against His people And He abhorred His inheritance.
41 Then He gave them into the hand of the nations, And those who hated them ruled over them.
42 Their enemies also oppressed them, And they were subdued under their power.
43 Many times He would deliver them; They, however, were rebellious in their counsel, And so sank down in their iniquity.
44 **Nevertheless** He looked upon their distress When He heard their cry;

⁴⁵ And He remembered His covenant for their sake, And relented according to the greatness of His lovingkindness.
⁴⁶ He also made them objects of compassion In the presence of all their captors.
⁴⁷ Save us, O LORD our God, And gather us from among the nations, To give thanks to Your holy name And glory in Your praise.
⁴⁸ Blessed be the LORD, the God of Israel, From everlasting even to everlasting. And let all the people say, "Amen." Praise the LORD!

(Psalm 106, NASB)

Read it and take notice of the large number of terrible deeds committed by Israel. But also notice the large number of times that "nevertheless" or "yet" or "still" come in to indicate that He "still" cared for them. Amazing!

In light of God's great acts toward Israel, you would have expected the nation to submit to Him and serve Him devotedly. Instead, they ungratefully rebelled again and again, and had to be disciplined many times. Before you judge them, however, consider whether you may be guilty of some of the same sins they committed.

Were it not for His covenant love (*hesed*), God would have destroyed them. But He forgave them once and again and allowed them to have many new beginnings. Finally, however, He had to disperse them among the Gentiles (v. 47). And yet even then He still did not cancel His covenant with them (Rom. 11:25–27).

Paul relates much of this sad story in 1 Cor. 10:1–13. The lesson is loud and clear: "These things happened to them as examples to us—that we might not desire the same things. They were written down for our instruction" (1 Cor. 10:6, 11). No matter how difficult the trial, He always steps in to provide us a "way of escape" (1 Cor. 10:13).

> *O Lord my God, I confess that I, along with all Your people through the ages, are unworthy of Your goodness, and especially because I do not live as remembering the examples of Your grace. May I never scorn the walk of trust and faithfulness before Your face, and so may I truly rejoice in Your praise and always bless Your holy name. AMEN.*

Psalm 107

"They Cried...He Saved"

Visitors to Israel, especially students in The Master's College IBEX program, often join in the singing of a Hebrew chorus taken directly from verse 1: *Hodu l'Adonai kee tove, kee l'olam hasdo*! "Give thanks to the LORD, for He is good, for his steadfast love is forever."

The heart of this psalm is the set of five word-pictures of human predicaments and divine interventions. These episodes and pictures are different ways of depicting the plight from which the nation had been delivered. The conclusion (vv. 33–43) enlarges on the great reversals of fortune which God delights to bring about in the affairs of men (Kidner).

107:1 Oh give thanks to the LORD, for He is good, For His lovingkindness is everlasting.
2 Let the redeemed of the LORD say so, Whom He has redeemed from the hand of the adversary
3 And gathered from the lands, From the east and from the west, From the north and from the south.
4 They wandered in the wilderness in a desert region; They did not find a way to an inhabited city.
5 They were hungry and thirsty; Their soul fainted within them.
6 Then they cried out to the LORD in their trouble; He delivered them out of their distresses.
7 He led them also by a straight way, To go to an inhabited city.
8 Let them give thanks to the LORD for His lovingkindness, And for His wonders to the sons of men!
9 For He has satisfied the thirsty soul, And the hungry soul He has filled with what is good.
10 There were those who dwelt in darkness and in the shadow of death, Prisoners in misery and chains,
11 Because they had rebelled against the words of God And spurned the counsel of the Most High.
12 Therefore He humbled their heart with labor; They stumbled and there was none to help.
13 Then they cried out to the LORD in their trouble; He saved them out of their distresses.
14 He brought them out of darkness and the shadow of death And broke their bands apart.

15. Let them give thanks to the LORD for His lovingkindness, And for His wonders to the sons of men!
16. For He has shattered gates of bronze And cut bars of iron asunder.
17. Fools, because of their rebellious way, And because of their iniquities, were afflicted.
18. Their soul abhorred all kinds of food, And they drew near to the gates of death.
19. Then they cried out to the LORD in their trouble; He saved them out of their distresses.
20. He sent His word and healed them, And delivered them from their destructions.
21. Let them give thanks to the LORD for His lovingkindness, And for His wonders to the sons of men!
22. Let them also offer sacrifices of thanksgiving, And tell of His works with joyful singing.
23. Those who go down to the sea in ships, Who do business on great waters;
24. They have seen the works of the LORD, And His wonders in the deep.
25. For He spoke and raised up a stormy wind, Which lifted up the waves of the sea.
26. They rose up to the heavens, they went down to the depths; Their soul melted away in their misery.
27. They reeled and staggered like a drunken man, And were at their wits' end.
28. Then they cried to the LORD in their trouble, And He brought them out of their distresses.
29. He caused the storm to be still, So that the waves of the sea were hushed.
30. Then they were glad because they were quiet, So He guided them to their desired haven.
31. Let them give thanks to the LORD for His lovingkindness, And for His wonders to the sons of men!
32. Let them extol Him also in the congregation of the people, And praise Him at the seat of the elders.
33. He changes rivers into a wilderness And springs of water into a thirsty ground;
34. A fruitful land into a salt waste, Because of the wickedness of those who dwell in it.
35. He changes a wilderness into a pool of water And a dry land into springs of water;
36. And there He makes the hungry to dwell, So that they may establish an inhabited city,
37. And sow fields and plant vineyards, And gather a fruitful harvest.
38. Also He blesses them and they multiply greatly, And He does not let their cattle decrease.
39. When they are diminished and bowed down Through oppression, misery and sorrow,
40. He pours contempt upon princes And makes them wander in a pathless waste.
41. But He sets the needy securely on high away from affliction, And makes his families like a flock.
42. The upright see it and are glad; But all unrighteousness shuts its mouth.
43. Who is wise? Let him give heed to these things, And consider the lovingkindnesses of the LORD.

(Psalm 107, NASB)

PSALM 107

How easy it is to take God's mercy and lovingkindness for granted! Ingratitude seems to be natural to the sinful human heart (vv. 8, 15, 21, 31; Rom. 1:21–28). Wiersbe effectively describes five types of people who received God's mercy, and how they responded.

Travelers (vv. 4–9) Being lost in the wilderness without food or drink would be a frightful experience. God not only saved them but led them to the safety of the city. **Did they take time to thank Him?**

Prisoners (vv. 10–16). They were in prison because they had rebelled against God's will, so they deserved to suffer. But when they cried out to God, He heard them and set them free. **Did they take time to thank Him?**

Sufferers (vv. 17–22). We move from the prison to the hospital where people were dying because of their foolish way of life. They had "made their own bed" and should lie in it, but God mercifully healed them. **Did they take time to show their appreciation?**

Sailors (vv. 23–32). Dangers on the water usually exceed dangers on the land, for where can you go for help in the midst of a violent storm? You can only look up, which is what they did, and the Lord rescued them. He calmed the storm, and He brought them to safety (John 6:15–21).

Farmers (vv. 33–38). Only God can send the rain that turns the wilderness into a garden, and only God can make the cattle multiply. We eat and are full, but **do we take time to thank the Lord** for giving us food (Deut. 2:10–13)?

Hodu l'Adonai kee tove, kee l'olam hasdo! O give thanks to the LORD, because He is good, because His hesed endures forever! LORD, I thank You for Your faithful love! AMEN.

Psalm 108

"We Shall Do Valiantly"

The last few psalms have been long. This one is a bit shorter and may sound familiar. See if you recall anything you have recently read from the Psalms.

A Song. A Psalm of David.
108:1 My heart is steadfast, O God; I will sing, I will sing praises, even with my soul.
2 Awake, harp and lyre; I will awaken the dawn!
3 I will give thanks to You, O Lord, among the peoples, And I will sing praises to You among the nations.
4 For Your lovingkindness is great above the heavens, And Your truth reaches to the skies.
5 Be exalted, O God, above the heavens, And Your glory above all the earth.
6 That Your beloved may be delivered, Save with Your right hand, and answer me!
7 God has spoken in His holiness: "I will exult, I will portion out Shechem And measure out the valley of Succoth.
8 "Gilead is Mine, Manasseh is Mine; Ephraim also is the helmet of My head; Judah is My scepter.
9 "Moab is My washbowl; Over Edom I shall throw My shoe; Over Philistia I will shout aloud."
10 Who will bring me into the besieged city? Who will lead me to Edom?
11 Have not You Yourself, O God, rejected us? And will You not go forth with our armies, O God?
12 Oh give us help against the adversary, For deliverance by man is in vain.
13 Through God we will do valiantly, And it is He who shall tread down our adversaries.

(Psalm 108, NASB)

This psalm is adapted with a few variations from Psalm 57:7–11 (v. 1–5) and Psalm 60:5–12 (vv. 6–13). It is the song of a warrior, and the warrior David makes three firm affirmations that clearly declare his resolve.

"I will praise You with all my *heart*" (vv. 1–6). A steadfast heart is a singing heart because confidence in God gives you something to sing about. David arose early in the morning to sing to the Lord. Worship is good preparation for warfare.

"I will obey You with all my *soul*" (vv. 7–9). God heard the voice of David, and then David listened to the voice of God. It was a word of assurance as the king went out to battle: "All nations are mine, and I can do with them as I please."

"I will face the enemy with all my *strength*" (vv. 10–13). God leads us into the battle, helps us capture the enemy's strongholds, and gives us the victory. Verse 13 is David's version of Phil. 4:13. If it was true for him, how much more is true for you today when you can experience the power of the Resurrected Son of David!

David loved God with his whole heart and soul and strength while obeying the Shema in Deut. 6:4–6. That command is illustrated in no better place than in this psalm. Each of the components of the human personality is best conveyed simply as "love God with your whole being." I remind you, however, that such a command was not just for ancient Israel. It also is embodied in what I call the "Jesus Creed" (Matt. 22:37). "Love God and Love others." How simple but profound!

> *O God, You use the songs of Your people to awaken Your dawn over all the earth. May I hold fast to Your promises during all my trials, so that I may not hesitate to undertake bold tasks by the strength of Your Spirit. AMEN.*

Psalm 109

With Yahweh at Hand

These three psalms of David (108–110) share a common perspective: the oppression of God's people at the hands of their enemies and their divine deliverance through the coming of the Lord's Messiah. Before Psalm 109 is a psalm of orientation, filled with the Lord's Adoration (Psalm 108). Following it is a Messianic Psalm, filled with the Lord's Anointed (Psalm 110). What distinguishes Psalm 109, however, is the very strong language used about David's enemies. Read it and wince:

For the choir director. A Psalm of David.

109:1 O God of my praise, Do not be silent!
2 For they have opened the wicked and deceitful mouth against me; They have spoken against me with a lying tongue.
3 They have also surrounded me with words of hatred, And fought against me without cause.
4 In return for my love they act as my accusers; But I am in prayer.
5 Thus they have repaid me evil for good And hatred for my love.
6 Appoint a wicked man over him, And let an accuser stand at his right hand.
7 When he is judged, let him come forth guilty, And let his prayer become sin.
8 Let his days be few; Let another take his office.
9 Let his children be fatherless And his wife a widow.
10 Let his children wander about and beg; And let them seek sustenance far from their ruined homes.
11 Let the creditor seize all that he has, And let strangers plunder the product of his labor.
12 Let there be none to extend lovingkindness to him, Nor any to be gracious to his fatherless children.
13 Let his posterity be cut off; In a following generation let their name be blotted out.
14 Let the iniquity of his fathers be remembered before the Lord, And do not let the sin of his mother be blotted out.
15 Let them be before the Lord continually, That He may cut off their memory from the earth;
16 Because he did not remember to show lovingkindness, But persecuted the afflicted and needy man, And the

despondent in heart, to put them to death.

17 He also loved cursing, so it came to him; And he did not delight in blessing, so it was far from him.

18 But he clothed himself with cursing as with his garment, And it entered into is body like water And like oil into his bones.

19 Let it be to him as a garment with which he covers himself, And for a belt with which he constantly girds himself.

20 Let this be the reward of my accusers from the LORD, And of those who speak evil against my soul.

21 But You, O GOD, the Lord, deal kindly with me for Your name's sake; Because Your lovingkindness is good, deliver me;

22 For I am afflicted and needy, And my heart is wounded within me.

23 I am passing like a shadow when it lengthens; I am shaken off like the locust.

24 My knees are weak from fasting, And my flesh has grown lean, without fatness.

25 I also have become a reproach to them; When they see me, they wag their head.

26 Help me, O LORD my God; Save me according to Your lovingkindness.

27 And let them know that this is Your hand; You, LORD, have done it.

28 Let them curse, but You bless; When they arise, they shall be ashamed, But Your servant shall be glad.

29 Let my accusers be clothed with dishonor, And let them cover themselves with their own shame as with a robe.

30 With my mouth I will give thanks abundantly to the LORD; And in the midst of many I will praise Him.

31 For He stands at the right hand of the needy, To save him from those who judge his soul.

(Psalm 109, NASB)

If there ever was a composition that deserved Brueggeman's classification as a "psalm of disorientation," it is Psalm 109. While not as pessimistic as Psalm 88, its realistic language sometimes shocks our sensibilities. But this is because we have allowed our sensibilities to become too dull to the real nature of evil. It is precisely because the Biblical writers understood both the nature of evil and the nature of God, that they could write with such searing honesty.

Sailhamer believes that the strong language here should be understood as poetic overstatements and exaggerated metaphors. While there is something to that approach (see the figurative language used in verses 22–23), we can't just explain this psalm away as poetic imagery that is not to be taken literally. These were real people who were flouting the real law of a real God.

It is better to view this language as covenantal, describing God's punishments on evil-doers which He had already promised would happen (Deut. 27:15–26; 28:15–46). Furthermore, **many of these statements** about David's enemy find their fullest expression in the enemy of the Son of David, namely Judas Iscariot (v. 3; John 15:25; Ps. 109:8; Acts 1:20).

That great word (hesed) again is used of God's "steadfast love" or "lovingkindness" promised to David (vv. 21, 26). It is in this Messianic perspective that the final verse takes on added meaning. "For He stands at the right hand of the needy one to save Him from those who would condemn him" (v. 31).

The Lord's promise to stand at the right hand of David and his great descendant prepares the reader for the following psalm (v. 5). What is so remarkable is that David's Lord will also be elevated to Yahweh's right hand (v. 1)! But that is in the next psalm!

> *O God my praise, help me to repent of my sinful desires, my acts of betrayal, and my share in the emotional suffering of Your precious children. Forgive my harshness and lack of gentleness for the sake of Him who has undone the ancient curse, my Savior Jesus Christ.*
> *AMEN.*

Psalm 110

The LORD and My Lord

Well, I have finally arrived at my favorite psalm and I almost don't know where to begin, much less where to end! Psalm 110 has the distinction of not only being the most quoted psalm in the NT, it is also the OT passage that is alluded to more often than any other in the entire Hebrew Bible! We have read both short and long psalms in our journey, but there is none more important or strategic than this short masterpiece of only seven verses.

> *A Psalm of David.*
> 110:1 The LORD says to my Lord: "Sit at My right hand Until I make Your enemies a footstool for Your feet."
> 2 The LORD will stretch forth Your strong scepter from Zion, saying, "Rule in the midst of Your enemies."
> 3 Your people will volunteer freely in the day of Your power; In holy array, from the womb of the dawn, Your youth are to You as the dew.
> 4 The LORD has sworn and will not change His mind, "You are a priest forever according to the order of Melchizedek."
> 5 The Lord is at Your right hand; He will shatter kings in the day of His wrath.
> 6 He will judge among the nations, He will fill them with corpses, He will shatter the "head" over a broad country.
> 7 He will drink from the brook by the wayside; Therefore He will lift up His head.
>
> (Psalm 110, NASB)

The psalm focuses on the Messianic promises that God made to David in 2 Samuel 7:12–16 (see also Psalms 2 and 72). The focus is not just on the Kingship of the Davidic Son ("scepter" "rule"), for it also develops the priesthood of his descendant ("You are a priest forever—like Melchizedek"). Like that ancient "mystery-man," the Messiah will also be a "king-priest."

No other psalm is so clear about the identity of the Promised Seed as Psalm 110. It was destined to form the basis of the New Testament teaching on the exaltation, heavenly session and royal priesthood of the Messiah. He is described in three specific roles:

The Messiah as King (vv. 1–3).
The Messiah as Priest (v. 4).
The Messiah as Warrior (vv. 5–7).

Jesus Himself reminded the Pharisees that David called the Messiah "my Lord." If Messiah is *only* a descendant of David, how could David call him "my Lord"? The ascension is implied because David's Lord is described as seated beside the right hand of Yahweh (the LORD).

There is so much more! I have a chapter in my book, *The Messiah: Revealed, Rejected, Received*, that explores this psalm in depth, with attention given to its implications for Jewish belief in the Messiah. You may also be surprised that His punishment of the Antichrist is even described in verse 6.

> *Lord Jesus, divine Son, eternal priest, and my Messiah, deepen my love for You as You intercede for me at Your Father's side. Then infuse me with confidence in Your final conquest of evil, and grant that daily on my way I may drink of the brook of eternal life, and so find courage to face all adversities. AMEN.*

A Student's Psalm

This lovely song begins like a psalm ("Hallelujah! I will praise the Lord ...") and it ends like a proverb ("The fear of the Lord is the beginning of wisdom ..."). Psalms 111–113 all begin with Hallelujah, and there is a close bond between Psalms 111 and 112. These two are acrostics, each having 22 lines, the number of letters in the Hebrew alphabet. They are also a matched pair in their contents: while **Psalm 111 describes the works of God, Psalm 112 describes the man of God.**

> 111:1 Praise the Lord! I will give thanks to the Lord with all my heart, In the company of the upright and in the assembly.
> 2 Great are the works of the Lord; They are studied by all who delight in them.
> 3 Splendid and majestic is His work, And His righteousness endures forever.
> 4 He has made His wonders to be remembered; The Lord is gracious and compassionate.
> 5 He has given food to those who fear Him; He will remember His covenant forever.
> 6 He has made known to His people the power of His works, In giving them the heritage of the nations.
> 7 The works of His hands are truth and justice; All His precepts are sure.
> 8 They are upheld forever and ever; They are performed in truth and uprightness.
> 9 He has sent redemption to His people; He has ordained His covenant forever; Holy and awesome is His name.
> 10 The fear of the Lord is the beginning of wisdom; A good understanding have all those who do His commandments; His praise endures forever.
>
> (Psalm 111, NASB)

This is a student's psalm. If you study, then do it this way.

Start your study with worship (v. 1). All truth is God's truth, wherever it is found. Therefore, thank Him for how He is revealed in the Book of Creation and also in the Book of the Word.

Study God's works (vv. 2–6). Whether it is science or history, you are examining God's works in His world. His works are great and glorious, revealing His power and wisdom. To see the creation but ignore the Creator is to move into idolatry and sin (Rom. 1:18–30).

Study God's Word (vv. 7–9). Truth, justice, uprightness, redemption, steadfast love, and covenant are all themes of the Word. The book of the word and the book of nature do not contradict each other, for the same Author wrote them. Read Psalm 19:1–11.

Obey what you study (v. 10). The search into truth is not just an academic exercise of your mind, but must involve your whole person. If you are willing to "do" God's truth, He will teach you (John 7:17). If you love truth, learn truth, and live truth, the truth will set you free (John 8:31–32).

Through the process of continual remembering described in this psalm, the fear of the Lord becomes natural and habitual and proves itself the beginning of wisdom, becoming known also as a fountain of life (Pr. 14:27).

> *O Lord and my Redeemer, increase in me that fear of Your name which is found to be the beginning and chief part of wisdom. While sharing in the fellowship of praise and communion, may I ever delight in Your wonders and be nourished with Your sustenance.*
> *AMEN.*

A God-Fearer

I grew up in the South. Although I did not come to faith until I was seventeen, I remember hearing often the sentence "He is a God-fearing man." Today it seems like we almost apologize for the Biblical expression, "to fear the Lord." Is it because of our own "fear" that such an emotion is bad? And yet, "fearing the Lord" is the expression used more than any other in the Old Testament to describe one who follows (and loves!) the Lord. In its many forms it used over a hundred times in the Old Testament to describe a believer's proper relationship to God. And the New Testament often uses it this way as well (Acts 9:31; Heb. 12:28; 1 Pet. 1:17).

Psalm 112 follows up on its sister, Psalm 111, by applying to everyday life that psalm's strong emphasis on praising and worshipping Yahweh. Verse 9 ends with the statement, "The fear of the LORD is the beginning of wisdom." The psalm then describes what the person who fears the Lord actually looks like. Read it in that light:

> 112:1 Praise the LORD! How blessed is the man who fears the LORD, Who greatly delights in His commandments.
> 2 His descendants will be mighty on earth; The generation of the upright will be blessed.
> 3 Wealth and riches are in his house, And his righteousness endures forever.
> 4 Light arises in the darkness for the upright; He is gracious and compassionate and righteous.
> 5 It is well with the man who is gracious and lends; He will maintain his cause in judgment.
> 6 For he will never be shaken; The righteous will be remembered forever.
> 7 He will not fear evil tidings; His heart is steadfast, trusting in the LORD.
> 8 His heart is upheld, he will not fear, Until he looks with satisfaction on his adversaries.
> 9 He has given freely to the poor, His righteousness endures forever; His horn will be exalted in honor.
> 10 The wicked will see it and be vexed, He will gnash his teeth and melt away; The desire of the wicked will perish.
>
> (Psalm 112, NASB)

Let me simply list the character traits in this psalm that God-fearing men and women possess, so you can measure your own life against them.

1. They delight in God's commands
2. Their descendants will be blessed
3. Their needs will be met
4. They share what God has given them
5. They are secure about the future
6. They can handle whatever "bad" stuff happens to them
7. They are victorious in the end

In the Christian experience the fear of the Lord is the fruit of the Incarnation, the Word becoming flesh so that those who receive Him may become children of God (John 1:12). The disciple is called to be an imitator of God, a child who walks in his love (Eph. 4:32–5:2).

> *O Jesus the light of the world, renew my heart to fear You and delight in Your commandments, so that I too may walk in love, even as You loved me and gave Yourself for me. AMEN.*

Psalm 113

Hallel!

A brief but wonderful hymn of praise for God's gracious care for His people, this psalm focuses on God's choosing a leader for those people by raising him out of humble circumstances. It is the first of the "Hallel Psalms" (113–118) which Jewish people for years have sung at Passover. Each of these psalms begins and ends with *Hallelujah*!

> 113:1 Praise the LORD! Praise, O servants of the LORD, **Praise the name of the LORD.**
> 2 Blessed be the name of the LORD From this time forth and forever.
> 3 From the rising of the sun to its setting The name of the LORD is to be praised.
> 4 The LORD is high above all nations; His glory is above the heavens.
> 5 Who is like the LORD our God, Who is enthroned on high,
> 6 Who humbles Himself to behold The things that are in heaven and in the earth?
> 7 He raises the poor from the dust And lifts the needy from the ash heap,
> 8 To make them sit with princes, With the princes of His people.
> 9 He makes the barren woman abide in the house As a joyful mother of children. Praise the LORD!
>
> (Psalm 113, NASB)

This hymn eloquently uses elements characteristic of praise psalms, especially the call to praise (vv. 1–3), the reasons for praise (v. 4), a rhetorical question expressing the uniqueness of the Lord (v. 5), and a series of four Hebrew participles (vv. 6–9) expressing the Lord's attributes and continuing actions. It is likely to have originally accompanied a great occasion of worship, the congregation being addressed as "servants of the Lord" (v. 1).

John Sailhamer loves to see these psalms as celebrations of the promises of the Davidic Covenant in 2 Sam. 7:12–16. In that light he writes, "This must without doubt refer to David's words in 2 Samuel 7:18: 'Who am I, O Lord of Hosts, and what is my family, that you have brought me thus far'?" I don't want to argue with that. I just want to remind the reader of the concept of "the one and the many" which makes these statements about David and his ultimate Son also applicable to all of us who by grace are IN David and IN his Son by the gift of corporate solidarity. We are the sons because of the Son; we are the seed because of the Seed; we are the servants because of the Servant.

Hallelujah!

> *O Lord, I bless Your name, the name above all names, and I thank You that from Your throne You saw us wretched sinners and humbled Yourself to save us. Grant that Your mind will be in me, that I also will humble myself, and take my role as an obedient servant in Your great work of salvation. AMEN.*

Psalm 114

The Exodus and Us

More than any other psalm, this little gem concentrates together graphic figures of speech to portray the Exodus and the conquest. Kidner even remarks that it is "a masterpiece whose flights of verbal fancy would have excluded it from any hymn book but this." Similes, metaphors, apostrophes, personification—they all abound and spill over each other in a torrent that matches the power of the events the words describe. Read it and marvel at the beauty of the language—and then marvel in the great acts of redemption that those words convey.

> 114:1 When Israel went forth from Egypt, The house of Jacob from a people of strange language,
> 2 Judah became His sanctuary, Israel, His dominion.
> 3 The sea looked and fled; The Jordan turned back.
> 4 The mountains skipped like rams, The hills, like lambs.
> 5 What ails you, O sea, that you flee? O Jordan, that you turn back?
> 6 O mountains, that you skip like rams? O hills, like lambs?
> 7 Tremble, O earth, before the Lord, Before the God of Jacob,
> 8 Who turned the rock into a pool of water, The flint into a fountain of water.
> (Psalm 114, NASB)

"Tremble, O earth at His presence"—and well, you should! John saw in the Apocalypse before the great white throne that "the earth and sky fled away, and no place was found for them."

Here is the exodus, not as a familiar item in Israel's creed, but as an event as startling as a clap of thunder and as shattering as an earthquake. The tsunami turns back, the mountains quake, and water flows from a rock. But there is more here than just powerful language. Like Moses and Miriam and all Israel who witnessed the great miracle, we are to join them on the "other" side of the Red Sea, pull out our tambourines and begin to sing and dance! (See Ex. 15:20–21).

Because of the great redemption purchased by the Messiah our Passover Lamb, let us today joyously observe the festival of God's redemption (1 Cor. 5:7–8).

> *O God of both the storm and the still small voice, Lord of the trembling earth and the quiet heart, please become my refuge and strong tower in times of peril and danger. AMEN.*

Psalm 115

Soli Deo Gloria

The great Christian composer Johann Sebastian Bach added the initials "SDG" to the musical manuscripts of each of his cantatas and many of his other works. This dedication was also used by his contemporary George Frederic Handel. It stands for the Latin expression: "Soli Deo Gloria" ("to God alone be the glory"). These letters could also be written across the entire text of Psalm 115. R.E. Prothero (*The Psalms in Human Life*) tells us that the English Christian lawmaker, William Wilberforce, marked the passing of his bill to abolish the slave trade by meditating on the first verse of Psalm 115: "Not to us, Lord, not to us, but to your name give glory." Many more examples could be given of the impact of this psalm on different people.

Read it with those tributes in mind, as well as with the thanksgiving of a grateful Israel for God's great deeds on their behalf:

115:1 Not to us, O LORD, not to us, But to Your name give glory Because of Your lovingkindness, because of Your truth.
2 Why should the nations say, "Where, now, is their God?"
3 But our God is in the heavens; He does whatever He pleases.
4 Their idols are silver and gold, The work of man's hands.
5 They have mouths, but they cannot speak; They have eyes, but they cannot see;
6 They have ears, but they cannot hear; They have noses, but they cannot smell;
7 They have hands, but they cannot feel; They have feet, but they cannot walk; They cannot make a sound with their throat.
8 Those who make them will become like them, Everyone who trusts in them.
9 O Israel, trust in the LORD; He is their help and their shield.
10 O house of Aaron, trust in the LORD; He is their help and their shield.
11 You who fear the LORD, trust in the LORD; He is their help and their shield.
12 The LORD has been mindful of us; He will bless us; He will bless the house of Israel; He will bless the house of Aaron.
13 He will bless those who fear the LORD, The small together with the great.
14 May the LORD give you increase, You

and your children.
15 May you be blessed of the Lord, Maker of heaven and earth.
16 The heavens are the heavens of the Lord, But the earth He has given to the sons of men.
17 The dead do not praise the Lord, Nor do any who go down into silence;
18 But as for us, we will bless the Lord From this time forth and forever. Praise the Lord!

(Psalm 115, NASB)

The idols of earthly wealth and power, the blessings that people always make for themselves, these continue indeed to be widely worshipped and highly exalted today. Our psalm would see them still as degrading their "worshippers" and directs our trust only to the Lord of the heavens, in whose praise is the truest blessing in life.

There is much in this psalm for which to give God the glory. Since, however, it echoes many previous psalms, our meditation will focus on the final two verses: "It is not the dead who praise the LORD, nor any of those descending into the silence of death. But we will praise the LORD, both now and forever. Hallelujah!" (vv. 17–18). This statement is not meant to deny life after death for anyone, because it does not stop at verse 17 but concludes with the final sentence. And that affirmation may well be saying that we who serve the living God will ourselves live on, unlike the worshipers of lifeless objects (v. 8). If so, this stanza adds its witness about an afterlife alongside such passages as Psalm 73:23–24 and others like Psalm 11:7 and Psalm 16:9–11.

Therefore, this psalm has every reason to end, like its other "Hallel" neighbors, with a *Hallelujah*!

> **"The good *hand* of our God."** The Bible uses human illustrations to explain divine attributes. When God wanted to create a world, He merely had to use His *fingers* (Ps. 8:3). To save lost sinners, He had to bare His *arm* (Isa. 53:1). When He wants to accomplish a task, He uses His mighty *hand* (Ezra 7:6, 9, 28; Neh. 2:8)" (Wiersbe).

O Lord, my help and shield, unite Your ministers and Your people in the fear of Your name. Bless me with that trust that looks only to You for abundant life, and with a thankful heart may I praise and worship You alone. AMEN.

How Can I Say Thanks?

"There is an infectious delight and touching gratitude about this psalm, the personal tribute of a man whose prayer has found an overwhelming answer. He has come now to the temple to tell the whole assembly what has happened" (Kidner). The language describing a near-death experience is so like the prayer in Jonah 2 that the reluctant prophet must have been reciting it after he was "burped" up on the beach. Have you ever experienced such a close call?

Notice how the psalm moves back and forth from thanksgiving to God's deliverance and back again. Here it is:

116:1 I love the LORD, because He hears My voice and my supplications.
2 Because He has inclined His ear to me, Therefore I shall call upon Him as long as I live.
3 The cords of death encompassed me And the terrors of Sheol came upon me; I found distress and sorrow.
4 Then I called upon the name of the LORD: "O LORD, I beseech You, save my life!"
5 Gracious is the LORD, and righteous; Yes, our God is compassionate.
6 The LORD preserves the simple; I was brought low, and He saved me.
7 Return to your rest, O my soul, For the LORD has dealt bountifully with you.
8 For You have rescued my soul from death, My eyes from tears, My feet from stumbling.
9 I shall walk before the LORD In the land of the living.
10 I believed when I said, "I am greatly afflicted."
11 I said in my alarm, "All men are liars."
12 What shall I render to the LORD For all His benefits toward me?
13 I shall lift up the cup of salvation And call upon the name of the LORD.
14 I shall pay my vows to the LORD, Oh may it be in the presence of all His people.
15 Precious in the sight of the LORD Is the death of His godly ones.
16 O LORD, surely I am Your servant, I am Your servant, the son of Your handmaid, You have loosed my bonds.
17 To You I shall offer a sacrifice of thanksgiving, And call upon the name of the LORD.

¹⁸ I shall pay my vows to the Lord, Oh may it be in the presence of all His people,
¹⁹ In the courts of the Lord's house, In the midst of you, O Jerusalem. Praise the Lord!

(Psalm 116, NASB)

Thanksgiving (vv. 1–2). An emphatically placed "I love" opens the psalm. The psalmist's reason for the expression of endearment is motivated by answered prayer. The Lord has heard his "cry for mercy."

God the Deliverer (vv. 3–6a). In his terrible situation the psalmist resorted to his only hope: the "name" of the Lord. He is fully aware that the Lord is "gracious" in his forgiveness, "righteous" in keeping the covenant, and "full of compassion" in his understanding of the limits of his children.

Thanksgiving (vv. 6b–7). The description of the character of the Lord evokes from the psalmist an affirmation of how the Lord "saved" him. The psalmist called on the Lord, "Save me" (v. 4), and the Lord was true to his promise.

God the Deliverer (v. 8–11). Only the Lord can change "death," "tears," and "stumbling" into a "walk before the Lord" and a joyful celebration of life "in the land of the living." He saw that final help cannot come from "men" because they are "liars."

Vows of thanksgiving (vv. 12–14). The Lord was faithful, and the psalmist responds to His acts of goodness with a question that has only one answer. There is no adequate way to "repay" the Lord.

God the Deliverer (vv. 15–16). The psalmist confesses the great love of the Lord for His "saints" in that He does not lightly permit adversity or an early death. They are "precious" to Him.

Vows of thanksgiving (vv. 17–19). In the presence of the godly, the psalmist will show his gratitude to the Lord for his deliverance by presenting a "thank offering."

How appropriate that I am writing this devotional on Thanksgiving morning, 2010!

O Lord Jesus, my gracious redeemer, who made the costly sacrifice to save me from destruction, help me to walk in gratitude daily before Your face, to serve You with a heart of love, and gladly to raise my cup and proclaim Your name in the way of worship that You have appointed. AMEN.

Psalm 117

Let's Hear It For the Goyim!

This Psalm is small in size but stupendous in scope. Its message about God's plan for Gentiles (goyim) was not lost on Paul in Romans 15:8–12 where it closes his powerful argument about Jewish AND Gentile salvation.

> 117:1 Praise the LORD, all nations; Laud Him, all peoples!
> 2 For His lovingkindness is great toward us, And the truth of the LORD is everlasting. Praise the LORD!
> (Psalm 117, NASB)

When reading and singing this psalm, we too are challenged not to accept the idea that different peoples have a right to different faiths. The very diversity of God's subjects comes out in the expression "all nations and tribes." This reappears in the multitude of Rev. 7:9 "from every nation, and from all tribes and peoples and tongues" (Kidner).

The cause for praise is that his *hesed* or steadfast love "prevails"—a vivid word used of prevailing in battle (Ex. 17:11); or of the flood which 'prevailed ... mightily' (Gen. 7:18–20); or of our transgressions (Ps. 65:3); but also of God's blessings (Gen. 49:26) and His steadfast love (here and in Ps. 103:11). What is more surprising in this Gentile context is that the cause for rejoicing is God's goodness toward "us," meaning Israel. Yet in reality it makes excellent sense, for through Abraham all nations were to find blessing, and through Abraham's descendant they indeed ARE finding it! (Gen. 12:3; Gal. 3:8–12).

If His steadfast love is great, His faithfulness is eternal. Not that the two are set in contrast, for they are aspects of the same grace. **This is another**

psalm that expounds the virtues and attributes of Yahweh so clearly proclaimed in Exodus 34:6.

Such an exhortation for the whole world is also a summons, with the obligation to make its invitation heard beyond our walls and immediate circle. This psalm is another reminder that God's heart for world missions did not begin with Matt. 28:18–19! "The Spirit of Christ is the spirit of missions, and the nearer we get to Him the more intensely missionary we must become" (Henry Martyn).

This the shortest of all psalms thus proves to be one of the most potent and the most prophetic.

> *As You, O God, have dealt in steadfast love and faithfulness with me, give me the strength to deal with grace and mercy toward others. AMEN.*

Psalm 118

Luther's Favorite

This is the last of the "Hallel Psalms" (113–118), and in it the spirit of jubilant thanksgiving finds its fullest utterance. It begins and ends with that sentence that is celebrated in Israelite worship that we saw in Psalm 107:1: "Give thanks to the LORD, for He is good; His faithful love endures forever. *Hodu l'Adonai kee tove, kee l'olam hasdo*." The speaker is a representative of all Israel, and as Israel did on the shores of the Red Sea, so the people give thanks once more.

118:1 Give thanks to the LORD, for He is good; For His lovingkindness is everlasting.
2 Oh let Israel say, "His lovingkindness is everlasting."
3 Oh let the house of Aaron say, "His lovingkindness is everlasting."
4 Oh let those who fear the LORD say, "HIS lovingkindness is everlasting."
5 From my distress I called upon the LORD; The LORD answered me and set me in a large place.
6 The LORD is for me; I will not fear; What can man do to me?
7 The LORD is for me among those who help me; Therefore I will look with satisfaction on those who hate me.
8 It is better to take refuge in the LORD Than to trust in man.
9 It is better to take refuge in the LORD Than to trust in princes.
10 All nations surrounded me; In the name of the LORD I will surely cut them off.
11 They surrounded me, yes, they surrounded me; In the name of the LORD I will surely cut them off.
12 They surrounded me like bees; They were extinguished as a fire of thorns; In the name of the LORD I will surely cut them off.
13 You pushed me violently so that I was falling, But the LORD helped me.
14 The LORD is my strength and song, And He has become my salvation.
15 The sound of joyful shouting and salvation is in the tents of the righteous; The right hand of the LORD does valiantly.
16 The right hand of the LORD is exalted; The right hand of the LORD does valiantly.
17 I will not die, but live, And tell of the works of the LORD.
18 The LORD has disciplined me severely, But He has not given me over to death.
19 Open to me the gates of righteousness; I shall enter through them, I shall give thanks to the LORD.

²⁰ This is the gate of the Lord; The righteous will enter through it.
²¹ I shall give thanks to You, for You have answered me, And You have become my salvation.
²² The stone which the builders rejected Has become the chief corner stone.
²³ This is the Lord's doing; It is marvelous in our eyes.
²⁴ This is the day which the Lord has made; Let us rejoice and be glad in it.
²⁵ O Lord, do save, we beseech You; Lord, we beseech You, do send prosperity!
²⁶ Blessed is the one who comes in the name of the Lord; We have blessed you from the house of the Lord.
²⁷ The Lord is God, and He has given us light; Bind the festival sacrifice with cords to the horns of the altar.
²⁸ You are my God, and I give thanks to You; You are my God, I extol You.
²⁹ Give thanks to the Lord, for He is good; For His lovingkindness is everlasting.
(Psalm 118, NASB)

1. **All are bidden to praise Yahweh for His *hesed* (vv. 1–4).**
2. **He is the deliverer and strength of His people (vv. 5–9).**
3. **Nations have plotted against Israel in vain (vv. 10–14; Ps. 2:1–3).**
4. **Public thanksgiving renews their national life (vv. 15–18).**
5. **Worshipers approach the Temple with praise (vv. 19–24).**
6. **Hosannas and blessings consummate the worship (vv. 25–29).**

This was Martin Luther's favorite psalm. The great reformer remarked, "Though the whole Psalter and all Holy Scripture is dear to me, as my only comfort in life, this psalm has been of special service to me. It has helped me out of many great troubles, when neither Emperor nor kings nor wise men nor saints could help."

Many ideas abound about the specific occasion when the psalm was sung. The fact that we can't really know the occasion for certain makes it appropriate that we recite it on any occasion when our hearts are full of praise and thanksgiving for the abundant acts of God on our behalf. Gratitude follows grace like thunder follows lightning.

Because there is so much here to consider, we must write more about the role of Psalm 118 in the life of our Lord, especially during His Passion Week. You may be surprised at my proposal.

> *O Lord, although human comforts may fail, let me take refuge in Your steadfast love. When my way grows dark and I seem to be hemmed in, be my strength and my salvation.* AMEN.

Psalm 118 (part 2)

An Overlooked Messianic Text

We just looked at the jubilation expressed in Psalm 118, especially in a very public manner in the OT Temple. Today I want to explore an aspect of the psalm that is often overlooked—how it played a major role in the events of the Passion Week. **I suggest that Psalm 118 was on the mind of Jesus from His triumphal entry until His crucifixion.** The most relevant section in this regard is verses 22–27:

> 118:22 The stone that the builders rejected has become the cornerstone.
> 23 This is the LORD's doing; it is marvelous in our eyes.
> 24 This is the day that the LORD has made; let us rejoice and be glad in it.
> 25 Save us, we pray (Hosanna), O LORD! O LORD, we pray, give us success!
> 26 Blessed is he who comes in the name of the LORD! We bless you from the house of the LORD.
> 27 The LORD is God, and he has made his light to shine upon us. Bind the festal sacrifice with cords, up to the horns of the altar!
>
> (Psalm 118:22–27, NASB)

1. Verses 25 and 26 were cited by the crowds who welcomed Jesus into Jerusalem on "Palm Sunday" (Matt. 21:9; Mark 11:9).

2. Verse 22 was the punch line in a parable of the Lord Jesus during his confrontation with the Jewish leaders on Tuesday morning (Matt. 21:42).

3. Verse 26 was quoted by Jesus at the end of his pronouncement of "woes" on the scribes and Pharisees on Tuesday afternoon (Matt. 23:39).

4. Since Psalm 118 is sung at the end of the Passover Seder, this passage was on the lips of Jesus on that fateful Thursday night in the upper room, in the shadow of Calvary (Matt. 26:30). In that week the horns of the altar became the arms of the cross, and the festival found its fulfillment in "Messiah our Passover Lamb" (1 Cor. 5:7).

Today Christians often quote verse 24 as they face a new day or try to make the best of a bad day: "This is the day that the LORD has made; let us rejoice and be glad in it." In light of its Messianic use during Passion Week, however, the "day" was a redemptive one—**the day when the rejected Messianic stone became the chief stone of God's new temple!**

Now that is something we should rejoice and be glad about!

> *O Jesus, may I rejoice in the day of Your Passion and Resurrection. Grant that I also may trust in You and call upon Your name in every peril, and that I may recount Your deeds in the time of singing and salvation. AMEN.*

The Golden Alphabet

This longest among the Psalms displays the full flowering of that "delight in the law of the Lord" which was described in Psalm 1, and gives its extended witness to the multi-faceted qualities of Scripture described in Psalm 19. If those two are the prototype Wisdom Psalms, this one is all that they hoped for. It is an acrostic psalm, an alphabet of prayerful reflections on the word of God, giving each Hebrew letter its turn to introduce eight successive verses on the subject (Kidner). We will look at this psalm in nine segments, with this first one examining the psalm as a whole, then the following eight devotionals will examine each of the successive alphabet sections.

This is pre-eminently the Psalm of the Word, with nearly every verse mentioning the Word by one of eight synonymous terms. They are:

1. **"Law"** (*torah*) occurs 25 times. In the broad sense *torah* refers to any "instruction" flowing from the revelation of God as the basis for life and action. In the narrow sense it denotes the Law of Moses, or the Pentateuch.

2. **"Word"** (*davar*) occurs 28 times. *Davar* is any word that proceeds from the mouth of the Lord. It is a general designation for divine revelation.

3. **"Judgments"** (*mishpatim*) occurs 23 times. *Mishaptim* are particular legal issues that form the basis for Israel's legal system. God himself is the Great Judge.

4. **"Statute(s)"** (*edut/edot*) occurs 21 times. *Edot* comes from the word that means "witness" or "testimony" and is often synonymous with "covenant" (Ps. 25:10, 132:12). The observance of the "statutes" of the Lord signifies loyalty to the terms of the covenant between God and Israel.

5. **"Command(s)"** (*mitsvah/mitsvot*) occurs 22 times. *Mitsvot* is a frequent designation for anything that the Lord, the covenant God, has ordered.

6. "Decrees" (*huqqim*) appears 21 times. *Huqqim* is derived from the root for "engrave," "inscribe." God reveals his royal sovereignty by establishing his divine will in nature and in the covenant community.

7. "Precepts" or "statutes" (*piqqudim*) occurs 21 times. *Piqqudim* appears only in the book of Psalms and appears to be synonymous with "covenant" (Ps. 103:18) and with the revelation of God (Ps. 111:7).

8. "Word" or "promise" (*imrah*) appears 19 times. *Imrah* denotes anything God has spoken, commanded, or promised.

A remarkable observation is the balanced way in which these eight terms are used (19 to 28 times!). The beauty of this psalm lies not only in the psalmist's commitment to the Word, but in **his absolute devotion to the Lord shown by his delight in the Word**. That is the "Big picture" of this great psalm. Now how does the psalmist (Ezra?) further describe the function of that Word in his own words?

> *Your word, O LORD, is forever settled in the heaven and yet it is with us on the earth. May I constantly be occupied with Your Torah that was revealed at Sinai by Your word and displayed at Calvary by the Savior. AMEN.*

Psalm 119
vv. 1–24

Aleph, Bet, Gimel

We will list the text of each of the twenty-two sections (named by letters of the Hebrew alphabet) of this psalm along with the basic idea of the section. Then will follow a devotional thought drawn from the text. Try to notice in each section both the *qualities* of Scripture (dependable, unshakable, reliable) and then the *benefits* of Scripture (liberation, light, life). See Kidner (419-422).

Aleph
^{119:1} How blessed are those whose way is blameless, Who walk in the law of the LORD.
² How blessed are those who observe His testimonies, Who seek Him with all their heart.
³ They also do no unrighteousness; They walk in His ways.
⁴ You have ordained Your precepts, That we should keep them diligently.
⁵ Oh that my ways may be established To keep Your statutes!
⁶ Then I shall not be ashamed When I look upon all Your commandments.
⁷ I shall give thanks to You with uprightness of heart, When I learn Your righteous judgments.
⁸ I shall keep Your statutes; Do not forsake me utterly!
(Psalm 119:1–8, NASB)

Aleph - The Undivided Heart Psalm (vv. 1–8)

What is taught here and what is implied throughout the psalm is so important to note: Scripture is revered for being *His* sayings, and God's servants thereby seek Him, not the book for its own sake. "Beyond the sacred page, I seek thee, Lord."

Beth

119:9 How can a young man keep his way pure? By keeping it according to Your word.
10 With all my heart I have sought You; Do not let me wander from Your commandments.
11 Your word I have treasured in my heart, That I may not sin against You.
12 Blessed are You, O Lord; Teach me Your statutes.
13 With my lips I have told of All the ordinances of Your mouth.
14 I have rejoiced in the way of Your testimonies, As much as in all riches.
15 I will meditate on Your precepts And regard Your ways.
16 I shall delight in Your statutes; I shall not forget Your word.

(Psalm 119:9–16, NASB)

Bet - The Stored Treasure Psalm (vv. 9–16)

From the heartfelt prayers of the surrounding verses it would seem that the young man who cleanses his way by heeding the Word is the psalmist himself in the first place. He is praying rather than preaching. Prov. 2:10–12 and Col. 3:16 show that the mind which stores up Scripture has its taste and judgment trained by God (Kidner).

Gimel

119:17 Deal bountifully with Your servant, That I may live and keep Your word.
18 Open my eyes, that I may behold Wonderful things from Your law.
19 I am a stranger in the earth; Do not hide Your commandments from me.
20 My soul is crushed with longing After Your ordinances at all times.
21 You rebuke the arrogant, the cursed, Who wander from Your commandments.
22 Take away reproach and contempt from me, For I observe Your testimonies.
23 Even though princes sit and talk against me, Your servant meditates on Your statutes.
24 Your testimonies also are my delight; They are my counselors.

(Psalm 119:17–24, NASB)

Gimel - Solace in Loneliness (vv. 17–24)

"That I may live" is the first of many such prayers. While some of them could refer simply to surviving an illness or an attack, others clearly speak of a life that is worthy of the name, the life found in fellowship with God. It is a familiar Old Testament concept (Ps. 16:11, 36:9; Deut. 8:3). For the request to "open my eyes" (v. 18) compare the sight of Elisha's servant (2 Kings 6:17). The metaphor is that of removing a veil (2 Cor. 3:14–18) (Kidner).

"When you truly delight in the Word, you will have a desire to meditate on it and make it a part of your life. In Psalm 119, the writer connects "delight" and "meditation" (vv. 15–16, 23–24, 47–48, 77–78). Cultivate an appetite for the Word of God" (Wiersbe).

> *Be a light to my path, O Lord, and give me the desire to grow to maturity. Help me to do Your will in my time of confusion, and open my eyes to discern the correct path to follow. AMEN.*

Psalm 119
vv. 25–48

Dalet, Hay, Vav

Dalet

119:25 My soul cleaves to the dust; Revive me according to Your word.
26 I have told of my ways, and You have answered me; Teach me Your statutes.
27 Make me understand the way of Your precepts, So I will meditate on Your wonders.
28 My soul weeps because of grief; Strengthen me according to Your word.
29 Remove the false way from me, And graciously grant me Your law.
30 I have chosen the faithful way; I have placed Your ordinances before me.
31 I cling to Your testimonies; O LORD, do not put me to shame!
32 I shall run the way of Your commandments, For You will enlarge my heart.
(Psalm 119:25–32, NASB)

Dalet - **Revive Me! (vv. 25–32)**

The Word of God brings you the blessing of life (v. 25) because it has life (Heb. 4:12), imparts life (1 Pet. 1:23–25), and nourishes life (1 Pet. 2:1–3). God's Word revives and strengthens you (v. 28), even when you are in the dust. Nine times in this psalm the writer prayed for new life from the Lord (vv. 25, 37, 40, 88, 107, 149, 154, 156, 159). There is no need to stay in the wasteland when there is life for you in the Word!

He

119:33 Teach me, O LORD, the way of Your statutes, And I shall observe it to the end.
34 Give me understanding, that I may observe Your law And keep it with all my heart.
35 Make me walk in the path of Your commandments, For I delight in it.
36 Incline my heart to Your testimonies And not to dishonest gain.
37 Turn away my eyes from looking at vanity, And revive me in Your ways.
38 Establish Your word to Your servant, As that which produces reverence for You.
39 Turn away my reproach which I dread, For Your ordinances are good.
40 Behold, I long for Your precepts; Revive me through Your righteousness.
(Psalm 119:33–40, NASB)

He - Teach Me! (vv. 33–40)

Develop your set of values from the Word (Ps. 119:37). The psalmist would rather have God's Word than food (Ps. 119:103), sleep (Ps. 119:55, 62, 147–48), or money (Ps. 119:14, 72, 127, 162). People waste time, energy, and money on things that amount to nothing (Isa. 55:2). The Hebrew word translated "worthless things" means "that which is vanity because it is false." The same word is also used of idols. What your heart covets (Ps. 119:36), your eyes will see, and then you will make wrong decisions. Check out the danger of Lot's "visual values" in Gen. 13:10–13.

Vav
119:41 May Your lovingkindnesses also come to me, O LORD, Your salvation according to Your word;
42 So I will have an answer for him who reproaches me, For I trust in Your word.
43 And do not take the word of truth utterly out of my mouth, For I wait for Your ordinances.
44 So I will keep Your law continually, Forever and ever.
45 And I will walk at liberty, For I seek Your precepts.
46 I will also speak of Your testimonies before kings And shall not be ashamed.
47 I shall delight in Your commandments, Which I love.
48 And I shall lift up my hands to Your commandments, Which I love; And I will meditate on Your statutes.
(Psalm 119:41–48, NASB)

Vav - Words for Others (vv. 41–48)

God will also give you freedom if you love and obey His Word (v. 45), which is truth (v. 43), and the truth sets you free (John 8:32). Disobedience may seem like freedom, but it is really bondage (2 Pet. 2:19). When you obey God's Word, you enjoy true freedom because His Word is "the law of liberty" (Jas. 2:12). Law and liberty are not enemies. They are coworkers in your life to build character and to bring joy.

Forgive me, merciful Father, for my complaining and revive me according to Your word. Strengthen my priorities, O Lord, and keep me on the right path. I claim Your promises and Your steadfast love. May I walk in liberty, following Your path. AMEN.

Psalm 119
vv. 49–72

Zayin, Het, Tet

Zayin

119:49 Remember the word to Your servant, In which You have made me hope.
50 This is my comfort in my affliction, That Your word has revived me.
51 The arrogant utterly deride me, Yet I do not turn aside from Your law.
52 I have remembered Your ordinances from of old, O Lord, And comfort myself.
53 Burning indignation has seized me because of the wicked, Who forsake Your law.
54 Your statutes are my songs In the house of my pilgrimage.
55 O Lord, I remember Your name in the night, And keep Your law.
56 This has become mine, That I observe Your precepts.

(Psalm 119:49–56, NASB)

Zayin - Steadying Words (vv. 49–56)

The psalmist suffered affliction and persecution because of his faith, but the Word gave him comfort and hope. When the days are difficult and the nights are long, remember God's promises and God's name, and He will comfort you. See also Psalm 119:76, 82, and 92. "This is my practice: I obey Your precepts." "Although obedience does not earn these blessings, it turns us around to receive them" (Kidner).

Heth

119:57 The Lord is my portion; I have promised to keep Your words.
58 I sought Your favor with all my heart; Be gracious to me according to Your word.
59 I considered my ways And turned my feet to Your testimonies.
60 I hastened and did not delay To keep Your commandments.
61 The cords of the wicked have encircled me, But I have not forgotten Your law.
62 At midnight I shall rise to give thanks to You Because of Your righteous ordinances.
63 I am a companion of all those who fear You, And of those who keep Your precepts.
64 The earth is full of Your lovingkindness, O Lord; Teach me Your statutes.

(Psalm 119:57–64, NASB)

Heth - With all My Heart (vv. 57–64)

If you are true to God's Word, you will have friends who are worth having (v. 63). If you walk with the wicked, they will bind you (v. 61), but if you walk with God's people, they will help you to enjoy life and liberty. People who love the Word will be glad to see you (v. 74) and will turn to you and help you (v. 79). "LORD, the earth is filled with Your faithful love" is a good companion to other glimpses of the world as God's handiwork and Kingdom: Ps. 24:1; Ps. 33:5; Isa. 6:3; Hab. 2:14; 3:3.

Tet

119:65 You have dealt well with Your servant, O LORD, according to Your word.

66 Teach me good discernment and knowledge, For I believe in Your commandments.

67 Before I was afflicted I went astray, But now I keep Your word.

68 You are good and do good; Teach me Your statutes.

69 The arrogant have forged a lie against me; With all my heart I will observe Your precepts.

70 Their heart is covered with fat, But I delight in Your law.

71 It is good for me that I was afflicted, That I may learn Your statutes.

72 The law of Your mouth is better to me Than thousands of gold and silver pieces.

(Psalm 119:65–72, NASB)

Tet - Hard Lessons Learned (vv. 65–72)

God's word encourages you in times of affliction (v. 67). "What life does to you depends upon what life finds in you. If the Word is in your mind and heart, affliction can bring out the best in you. If not, it may bring out the worst in you" (Wiersbe). "It was good for me to be afflicted so that I could learn Your statutes" (v. 71). The school of suffering never graduates any students, so ask God to teach you the lessons He wants you to learn. On the psalmist's gratitude for bitter medicine, see also Psalm 119:75.

> *I thank You, Lord, that Your word is a comfort in my distress and that Your promises give me life. Therefore, be gracious to me according to those promises. You have dealt well with me, O Lord, and I have experienced Your goodness.* AMEN.

Yod, Kaf, Lamed

Yod

119:73 Your hands made me and fashioned me; Give me understanding, that I may learn Your commandments.

74 May those who fear You see me and be glad, Because I wait for Your word.

75 I know, O LORD, that Your judgments are righteous, And that in faithfulness You have afflicted me.

76 O may Your lovingkindness comfort me, According to Your word to Your servant.

77 May Your compassion come to me that I may live, For Your law is my delight.

78 May the arrogant be ashamed, for they subvert me with a lie; But I shall meditate on Your precepts.

79 May those who fear You turn to me, Even those who know Your testimonies.

80 May my heart be blameless in Your statutes, So that I will not be ashamed.

(Psalm 119:73–80, NASB)

Yod - Justice, Love, and Compassion (vv. 73–80)

God made you and knows best how you should manage your life so He has provided a how-to- do-it manual for making life work successfully (v. 73). This manual is based, not on pragmatism, but on those qualities mentioned in the title of this section—justice, love, compassion. He tells you how to use your body and mind, how to handle your time and money, and how to make right decisions. Obeying the manual can keep you from getting into trouble and hurting yourself and others. Don't be like me! I am the typical man who waits until things break down before I read the instructions!

Kaph

119:81 My soul languishes for Your salvation; I wait for Your word.

82 My eyes fail with longing for Your word, While I say, "When will You comfort me?"

83 Though I have become like a wineskin in the smoke, I do not forget Your statutes.

84 How many are the days of Your servant? When will You execute judgment on those who persecute me?

85 The arrogant have dug pits for me, Men who are not in accord with

Your law.
86 All Your commandments are faithful; They have persecuted me with a lie; help me!
87 They almost destroyed me on earth, But as for me, I did not forsake Your precepts.
88 Revive me according to Your lovingkindness, So that I may keep the testimony of Your mouth.
(Psalm 119:81–88, NASB)

Kaph - The Brink of Ruin (vs. 81–88)

Here the psalmist looks outward to those who are opposing his witness. He is at the very edge, but reminds us that the Word helped him (and us!) to get victory over those enemies (vv. 84–87). When your soul is fainting, the Word provides you strength and comfort. When it looks like the end has come, God's Word helps you start afresh. And remember that famous saying of the cartoon character, Pogo: "We have met the enemy, and he is us!" Your worst enemy is on the inside, so allow the Word to do its work inside your heart.

Lamedh
119:89 Forever, O LORD, Your word is settled in heaven.
90 Your faithfulness continues throughout all generations; You established the earth, and it stands.
91 They stand this day according to Your ordinances, For all things are Your servants.
92 If Your law had not been my delight, Then I would have perished in my affliction.
93 I will never forget Your precepts, For by them You have revived me.
94 I am Yours, save me; For I have sought Your precepts.
95 The wicked wait for me to destroy me; I shall diligently consider Your testimonies.
96 I have seen a limit to all perfection; Your commandment is exceedingly broad.
(Psalm 119:89–96, NASB)

Lamedh - The Great Certainties (vv. 89–96)

"A striking feature of these verses is the coupling of God's creative, world-sustaining word with his law for man. Both are the product of the same ordering mind; and not only men but 'all things' are his servants" (Kidner). Verse 96 ("I have seen a limit to all perfection") serves well as a reminder of the message of Ecclesiastes. In that sober reflection on life, every earthly enterprise has its day and comes to nothing, while only in God and his commandments do we get beyond these frustrating limits. Let us rejoice that while all else in life is temporal, the universe as a whole reveals the stability of our uncreated and universal God.

The Psalmists have learned in the midst of life's distractions that security comes from fixing our eyes on our Sovereign Lord and making God the exclamation point at the center of our lives.

> *O LORD, my soul longs for Your deliverance, but I still trust in Your promises. This is because Your faithfulness reaches to the heavens and all things in the earth and the heavens are Yours. I claim them in your name. AMEN.*

Psalm 119
vv. 97–120

Mem, Nun, Samek

Mem

119:97 O how I love Your law! It is my meditation all the day.
98 Your commandments make me wiser than my enemies, For they are ever mine.
99 I have more insight than all my teachers, For Your testimonies are my meditation.
100 I understand more than the aged, Because I have observed Your precepts.
101 I have restrained my feet from every evil way, That I may keep Your word.
102 I have not turned aside from Your ordinances, For You Yourself have taught me.
103 How sweet are Your words to my taste! Yes, sweeter than honey to my mouth!
104 From Your precepts I get understanding; Therefore I hate every false way.

(Psalm 119:97–104, NASB)

Mem - Heavenly Wisdom (vv. 97–104)

The NT illumines verses 98–100 by its plain statements that heavenly wisdom begins as a gift "to babies," hidden from the worldly-wise. This emerges clearly in the ministry of Christ (Luke 10:21), decisively at the crucifixion (1 Cor. 2:8), and consistently after that in the reactions of Bunyan's "Worldly-wise Man" to the gospel (1 Cor. 1:18–25). On the themes of these verses see also Acts 6:10 and 1 John 2:27. "Your word is sweeter than honey" (v. 103). The prophets also experienced this delectable reaction when they tasted the Word (Jer. 15:16; Ezek. 3:3) (Kidner).

Nun

119:105 Your word is a lamp to my feet And a light to my path.
106 I have sworn and I will confirm it, That I will keep Your righteous ordinances.
107 I am exceedingly afflicted; Revive me, O LORD, according to Your word.
108 O accept the freewill offerings of my mouth, O LORD, And teach me Your ordinances.
109 My life is continually in my hand, Yet I do not forget Your law.

¹¹⁰ The wicked have laid a snare for me, Yet I have not gone astray from Your precepts.
¹¹¹ I have inherited Your testimonies forever, For they are the joy of my heart.
¹¹² I have inclined my heart to perform Your statutes Forever, even to the end.
(Psalm 119:105–112, NASB)

Nun - Don't Lose Your Way (vv. 105–112)

This is not simply convenient guidance for one's career, but truth for moral choices, the most difficult choices on life's path. That includes the "traps" of the wicked in v. 110. The classic example of drawing on the light of Scripture in a time of darkness is in our Lord's temptation when He drew on that light for His own path (Matt. 4:1–10).

Samek
¹¹⁹:¹¹³ I hate those who are double-minded, But I love Your law.
¹¹⁴ You are my hiding place and my shield; I wait for Your word.
¹¹⁵ Depart from me, evildoers, That I may observe the commandments of my God.
¹¹⁶ Sustain me according to Your word, that I may live; And do not let me be ashamed of my hope.
¹¹⁷ Uphold me that I may be safe, That I may have regard for Your statutes continually.
¹¹⁸ You have rejected all those who wander from Your statutes, For their deceitfulness is useless.
¹¹⁹ You have removed all the wicked of the earth like dross; Therefore I love Your testimonies.
¹²⁰ My flesh trembles for fear of You, And I am afraid of Your judgments.
(Psalm 119:113–120, NASB)

Samek - No One Double-Minded (vv. 113–120)

In my commentary on James, I suggest that James invented the colorful Greek word "double-minded" (Jas. 1:8, 4:8). Even if that is true, he did not invent the *idea* that people often want to have it both ways—to follow both God and the world instead of exclusively choosing one. The Hebrew word in v. 114 is similar to Elijah's mocking of those who hobbled "first on one leg then on the other" (1 Kings 18:21). With a single purpose, the psalmist trembles exclusively before the Lord and fears His judgments (v. 120).

> *O my God, lighten my path through the dark stretches of life, and lead me to the true light of life. You are my hiding place and my shield. Therefore I hope in Your word. O Lord, help me not to falter. May I love You with a single purpose. AMEN.*

Psalm 119
vv. 121–144

Ayin, Pe, Tsade

Ayin

119:121 I have done justice and righteousness; Do not leave me to my oppressors.
122 Be surety for Your servant for good; Do not let the arrogant oppress me.
123 My eyes fail with longing for Your salvation And for Your righteous word.
124 Deal with Your servant according to Your lovingkindness And teach me Your statutes.
125 I am Your servant; give me understanding, That I may know Your testimonies.
126 It is time for the LORD to act, For they have broken Your law.
127 Therefore I love Your commandments above gold, yes, above fine gold.
128 Therefore I esteem right all Your precepts concerning everything, I hate every false way.

(Psalm 119:121–128, NASB)

Ayin - Pressure from the Godless (vv. 121–128)

We do not live our lives in ivory towers, because most of us are down and dirty in the mean streets. God's people are aliens in an enemy territory, and only the Word can protect them from the lies of the oppressor. The Word will enable you when you feel the oppression of the enemy (vv. 121–22). But you must accept all that God's Word says about these things. If you love the truth, you must also hate the false (v. 128). That key word in the Old Testament for God and His covenant (*hesed*) only appears seven times in this psalm, and one of them is here: "Deal with Your servant based on Your lovingkindness (*hesed*) and teach me Your statutes."

Pe

119:129 Your testimonies are wonderful; Therefore my soul observes them.
130 The unfolding of Your words gives light; It gives understanding to the simple.
131 I opened my mouth wide and panted, For I longed for Your commandments.
132 Turn to me and be gracious to me, After Your manner with those who love Your name.
133 Establish my footsteps in Your word, And do not let any iniquity have dominion over me.

¹³⁴ Redeem me from the oppression of man, That I may keep Your precepts.
¹³⁵ Make Your face shine upon Your servant, And teach me Your statutes.
¹³⁶ My eyes shed streams of water, Because they do not keep Your law.
(Psalm 119:129–136, NASB)

Pe - A Light in the Darkness (vv. 129–136)

Around Christmas each year we hear about the movie, "The Wonderful Life." At times, you may not feel very "wonderful," but your life can become wonderful because the Word of God is wonderful (v. 129). The Spirit shows you wonderful things in the Word and enables you to meditate on His wonderful works (119:27). God can transform your mind and enable you to escape the dull conformity of the world (Rom. 12:1–2). His light shines within you (v. 130) and His face shines upon you (v. 135, an echo of Num. 6:24–25), so that you become a light in a dark world (Phil. 2:14–16).

Tsadhe
119: ¹³⁷ Righteous are You, O LORD, And upright are Your judgments.
¹³⁸ You have commanded Your testimonies in righteousness And exceeding faithfulness.
¹³⁹ My zeal has consumed me, Because my adversaries have forgotten Your words.
¹⁴⁰ Your word is very pure, Therefore Your servant loves it.
¹⁴¹ I am small and despised, Yet I do not forget Your precepts.
¹⁴² Your righteousness is an everlasting righteousness, And Your law is truth.
¹⁴³ Trouble and anguish have come upon me, Yet Your commandments are my delight.
¹⁴⁴ Your testimonies are righteous forever; Give me understanding that I may live.
(Psalm 119:137–144, NASB)

Tsadhe - Everlasting Righteousness (vv. 137–144)

While it can be a loaded theological word, *righteousness* is simply "rightness"—an attribute of God which is to be reflected in us. No matter how zealous we may be for God's truth (v. 139), we must also have His righteousness if we are going to succeed. The Word helps us practice righteousness in a world that is not right. There is no substitute for integrity, which comes from loving the Word and obeying it.

> *Lord God, lift my vision, heal my spirit, and give me a heart of gratitude. I look at all my faults, so I appeal to Your steadfast love and look rather for Your gift of righteousness. AMEN.*

Psalm 119
vv. 145–168

Qof, Resh, Shin

Qof

119:145 I cried with all my heart; answer me, O LORD! I will observe Your statutes.
146 I cried to You; save me And I shall keep Your testimonies.
147 I rise before dawn and cry for help; I wait for Your words.
148 My eyes anticipate the night watches, That I may meditate on Your word.
149 Hear my voice according to Your lovingkindness; Revive me, O LORD, according to Your ordinances.
150 Those who follow after wickedness draw near; They are far from Your law.
151 You are near, O LORD, And all Your commandments are truth.
152 Of old I have known from Your testimonies That You have founded them forever.

(Psalm 119:145–152, NASB)

Qof - Insomnia (vv. 145–152)

Many psalms deal with the problem of sleeplessness (Ps. 6:6; 16:7; 22:2; 30:5; 42:3; 77:2; 88:1). Anxiety, dread, and worry can disturb and confound sleep. When persecutors drew near (v. 150), the psalmist rose before dawn, crying for help (vv. 147–48). Insomnia can be difficult to overcome. For many, however, something better than drugs is meditation on God's promises (v.148b) which are the sources of all life.

Resh

119:153 Look upon my affliction and rescue me, For I do not forget Your law.
154 Plead my cause and redeem me; Revive me according to Your word.
155 Salvation is far from the wicked, For they do not seek Your statutes.
156 Great are Your mercies, O LORD; Revive me according to Your ordinances.
157 Many are my persecutors and my adversaries, Yet I do not turn aside from Your testimonies.
158 I behold the treacherous and loathe them, Because they do not keep Your word.
159 Consider how I love Your precepts; Revive me, O LORD, according to Your lovingkindness.
160 The sum of Your word is truth, And every one of Your righteous ordinances is everlasting.

(Psalm 119:153–150, NASB)

Resh - Give Me Life (vv. 153–160)

There is a mounting sense of urgency in the thrice-repeated prayer, "Give me life" or "revive me."

1. Give me life according to Your promise. (v. 154)
2. Give me life according to Your rules. (v. 156)
3. Give me life according to Your *hesed*. (v. 159)

God's blessings are dispensed on the basis of His terms, not on the basis of our demands.

> "Our worst prayers may really be our best. God seems to speak to us most intimately when he catches us off guard" (C. S. Lewis).

Shin

161 Princes persecute me without cause, But my heart stands in awe of Your words.
162 I rejoice at Your word, As one who finds great spoil.
163 I hate and despise falsehood, But I love Your law.
164 Seven times a day I praise You, Because of Your righteous ordinances.
165 Those who love Your law have great peace, And nothing causes them to stumble.
166 I hope for Your salvation, O Lord, And do Your commandments.
167 My soul keeps Your testimonies, And I love them exceedingly.
168 I keep Your precepts and Your testimonies, For all my ways are before You.

(Psalm 119:161–168, NASB)

Shin - A Place of Peace (vv. 161–168)

Knowing and obeying God's word brings joy to your heart, the kind of joy you would feel if you found a buried treasure (v. 162) or if you inherited a fortune (vv. 111). But if wealth is the goal that "drives your engine," then God's Word will not be a joy to you. If you love the Word more than money (v. 127), you will have eternal spiritual treasures. Along with joy, you will experience love (vv. 163, 167), peace (v. 165), and hope (v. 166). These are treasures money simply cannot buy.

> *"O may my soul in Thee repose, and may sweet sleep mine eyelids close, sleep that shall me more vigorous make, to serve my God when I awake. AMEN." (hymn by Thomas Ken).*

Psalm 119
vv. 169–176

"Tav and the Sof"

Tav

119:169 Let my cry come before You, O LORD; Give me understanding according to Your word.

170 Let my supplication come before You; Deliver me according to Your word.

171 Let my lips utter praise, For You teach me Your statutes.

172 Let my tongue sing of Your word, For all Your commandments are righteousness.

173 Let Your hand be ready to help me, For I have chosen Your precepts.

174 I long for Your salvation, O LORD, And Your law is my delight.

175 Let my soul live that it may praise You, And let Your ordinances help me.

176 I have gone astray like a lost sheep; seek out Your servant, For I do not forget Your commandments.

(Psalm 119:169–176, NASB)

Ta - I Will Sing and Pray and Not Forget (vv. 169–176)

If you put the Word first in your list of priorities, you will have something to sing about (vv. 171, 172, 175). You will even find yourself singing God's Word and turning statutes into songs (v. 54)! When your heart delights in God's law (v. 174), your lips will declare God's praise (Matt. 12:34). People talk about the things that they love. When God's Word fills your heart, the right words will come out of your mouth (Col. 3:16).

How appropriate that, after all his marvelous prayers, the last thing on the lips of the psalmist is a confession and a plea for the Lord to be his Shepherd ("I have gone astray like a lost sheep. Seek out your servant"). How can we not look forward to the Good Shepherd who seeks and saves His sheep (John 10:35)?

> *Lord, hear the cry of the soul that melts away for heaviness, the soul that often cleaves to the dust, and also the soul who longs for Your judgments. That soul is me, O Lord. Therefore, let my plea enter into Your presence, and give me life according to the living Word, Your Son, my Savior Jesus Christ. AMEN.*

What is the Sof?

There is no letter *sof* in the Hebrew alphabet. *Sof* means "end" in Hebrew, and now we have arrived at the *end* of the Golden Alphabet in Psalm 119. What shall we now say? Kidner expresses aptly my own thoughts: "Like a ring of eight bells, eight synonyms for Scripture dominate the psalm, and the twenty-two stanzas ring the changes on them. They do it freely, not with a bell-ringer's elaborate formula, and they introduce an occasional extra term. But the synonyms belong together, and we should probably not look for each to show its distinct character at each occurrence, but rather to contribute, by its frequent arrival, to our total understanding of what Scripture is." For those terms for Scripture, I refer you back to my first comments on this psalm.

This is not just about getting more information in your head; it is about getting it in your heart and thus transforming your walk. You have been thinking about **what the Word of God does**. Now it is time to discover **what you must do with God's Word.** You should do more than simply read it, although that is necessary. You should also love it (v. 97), treasure it (v. 72), learn it (vv. 26–27), memorize it (v. 11), meditate on it (v. 15), believe it (v. 42), and practice it (vv. 1–4). The way you treat your Bible is the way you treat your Lord, for it is His Word to your heart.

For the "last word" on this great psalm, see *The Word of God in the Child of God* by George Zemek. For a more devotional treatment, see *The Golden Alphabet* by Charles Spurgeon.

Psalms 120–134

Introduction to the Psalms of Ascent

The next fifteen psalms (120–134) are known as "the Songs of Ascents." They are thought to be the songs that Jewish pilgrims sang when they went up to Jerusalem for the feasts three times each year (Ex. 23:14–17). Whoever made this selection chose four psalms by David and one by Solomon, while the other ten are anonymous.

The Hebrew word translated "ascents" also means "degrees," and for this reason some scholars also relate this special collection to King Hezekiah and his experience of the sun dial related in Isaiah 38. According to a rabbinic view, the fifteen psalms mark the fifteen years added to Hezekiah's life, and the ten anonymous psalms are a reminder of the shadow going back ten degrees (Isa. 38:5–8).

The emphasis in this "hymnal within the hymnal" is on trusting the God of Mount Zion, even in the midst of suffering and trial. The writers describe both the trials and the triumphs of the people of God and reveal that God is with His people no matter what the difficulty.

During my forty-six visits to Jerusalem I have always read some of these psalms as we went "up to Jerusalem." The air-conditioned comfort of the bus, however, is quite different from the perils faced by those ancient pilgrims as they ascended the hills to the Holy City (Ps. 121:5–8).

Try reading Psalms 121 and 122 on your own and in your own Bible, to get the feel of where we are going as we study these Pilgrim Psalms.

> *I need Your daily guidance, O my great Redeemer, because I am a pilgrim in this barren land. May I, like Pilgrim, always be making progress as I journey to the Heavenly City. AMEN.*

Depressed In the Diaspora

Not every psalm in the pilgrim psalms (120–134) was necessarily composed for the purpose of singing during a pilgrimage. The present psalm seems sharply personal, although in a pilgrim context it voices very well the homesickness of those who settled among strangers and enemies (Kidner). Where Jews lived outside Eretz Israel is the Greek word *diaspora*. The psalm, therefore, appropriately begins the series in a distant land, so that we join the pilgrims as they prepare to set out on a journey which will eventually bring "us" to Jerusalem in Psalm 122:1–2. In the last psalm of the group, they/we come to the ark, the priests and the temple servants who minister day and night at the house of the Lord (Ps. 134:1–3). Consider these things as we read Psalm 120:

> *A Song of Ascents.*
> 120:1 In my trouble I cried to the Lord, And He answered me.
> 2 Deliver my soul, O Lord, from lying lips, From a deceitful tongue.
> 3 What shall be given to you, and what more shall be done to you, You deceitful tongue?
> 4 Sharp arrows of the warrior, With the burning coals of the broom tree.
> 5 Woe is me, for I sojourn in Meshech, For I dwell among the tents of Kedar!
> 6 Too long has my soul had its dwelling With those who hate peace.
> 7 I am for peace, but when I speak, They are for war.
>
> (Psalm 120, NASB)

Meschech was far to the north of Israel (Gen. 10:2) and *Kedar* far to the south (Gen. 25:13). It appears that the psalmist had been a sojourner in the exile for "too long." He had discovered that his offers of peace were met by words of war and lying lips. While you may identify with this at your work or school, think of Jews who had experienced this for years in the *diaspora*! Pilgrims longing to leave hostile environments for the joys of worship in the Holy City must have often chanted this pilgrim psalm.

PSALM 120

"In Christian use, the psalm has inaugurated the steps of ascent to God; the one who begins this upward journey is at once beset by much antagonism and many hostile tongues. From the follies of his own tongue also he prays for deliverance, and would be taken into the peace of Jesus, to whom the words of verse 7a are appropriate (literally 'I am peace')" (Eaton).

> *O my good and gracious Lord, deliver me from lying lips and a deceitful tongue. Grant that I may never tire of speaking peace to those intent on war, through Him who is my peace and the dwelling place of my soul, Jesus Your Son. AMEN.*

The Keeper

Here the pilgrim role of these Psalms of Ascents comes clearly into view. The psalmist affirms that he will lift up his eyes to the hills. Both in these psalms and elsewhere, the Holy City Jerusalem is up in the hills (2800 feet above sea level), yet it still surrounded by even higher hills (Mounts Scopus and Olives). See Psalm 125:2.

It is at this point in verse one, however, that the old Authorized Version introduces a translation that is a bit misleading. In that venerable version, verse one reads: "I will lift up mine eyes unto the hills, from which cometh my help" (made famous further by the Mother Superior quoting it in "The Sound of Music"!). This gives the impression that our help comes from the hills. This part of the verse, however, is actually a question: "From where does my help come?" The answer is clearly given in verse 2: "My help comes from the Lord."

Now that the translation is clarified, let's read the psalm. Note also the many references to the "keeper" theme. I have highlighted them in the text of the psalm.

> *A Song of Ascents.*
> 121:1 I will lift up my eyes to the mountains; From where shall my help come?
> 2 My help comes from the Lord, who made heaven and earth.
> 3 He will not allow your foot to slip; He who **keeps** you will not slumber.
> 4 Behold, He who **keeps** Israel will neither slumber nor sleep.
> 5 The Lord is your **keeper**; The Lord is your shade on your right hand.
> 6 The sun will not smite you by day, nor the moon by night.
> 7 The Lord will **keep** you from all evil; He will **keep** your soul.
> 8 The Lord will **keep** your going out and your coming in from this time forth and forever.
>
> (Psalm 121, NASB)

The word for "keeper" is *shomer*, which is the term for "guardian." Yahweh will guard His people from every danger along the pilgrim path.

While sentries may fall asleep, Yahweh "neither slumbers nor sleeps." Satan's wrong use of a similar promise (Matt. 4:6) should not cause us to think that this promise is an empty one. "We are immortal until our work is finished."

The especially glowing promises here (and also in Psalm 91) seem to come from the royal ideal. So their deepest fulfillment is to be sought in the Messiah. The disciples of Christ, however, expect to suffer with Him, yet we are guarded by God in deepest mystery, until the secret of that faithful guarding is fully revealed.

> *Grant it, Lord, when I lift up my eyes to the hills in longing for Your help, that I may hear and take to my heart the promise of Your unfailing care. May I know as I go out and as I come that you are guarding me day and night. In my deepest heart may I recognize that whatever is my share in the sufferings of the cross, that You are my shade and my savior, now and for evermore. AMEN.*

Let's Go

At last Jerusalem and the house of the Lord come into sight, and we have arrived! Catch the sheer delight of verse 2: "And now our feet are standing within your gates, O Jerusalem." The trials of an expatriate (Ps. 120) and the hazards of travel (Ps. 121) are eclipsed now by the joy which had first drawn the pilgrims on their journey (Kidner).

> *A Song of Ascents, of David.*
> 122:1 I was glad when they said to me, "Let us go to the house of the LORD."
> 2 Our feet are standing Within your gates, O Jerusalem,
> 3 Jerusalem, that is built As a city that is compact together;
> 4 To which the tribes go up, even the tribes of the LORD—An ordinance for Israel—To give thanks to the name of the LORD.
> 5 For there thrones were set for judgment, The thrones of the house of David.
> 6 Pray for the peace of Jerusalem: "May they prosper who love you.
> 7 "May peace be within your walls, And prosperity within your palaces."
> 8 For the sake of my brothers and my friends, I will now say, "May peace be within you."
> 9 For the sake of the house of the LORD our God, I will seek your good.
> (Psalm 122, NASB)

I like Wiersbe's treatment of this psalm, some of which I have adapted as follows:

"Let us proceed" (v. 1). Do you really rejoice when you have opportunity to go to God's house and worship Him? We today can travel easily to a place of worship but the ancient Israelites had to sometimes walk a great distance, especially on a pilgrimage. Yet the pilgrim was happy to go to God's house.

"Let us praise" (vv. 2–5). How the people loved Jerusalem! It was a **holy** place because the temple was there, an **honored** place because David's throne was there, and a **happy** place because the tribes were there to celebrate the greatness and goodness of God.

PSALM 122

"Let us pray" (vv. 6–9). Do you pray for the peace and prosperity of the people in your local "house of God"? Do you also pray for God's people Israel? There can be no peace in our world until the Prince of Peace rules His people from His throne of peace in Jerusalem.

> *O Lord my God, may I ever be glad to go to Your house, and in the power of the Spirit find myself before Your presence, bound in fellowship with all Your worshippers. May I be renewed both by Your judgment and Your mercy. Help me to persevere in prayer for Your church, the Body who embraces me in Your new creation.*
> *AMEN.*

Psalm 123

Desiring God's Favor

These pilgrim songs preserve many moods, reflecting the turbulent history of the Jewish people, a history which continues in the story of the church. The psalmist's cry from the heart here can still speak for our brothers under persecution. In the 1970's, James and Marty Hefly concluded that more Christians had died for their faith in the 20th century than in all the previous centuries combined! Let us not forget them. "Blessed are the dead who die in the Lord..." (Rev. 14:13).

A Song of Ascents.
123:1 To You I lift up my eyes, O You who are enthroned in the heavens!
2 Behold, as the eyes of servants look to the hand of their master, As the eyes of a maid to the hand of her mistress, So our eyes look to the LORD our God, Until He is gracious to us.
3 Be gracious to us, O LORD, be gracious to us, For we are greatly filled with contempt.
4 Our soul is greatly filled With the scoffing of those who are at ease, And with the contempt of the proud.
(Psalm 123, NASB)

The psalm begins with an individual speaking (v. 1), but in the rest of the psalm (vv. 2–4), the group speaks. "I lift my eyes to You" represents the posture of prayer. For the figure of Yahweh's throne in heaven, see Psalm 2:4 and 11:4. It seems best to take the language as a figure of trust and dependence. With such an attitude the people look to Yahweh their God for his mercy. The sense is: "We will keep looking to you, Lord, our God, until you have mercy on us. We will do this as a servant or a maid looks to the one in charge of them."

In the prayer for mercy (vv. 3–4) the people complain of the contempt and scorn to which they have been subjected. In this same verse those with "more than enough contempt" are the rich, self-satisfied people who have all they want and are happy with things as they are (Amos 6:1). The NKJV describes them as "the complacent."

Throughout their history, Jews have often had to endure the scorn and contempt of their enemies. The world has never loved God's people, for they represent a life style that is a threat to their complacency. "As we make our way on the narrow road that leads to Zion, we run up against a crowd going in the other direction" (Wiersbe).

In summary, these pilgrims are people returning home from exile in a foreign country. After expressing their humble submission to Yahweh (vv. 1–2), the group prays for his mercy (vv. 3–4). This is a simple but wise model to follow when we are opposed.

If Christianity ever becomes illegal, will there be enough evidence in your life to convict you?

> *O LORD, this world is not my home, but I still pray for the country where I live. May the "powers that be" restrain evil and promote righteousness, and may what we experience now be a foretaste of the righteousness which someday will fill the whole earth. AMEN.*

What If The Lord Wasn't There?

In this thanksgiving hymn, David thanks God, on behalf of his people, for rescuing them from Israel's enemies. The psalm opens with David asking the people what would have happened if Yahweh had not defended them (v. 1). The answer is obvious (v. 5), after which the people express their thanks to Yahweh for His help (vv. 6–8).

A Song of Ascents, of David.
124:1 "Had it not been the Lord who was on our side," Let Israel now say,
2 "Had it not been the Lord who was on our side When men rose up against us,
3 Then they would have swallowed us alive, When their anger was kindled against us;
4 Then the waters would have engulfed us, The stream would have swept over our soul;
5 Then the raging waters would have swept over our soul."
6 Blessed be the Lord, Who has not given us to be torn by their teeth.
7 Our soul has escaped as a bird out of the snare of the trapper; The snare is broken and we have escaped.
8 Our help is in the name of the Lord, Who made heaven and earth.
(Psalm 124, NASB)

David's authorship should not be overlooked, for this gives us an insight into the early peril of his rule, particularly from the Philistines, who had thought to see the last of Israel when they shattered the kingdom of Saul. 2 Sam. 5:17–25 shows how serious the threat was, and how little confidence David placed in his own power to survive it. This was not simply one of the occasional Philistine raids to gain territory (Kidner). It was an invasion meant to put an end to David and the future hope of Israel. But David had an ally that his enemies did not have (v. 8).

Metaphors of danger ranging from turbulent waters to vicious animals abound in the psalm. That of a wild animal in verse 6 presents the ordeal as one that was already far advanced, while the enemy's grip is a present fact with its army in a dominating position (cf. 2 Sam. 5:18). These figures make the psalm all the more accessible to Christians as a vehicle of our own praise. Like David we are captives released from the den of a deadly lion who still threatens us (1 Pet. 5:8).

We thank God for the saving help that has come in the name of Jesus, the Word of creation. He has shown himself to be with us and for us. Who then can prevail against us? We are more than conquerors through Him and his love! (Rom. 8:31, 37).

> *O Lord, in whose name alone is my help, I pray that You will defend me against the assaults that come unexpectedly upon me, and the unseen snare that sometimes entraps my souls. May I bless You and sing of You as the Savior who has set me free. AMEN.*

Psalm 125

Mountains Around The City

The hills and the holy city, much in mind and finally much in view to the pilgrims, make their presence felt again (Ps. 121:1–2). While Jerusalem sits atop the Central Mountains of Judea, it is often overlooked that the Temple on Mount Moriah was still lower than the hills around it. The first view of the city by pilgrims was most often from the crest of the Mount of Olives, which still offers that breathtaking view to the modern Jerusalem "pilgrim." Hills are really just that—big piles of dirt and rocks—but they assume a symbolic representation of the Strong Lord, who is really the ultimate goal of pilgrims, both then and now.

A Song of Ascents.
125:1 Those who trust in the Lord Are as Mount Zion, which cannot be moved but abides forever.
2 As the mountains surround Jerusalem, So the Lord surrounds His people From this time forth and forever.
3 For the scepter of wickedness shall not rest upon the land of the righteous, So that the righteous will not put forth their hands to do wrong.
4 Do good, O Lord, to those who are good And to those who are upright in their hearts.
5 But as for those who turn aside to their crooked ways, The Lord will lead them away with the doers of iniquity. Peace be upon Israel.

(Psalm 125, NASB)

Trusting the Lord brings security (vv. 1–2). Built on Mount Zion and surrounded by the mountains, Jerusalem was secure. Pilgrims felt safe when they arrived there after their dangerous journey. As a citizen of the heavenly Zion, you are safe in the Lord's care (Heb. 12:22).

Trusting the Lord implies sovereignty (v. 3). This leads to bowing before the God who holds the righteous scepter. Wickedness in our world is a temptation even to the righteous, so keep submitting to the Sovereign's just and righteous rule.

Trusting the Lord leads to sanctity (vv. 4–5). When you walk by faith with eyes on the Lord, you avoid dangerous detours that lead you away from the path of righteousness. God has made you safe so that you might be submitted and live a life of "doing good."

That last sentence of the psalm, "Peace be with Israel" (*Shalom al Yisrael*), has been found in the mosaic floors of ancient synagogues in Israel. It is a prayer for peace that seems so elusive today, but will find an answer when both sides submit to the gracious rule of the Prince of Peace.

This message of peace is not easy to convey in a situation when crooked and violent ways seem so often to prosper. But the psalmist challenges us to see through to the deepest truth, to believe in the Lord's steadfastness and so to become steadfast, so we can be a stronghold for good in a bad world, by being surrounded by the savior's power.

> *O God, my eternal King and mountain of strength, let not evil have dominion over Your people, but grant that as we are supported by Your goodness, we may reject all crooked ways, and with steadfast hearts ever rejoice in Your peace.* AMEN.

Psalm 126

From Joy to Tears to Joy

The mood in the first half of this song (vv. 1–3) is one of delirious happiness and relief. But it seems to be only a memory, and the psalm turns into a prayer for the transformation of a barren and cheerless scene (vv. 4–6) (Kidner). The kind of deliverance that God will yet give is described by the promises of reaping through tears. This then concludes a psalm that moves from joy to tears and back again to joy.

> *A Song of Ascents.*
> 126:1 When the Lord brought back the captive ones of Zion, We were like those who dream.
> 2 Then our mouth was filled with laughter And our tongue with joyful shouting; Then they said among the nations, "The Lord has done great things for them."
> 3 The Lord has done great things for us; We are glad.
> 4 Restore our captivity, O Lord, As the streams in the South.
> 5 Those who sow in tears shall reap with joyful shouting.
> 6 He who goes to and fro weeping, carrying his bag of seed, Shall indeed come again with a shout of joy, bringing his sheaves with him.
> (Psalm 126, NASB)

In my earliest days as a Christian, this little jewel was always presented to me as "the soul-winner's psalm." While that is certainly a possible application, there seems to be so much more here than witnessing to others. The main point in this beautiful song is best found in verse 4—a prayer that the person's exhausted life may be renewed. By way of support for this prayer, it is preceded by recollection of a past renewal (vv. 1–3) and followed then by proverbs style thoughts of suffering turned to joy (vv. 5–6).

God always wants to make us rivers of blessing, like the dry wadis in the Israeli desert that become rushing torrents in the rainy season. If God sends you "showers of blessing," share the blessing with others through both words and deeds.

PSALM 126

He also wants you to get to work in the harvest. Whether it is plowing the field (Luke 9:62), sowing the seed, or reaping the sheaves, God has a ministry for you. If you water the seed with your tears, you will one day rejoice as you bring in the sheaves. This is the formula for a harvest: **going, weeping, sowing, reaping**. It is more than a rhyme. It is a path for life and blessing!

> *Lord, as You send rain and flowers even to the wilderness, renew my often dry existence by Your Holy Spirit. Help me to sow good seed in all times of adversity, and so live that I may rejoice in Your good harvest both now and at the end of the age. AMEN.*

Psalm 127

A Quiver Full of Arrows

This short poem singles out three of our most universal activities—building, security, raising a family—and asks us who insures the success of each. The psalm is ascribed to Solomon, and has perhaps a concealed signature in the expression "his *beloved*" (v. 2), which is the word from which *Jedidiah*, his personal name from God, was formed (2 Sam. 12:25). Like much of Solomon's wisdom, however, the lessons of this psalm were mostly lost on him. His building, both literal and figurative, became reckless (1 Kings 9:10, 19), his kingdom a ruin (1 Kings 11:11) and his marriages a disastrous denial of God (1 Kings 11:1) (Kidner).

The two parts of the psalm are well marked. Both parts proclaim that only what is from God is truly strong: **the city-house (vv. 1–2) and the family-house (vv. 3–5)**. The two senses of the word "house" (a dwelling or a family) make a well-known wordplay in the OT, leading to the similarity of the Hebrew words *bōnîm*, "builders" (v. 1), and *bānîm*, "sons" (v. 3).

Read Psalm 127, looking for those features.

> *A Song of Ascents, of Solomon.*
> 127:1 Unless the Lord builds the house, They labor in vain who build it; Unless the Lord guards the city, The watchman keeps awake in vain.
> 2 It is vain for you to rise up early, To retire late, To eat the bread of painful labors; For He gives to His beloved even in his sleep.
> 3 Behold, children are a gift of the Lord, The fruit of the womb is a reward.
> 4 Like arrows in the hand of a warrior, So are the children of one's youth.
> 5 How blessed is the man whose quiver is full of them; They will not be ashamed When they speak with their enemies in the gate.
> (Psalm 127, NASB)

Whether the building is on a large scale, within a city (vv.1–2), or on a small scale, within a home (vv. 3–5), it is the Lord who insures the protection

Psalm 127

and blessing of the "house." Children in a God-centered home are compared to arrows in the bag ("quiver") of an ancient warrior. We don't really know how large a quiver was or how many arrows it could hold. Some fathers are proud of their large quivers. I once preached on this text and a proud father of eight pumped my hand at the door afterward in gratitude, for he thought that I was affirming his masculinity and virility! His tired looking wife then told me that she wanted to paraphrase the text: "Blessed is the man who knows *when* his quiver is full!"

So check out how this little psalm best applies to you!

> Lord Jesus, You taught me to consider Your provision for the birds and how You provide beautiful garments for the flowers. I thank You for all that you provide for me as I rest in You. Now I pray that You will strengthen me by Your grace against all adversity. AMEN.

Psalm 128

Kids as House Plants

The blessings of a godly life are traced from the center outwards in this psalm, as the focus moves from the godly man to his family and finally to all Israel. Portrayed here is a simple piety with its fruit of stability, fruitfulness, and peace.

> *A Song of Ascents.*
> 128:1 How blessed is everyone who fears the LORD, Who walks in His ways.
> 2 When you shall eat of the fruit of your hands, You will be happy and it will be well with you.
> 3 Your wife shall be like a fruitful vine Within your house, Your children like olive plants Around your table.
> 4 Behold, for thus shall the man be blessed Who fears the LORD.
> 5 The LORD bless you from Zion, And may you see the prosperity of Jerusalem all the days of your life.
> 6 Indeed, may you see your children's children. Peace be upon Israel!
> (Psalm 128, NASB)

A man before his Father (vv. 1–2). The ingredients of true happiness (for the psalm opens with the word "Happy"), are easy to discover. Note the inclusio about the one "who fears the Lord" in verse 1 and verse 4. His character is summed up by the qualities of reverence (the right relationship to God, v. 1a) and obedience. Hard work is taken for granted, but this psalm makes it clear (as did its sister Psalm 127) that enjoyment of its fruits is a gift from God.

A man before his family (vv. 3–4). The vine was a symbol of both fruitfulness and festivity (Judg. 9:13). The children around your table are the hope and promise of the future. The simile of olive shoots is similar to the simile of the "arrows" in Psalm 127:4. "In the two psalms these two aspects or stages of youth, as tender growth to be nurtured and as the embodiment of fiery zeal, make a complementary pair" (Kidner).

A man before his future (vv. 5–6). The Godly man and his family's future is bound up in Zion's welfare and that of Israel. There is a New Testament echo of the last prayer, "Peace be upon Israel," in Galatians 6:16. It sums up the concern of Paul that God's people should not put up barriers against each other, but show themselves true citizens of "the Jerusalem above" (Gal. 4:26). It is still a prayer that we should pray.

For a congregation largely of farmers, the Psalmist teaches that profound happiness would be granted them when they revered the Lord and walked by His guidance. Their work would not be wasted and their family life would be richly blessed. He then added his prayer that with their own blessing they would see peace extend from the sanctuary to cover all of their society. But even if you are not a farmer, you who hear this song can take from it the conviction that in walking with the Lord lies the secret of happiness.

> *O God, my Creator, may I know the happiness of fearing You and walking in Your paths. May I know in my work and in my home the fruit of the Spirit, and grant blessing on Your church and peace upon all Your people. AMEN.*

Psalm 129

Anti-Semitism, Then and Now

Anti-Semitism, as old as the patriarchs and as modern as some Arabic textbooks, is the theme of this psalm. The curses pronounced are also as old as the promise to Abram, "Whoever curses you I will curse" (Gen. 12:3). The enemies' attempts to destroy Israel while God protects her are in verses 1–4. The judgment on those would be destroyers is described in verses 5–8a. A contrasting blessing on Israel concludes the psalm in verse 8b.

A Song of Ascents.

129:1 "Many times they have persecuted me from my youth up," Let Israel now say,
2 "Many times they have persecuted me from my youth up; Yet they have not prevailed against me.
3 "The plowers plowed upon my back; They lengthened their furrows."
4 The LORD is righteous; He has cut in two the cords of the wicked.
5 May all who hate Zion Be put to shame and turned backward;
6 Let them be like grass upon the housetops, Which withers before it grows up;
7 With which the reaper does not fill his hand, Or the binder of sheaves his bosom;
8 Nor do those who pass by say, "The blessing of the LORD be upon you; We bless you in the name of the LORD."
(Psalm 129, NASB)

Most nations look back on what they have achieved; Israel reflects on what she has survived. It could be a disheartening exercise, for Israel today still has her ill-wishers. The psalmist takes courage from the past, facing God with gratitude and his enemies with defiance (Kidner). So, you are not Jewish, you say! How often it happens that we can recognize the blessing of God upon those who have suffered deeply, and from them others can receive great blessing in the name of the Lord!

Israel's afflictions are compared to the plowing of a field. Think of what it would feel like to be face down in the dirt while a plow goes down your back! How do you handle a situation like that? With Jesus and Paul as additional

PSALM 129

guides—you wait for the Lord to judge your enemies. He will put them to shame and make them wither like grass on a sod roof (see Rom. 12:19–21). On the other hand, God's people will hear God's blessing in their ears and have God's blessing in their hands. Plowing times can be productive times.

> *Lord Jesus, who bore the sin of the world and gathered up the pain of all the ages, I thank You for all who have joined their afflictions to Your own. I ask that Yours and their blessing may fall upon me, so that I may also rejoice with them in the harvest of Your Holy Spirit.*
>
> *"From war's alarms, from deadly pestilence, be Your strong arm, O Lord, our ever sure defense. Your true religion in our hearts increase. Your bounteous goodness nourish us in peace. Refresh your people on their toilsome way. Lead us from night to everlasting day. Fill all our hearts with heaven-born love and grace, until at last we meet before Your face" ("God of Our Fathers"). AMEN.*

Out of the Depths

The first words provide a fitting title for this psalm. The psalmist saw himself in four different situations, and claimed the mercy (*hesed*) of Yahweh to deliver him from each dangerous place.

A Song of Ascents.
130:1 Out of the depths I have cried to You, O LORD.
2 Lord, hear my voice! Let Your ears be attentive To the voice of my supplications.
3 If You, LORD, should mark iniquities, O Lord, who could stand?
4 But there is forgiveness with You, That You may be feared.
5 I wait for the LORD, my soul does wait, And in His word do I hope.
6 My soul waits for the Lord More than the watchmen for the morning; Indeed, more than the watchmen for the morning.
7 O Israel, hope in the LORD; For with the LORD there is lovingkindness, And with Him is abundant redemption.
8 And He will redeem Israel from all his iniquities.

(Psalm 130, NASB)

As you read it, consider yourself in these four places:

You are in the depths (vv. 1–2). The depths of despair can overwhelm you. You are drowning, and all you can do is cry out to God. He hears—and He rescues you! What is clear in all such passages is that self-help is no answer to the depths of distress, however useful it may be in the shallows of self-pity.

You are in the court (vv. 3–4). Now the nature of the trouble comes out, as something different from the depression of illness, homesickness or persecution seen in some other psalms (Psalms 6, 42, 69). Here the trouble is our guilt. For all that, the fact of forgiveness (v. 4) is not in doubt. You are on trial, facing your sins, and you have no defense. But the Judge pays the penalty, and you are forgiven!

You are in the dark (vv. 5–6). It is the Lord Himself, not simply escape from punishment, for which the writer longs. In plain terms, he speaks of a promise ("His Word") to cling to, and with the word, "watchmen," he chooses as his simile a hope that will not fail. Night may seem endless, but morning is certain and its time determined. The sun rises and God gives you the dawning of a new day!

You are on the block (vv. 7–8). You are a slave, bound by your own sins, and you are about to sell yourself to a terrible master. But the Savior comes and purchases you and sets you free! Coverdale's beautiful expression, *plenteous redemption,* in the Psalter of the Book of Common Prayer, was retained by the KJV. It shines brightly against the darkness of the psalm's beginning.

That wonderful word, *hesed,* so prevalent throughout the Psalms, is the answer again to both the psalmist's and to your own guilt (v. 7). "Lovingkindness!" "Steadfast love!" What a wonderful salvation we have! "Where sin abounded, grace super-abounded" (Rom. 5:20).

> *Father, I commend to Your faithful and steadfast love those who are crying from the depths in areas of the world I know not. Help them to watch and pray through their time of darkness, in the sure hope of the dawn of Your forgiveness and redemption. AMEN.*

Psalm 131

A Calm and Quiet Soul

David's name at the head of this psalm has its ironies in the light of his middle and later years, but it also awakens memories of his early modesty, simplicity and lack of revenge—some of the qualities which made him great as a man after God's heart. The precious little psalm anticipates the object lesson of Matt. 18:1–4, where Jesus called a child to him to answer the question, "Who is the greatest in the kingdom of heaven?" (Kidner).

> *A Song of Ascents, of David.*
> 131:1 O LORD, my heart is not proud, nor my eyes haughty; Nor do I involve myself in great matters, Or in things too difficult for me.
> 2 Surely I have composed and quieted my soul; Like a weaned child rests against his mother, My soul is like a weaned child within me.
> 3 O Israel, hope in the LORD From this time forth and forever.
> (Psalm 131, NASB)

The singer's theme of humility and quiet trust here has national relevance (v. 3). As in the previous psalm, however, we best take this individual as playing a representative role. He takes the lead in the attitude he describes (vv. 1–2) and then turns to encourage his assembly in such trust. His song may have been inspired in circumstances of hardship for the people, but the time period cannot be clearly determined. So its application is for all times!

The following thoughts are freely adapted from Warren Wiersbe.

Most children resist weaning because they want to continue receiving the special attention of mother and the security it brings. Children do not realize that the traumatic experience of weaning is the first step toward maturity and freedom. From birth to death, life is a series of weanings, and God never takes anything from you without giving you something better. You may weep and try to hold on to the past, but God tenderly leads you toward the future.

Weaned children discover who they are and what they can do. They have quiet hearts and no desire to go back to babyhood. They live for the future and watch for the special things that come to children growing up. They learn to obey, for only then can they fully experience all that the Father has for them.

As you mature in the Lord, you must "put away childish things" (1 Cor. 13:11). When God weans you away from something, do not fret. He has something better to take its place.

> "Trust the past to God's mercy, the present to God's love, and the future to God's providence" (Augustine).

Grant to me, Lord, a quiet and patient spirit, that I may always hope in You, and wait upon Your wisdom and Your goodness. In the name of the One who invited little children to come to Him
AMEN.

Psalm 132

David – Messianic King

When the ark was moved from Kiriath-jearim to the newly captured Jebus/Jerusalem/City of David, it was the climax of a journey that began centuries earlier at Mt. Sinai. At least two other psalms bring this event vividly to mind: Psalm 24, as awestruck at the holiness of the King of glory, and Psalm 68, as exultant at God's choice of little Zion to be His royal throne. In Psalm 132 another pattern comes into view. It is the place of David in this whole Divine plan. The first half reveals his sworn resolve to see the matter through and relives the great occasion. The second half reveals God's oath to stand by David's dynasty and by His own choice of Zion (Kidner).

A Song of Ascents.

132:1 Remember, O LORD, on David's behalf, All his affliction;

2 How he swore to the LORD And vowed to the Mighty One of Jacob,

3 "Surely I will not enter my house, Nor lie on my bed;

4 I will not give sleep to my eyes Or slumber to my eyelids,

5 Until I find a place for the LORD, A dwelling place for the Mighty One of Jacob."

6 Behold, we heard of it in Ephrathah, We found it in the field of Jaar.

7 Let us go into His dwelling place; Let us worship at His footstool.

8 Arise, O LORD, to Your resting place, You and the ark of Your strength.

9 Let Your priests be clothed with righteousness, And let Your godly ones sing for joy.

10 For the sake of David Your servant, Do not turn away the face of Your anointed.

11 The LORD has sworn to David A truth from which He will not turn back: "Of the fruit of your body I will set upon your throne.

12 "If your sons will keep My covenant And My testimony which I will teach them, Their sons also shall sit upon your throne forever."

13 For the LORD has chosen Zion; He has desired it for His habitation.

14 "This is My resting place forever; Here I will dwell, for I have desired it.

Psalm 132

¹⁵ "I will abundantly bless her provision; I will satisfy her needy with bread.
¹⁶ "Her priests also I will clothe with salvation, And her godly ones will sing aloud for joy.
¹⁷ "There I will cause the horn of David to spring forth; I have prepared a lamp for Mine anointed.
¹⁸ "His enemies I will clothe with shame, But upon himself his crown shall shine."

(Psalm 132, NASB)

The psalm is the centerpiece of the Ascent Psalms. **It follows closely the account of the Davidic Covenant in 2 Sam. 7:1–16.** David wanted a place for God to dwell (vv. 2–10) and received an oath from the Lord that his descendants would rule on his throne forever (vv. 11–12). His descendants, however, were not faithful, and were thus removed from the throne. But God had chosen David and Zion, so **He thus promised to raise up a future descendant, the Anointed One, i.e., the Messiah (vv. 13–17).**

Psalm 132 is a reminder that God's promise remains firm and is the basis on which the future hope of Israel lies. When that chosen seed comes, and He has (Luke 1:32–33), the promise is that "I will clothe his enemies with shame, but the crown on his head will be glorious" (v. 18). In the era when the Psalter was edited, the inclusion of this psalm among the Ascent Psalms shows the editors' faith that someday God will renew the Davidic line. And He did! See the clear reference to this psalm in Acts 2:30–31.

> "The church has continued to sing this colorful psalm, praying that God's ministers be clothed with salvation and his faithful sing for joy, for through Jesus they enter the dwelling-place of the Lord, bow low before his footstool, and are abundantly blessed with the gifts of eternal life" (Eaton).

Almighty God, grant that I may seek a resting place for Your presence in my heart, so that from all my labor and prayers Your blessing may go out to comfort the needy and bring light to those who sit in darkness. This is for the sake of Him who by His humility and suffering established the sanctuary of my eternal salvation.
AMEN.

Psalm 133

Unity, O to Dwell In Unity

This vivid little psalm ascribed to David apparently marked the moment he had waited for, when at last all Israel had rallied to him, and God had given him Jerusalem (2 Sam. 5:1–10) (Kidner).

A Song of Ascents, of David.
133:1 Behold, how good and how pleasant it is For brothers to dwell together in unity!
2 It is like the precious oil upon the head, Coming down upon the beard, Even Aaron's beard, Coming down upon the edge of his robes.
3 It is like the dew of Hermon Coming down upon the mountains of Zion; For there the Lord commanded the blessing—life forever.
(Psalm 133, NASB)

It is one thing for a group of people to journey together to Jerusalem for a yearly festival and something else for them to live together day after day. The accounts of Abraham and Lot, Isaac and his family, Jacob and Laban, and Joseph's brothers remind us that brethren do not always dwell together in unity!

Unity must come down from above, like the oil running down Aaron's beard and bathing the twelve jewels on the breastplate (Ex. 29:5–7). It is also like the dew descending on Mount Hermon, the source of the Jordan River, with its water eventually descending south through Israel (Jordan means "descending"). You can manufacture uniformity by manipulating people and exerting pressure, but true unity can come only from God by His Spirit.

Unity is pleasant and produces a lovely fragrance like scented oil. It is good and produces fruitfulness like the dew. On the other hand, divisions among God's people produce strife and disorder (Jas. 3:13–18). Have you heeded the admonition of Eph. 4:1–3?

Psalm 133

A popular folk sung in Israel consists in singing the Hebrew of verse 1: *Hinei mah tov umah na'im, shevet achim gam yachad.* I encourage you to sing it with me followed by singing it also in English: "Behold how good and how pleasant it is for brethren to dwell together. In unity to dwell in unity. Lalalalalalalalala."

> *O Lord, richly bless my _____. Make it a haven of peace and a place of joy and comfort. AMEN. (You fill in the blank with church, family, club, class, Bible study, etc.)*

Psalm 134

Blessings 24/7

This precious little psalm works like a final benediction for the Ascent Psalms. These Songs, which began in the foreign surroundings of Meshech and Kedar (Ps. 120), end fittingly on the note of servants blessing God "unceasingly within His temple."

> *A Song of Ascents.*
> 134:1 Behold, bless the LORD, all servants of the LORD, Who serve by night in the house of the LORD!
> 2 Lift up your hands to the sanctuary And bless the LORD.
> 3 May the LORD bless you from Zion, He who made heaven and earth.
> (Psalm 134, NASB)

We learn from 1 Chronicles 9:33 that Levitical singers were on duty "day and night." The law of Moses had summed up the role of this tribe in the words "to carry the ark ... to stand before the Lord to minister ... and to bless in His name" (Deut. 10:8). When the ark found its resting-place, David gave them new responsibilities, but worship still remained paramount: "they shall stand every morning, thanking and praising the Lord, and likewise at evening" (1 Chron. 23:30).

The phrase, "in the holy place," translates a single word, "holiness." It is here used adverbially. So it may speak of worshiping "in holiness" and be the passage underlying 1 Tim. 2:8, "lifting up holy hands."

The word *bless* is perhaps the key-note of the psalm, mentioned as it is in each verse. First it is directed Godward, and then it returns from God to man. To bless God is to acknowledge gratefully what he is. To bless man God must make of him what he is not, and give him what he has not. God blesses people by conferring good on them. We bless God by praising the good in Him.

A word about the place God has for his blessing. As the one who made heaven and earth, He gives without measure, and His ways are past finding out. Yet His blessing is from Zion, a particular place to which the Israelite could get up and go. Like His commandment, His blessing is not "far off" nor "beyond the sea" but "very near you" (Deut. 30:11–14; Rom. 10:6–10). His true Mount Zion, as **Hebrews 12:22–24 shows is, where "Jesus, the mediator of a new covenant" reigns in the midst of His people**. In the words of the previous psalm: **"There the Lord has commanded the blessing, life forevermore."** Derek Kidner has again influenced these thoughts.

> *O Lord, maker of heaven and earth, I bless Your holy name. Some people would think me weird if I raised my hands in worship as the psalmist told me to do. So I raise them now to You seeking Your blessing on this unworthy servant. AMEN.*

Psalm 135

God Is Great, God is Good

"God is great, God is good, and we thank Him for our food." So goes the prayer before meals that many of us were taught as children, and the prayer that many of us have taught our own children. Reminding us of God's goodness and greatness is what this psalm is all about. It even echoes the above statements in verses 3 and 5!

135:1 Praise the Lord! Praise the name of the Lord; Praise Him, O servants of the Lord,

2 You who stand in the house of the Lord, In the courts of the house of our God!

3 Praise the Lord, for the Lord is good; Sing praises to His name, for it is lovely.

4 For the Lord has chosen Jacob for Himself, Israel for His own possession.

5 For I know that the Lord is great And that our Lord is above all gods.

6 Whatever the Lord pleases, He does, In heaven and in earth, in the seas and in all deeps.

7 He causes the vapors to ascend from the ends of the earth; Who makes lightnings for the rain, Who brings forth the wind from His treasuries.

8 He smote the firstborn of Egypt, Both of man and beast.

9 He sent signs and wonders into your midst, O Egypt, Upon Pharaoh and all his servants.

10 He smote many nations And slew mighty kings,

11 Sihon, king of the Amorites, And Og, king of Bashan, And all the kingdoms of Canaan;

12 And He gave their land as a heritage, A heritage to Israel His people.

13 Your name, O Lord, is everlasting, Your remembrance, O Lord, throughout all generations.

14 For the Lord will judge His people And will have compassion on His servants.

15 The idols of the nations are but silver and gold, The work of man's hands.

16 They have mouths, but they do not speak; They have eyes, but they do not see;

17 They have ears, but they do not hear, Nor is there any breath at all in their mouths.

> ¹⁸ Those who make them will be like them, Yes, everyone who trusts in them.
> ¹⁹ O house of Israel, bless the Lord; O house of Aaron, bless the Lord;
> ²⁰ O house of Levi, bless the Lord; You who revere the Lord, bless the Lord.
> ²¹ Blessed be the Lord from Zion, Who dwells in Jerusalem. Praise the Lord!
> (Psalm 135, NASB)

The psalmist opens his song by praising the Lord four times (vv. 1–3), and he ends it by blessing the Lord four times (vv. 19–21). In between, he gives four excellent reasons why the Lord deserves your heartfelt praise.

He is the God of salvation (v. 4). By His grace, He chose you. By His mercy, He made you His special treasure. You belong to Him. He values you and He loves you.

He is the God of creation (vv. 5–7). He provides for you day after day and gives you the things you need. He is in charge of the storms and uses them to accomplish His perfect will.

He is the God of redemption (vv. 8–14). God worked especially on behalf of the Jewish people. He worked for Israel and through Israel to bring about His great plan of salvation.

He is the God of celebration (vv. 15–18). These verses parallel Psalm 115 and show the greatness of the living God in contrast to the dead idols of the nations. Celebrate the Lord today!

House of Israel, bless the Lord! House of Aaron, bless the Lord! House of Levi, bless the Lord! (ALL): Bless His holy name!

Psalm 136

First the Boys, Then the Girls

This is what we call an "antiphonal psalm" with two choirs singing. One choir sang the first line of each verse, and the other choir answered, "For His mercy endures forever" (*kee laolam hasdo*). Another rendering is "His love is eternal" (HCSB). This was not vain repetition (Matt. 6:7), for the second choir was offering inspired praise to the Lord. You can never sing too much about God's *hesed*!

Read it and respond in your heart.

136:1 Give thanks to the LORD, for He is good, For His lovingkindness is everlasting.
2 Give thanks to the God of gods, For His lovingkindness is everlasting.
3 Give thanks to the Lord of lords, For His lovingkindness is everlasting.
4 To Him who alone does great wonders, For His lovingkindness is everlasting;
5 To Him who made the heavens with skill, For His lovingkindness is everlasting;
6 To Him who spread out the earth above the waters, For His lovingkindness is everlasting;
7 To Him who made the great lights, For His lovingkindness is everlasting:
8 The sun to rule by day, For His lovingkindness is everlasting,
9 The moon and stars to rule by night, For His lovingkindness is everlasting.
10 To Him who smote the Egyptians in their firstborn, For His lovingkindness is everlasting,
11 And brought Israel out from their midst, For His lovingkindness is everlasting,
12 With a strong hand and an outstretched arm, For His lovingkindness is everlasting.
13 To Him who divided the Red Sea asunder, For His lovingkindness is everlasting,
14 And made Israel pass through the midst of it, For His lovingkindness is everlasting;
15 But He overthrew Pharaoh and his army in the Red Sea, For His lovingkindness is everlasting.
16 To Him who led His people through the wilderness, For His lovingkindness is everlasting;
17 To Him who smote great kings, For His lovingkindness is everlasting,
18 And slew mighty kings, For His

lovingkindness is everlasting:
19. Sihon, king of the Amorites, For His lovingkindness is everlasting,
20. And Og, king of Bashan, For His lovingkindness is everlasting,
21. And gave their land as a heritage, For His lovingkindness is everlasting,
22. Even a heritage to Israel His servant, For His lovingkindness is everlasting.
23. Who remembered us in our low estate, For His lovingkindness is everlasting,
24. And has rescued us from our adversaries, For His lovingkindness is everlasting;
25. Who gives food to all flesh, For His lovingkindness is everlasting.
26. Give thanks to the God of heaven, For His lovingkindness is everlasting.

(Psalm 136, NASB)

In Jewish tradition this psalm is often known as the Great *Hallel* ("the Great Psalm of Praise"). It tells us that God reveals His mercy by giving us a wonderful creation to use and to enjoy (vv. 4–9). He had everything ready for our first parents when He made them! It is too bad that many people are such poor stewards of God's creation gifts. Never take for granted the wonderful world God made and allows us to live in.

He reveals His *hesed* in His care for you, helping you fight your battles and defeat your enemies (vv. 10–25). Israel was not always faithful to God, but that is where His *hesed* comes in! He was faithful to them. The God of heaven is caring for you on earth! His *hesed* endures forever!

Try singing or chanting this psalm with your Bible study or small group, or with your family! Have the guys affirm the first lines, with the girls responding. Then switch around about half way through—just for variety. Welcome to the ancient Temple!

"A Bible that is falling apart usually belongs to someone who isn't."

> *O God, You that made me, gave me my daily bread, and rescued me from many dangers, grant that in all times of trouble I may recognize that Your faithfulness is forever, and give thanks for Your goodness, through Him who is Your Wisdom and Your Word, Jesus Christ my Savior. AMEN.*

Psalm 137

By The Rivers of Babylon

A title for this psalm is easy to find. The first sentence says it all. Every line of the psalm is alive with pain, and the intensity of the pain grows with each additional line all the way to the shocking climax.

> 137:1 By the rivers of Babylon, There we sat down and wept, When we remembered Zion.
> 2 Upon the willows in the midst of it We hung our harps.
> 3 For there our captors demanded of us songs, And our tormentors mirth, saying, "Sing us one of the songs of Zion."
> 4 How can we sing the Lord's song In a foreign land?
> 5 If I forget you, O Jerusalem, May my right hand forget her skill.
> 6 May my tongue cling to the roof of my mouth If I do not remember you, If I do not exalt Jerusalem Above my chief joy.
> 7 Remember, O Lord, against the sons of Edom The day of Jerusalem, Who said, "Raze it, raze it To its very foundation."
> 8 O daughter of Babylon, you devastated one, How blessed will be the one who repays you With the recompense with which you have repaid us.
> 9 How blessed will be the one who seizes and dashes your little ones Against the rock.
>
> (Psalm 137, NASB)

The psalm is intensely national and expressive of Israel's pain in exile. How do we adapt it to our lives? It helps us to take inventory by asking some personal questions.

What makes us weep (v. 1)? Jews wept as they remembered the past, but they did not weep over their sins. They wept because their sins caught up with them, not because they had sinned.

What makes us sing (vv. 2–4)? They lost their song, so they hung up their harps. David had a similar experience (Ps. 32:1–7). Can you sing praises to God in a difficult place (Acts 16:25)? Can you praise the Lord at all times?

What makes us yearn (vv. 5–6)? What is the ache in your heart? What do you long for more than anything else? Is it in God's will?

What makes us angry (vv. 7–9)? God promised to judge Babylon (Isa. 13:16), so they were praying in His will. If you love the Lord, you must hate evil (Ps. 97:10; Rom. 12:9) but you must still leave the judgment to the Lord (Rom. 12:17–21).

The psalmist does not mention the covenantal promises of restoration. If Israel's promised covenant curses were fulfilled literally, their promised covenant blessings will also be fulfilled literally (Rom. 11:25–27).

Some Christians have seen Babylon as a symbol of wickedness with her children as our evil thoughts, to be crushed at the outset. Others have found value in the prophetic aspect, which can be heard as a warning that evil deeds rebound upon the perpetrators.

> *Lord, I pray for scattered Israel as the apple of Your eye. Enable me, Lord, to dedicate my efforts to care for those who suffer both without and within the Church. Grant that in times of humiliation I may be strong in prayer, both for Israel's restoration and for the repentance of her adversaries. AMEN.*

Psalm 138

Goodness Beyond Measure

The last group of eight Davidic psalms (out of a total of 75) commences with David being intimately aware of the presence of his enemies. Although he is much threatened, he is also much protected.

> *A Psalm of David.*
> 138:1 I will give You thanks with all my heart; I will sing praises to You before the gods.
> 2 I will bow down toward Your holy temple And give thanks to Your name for Your lovingkindness and Your truth; For You have magnified Your word according to all Your name.
> 3 On the day I called, You answered me; You made me bold with strength in my soul.
> 4 All the kings of the earth will give thanks to You, O LORD, When they have heard the words of Your mouth.
> 5 And they will sing of the ways of the LORD, For great is the glory of the LORD.
> 6 For though the LORD is exalted, Yet He regards the lowly, But the haughty He knows from afar.
> 7 Though I walk in the midst of trouble, You will revive me; You will stretch forth Your hand against the wrath of my enemies, And Your right hand will save me.
> 8 The LORD will accomplish what concerns me; Your lovingkindness, O LORD, is everlasting; Do not forsake the works of Your hands.
>
> (Psalm 138, NASB)

At least three forces in David's life compete against the sovereignty of God.

First, he says that he will sing praise to Yahweh before the "gods" (v. 1). Worshiping the one God was the unique mark of the faithful Israelite, just as it is the mark of the faithful Christian amidst today's paganism. Putting away all other "idols" is the sanctifying work of a lifetime.

Second, the rule of "secular authority" can actually compete against the God who ordains it! (v. 4). Such earthly glories are but a faint reflection of the glory of the heavens and exist only as subjects of heaven's authority. All kings will eventually kneel before the King of Kings.

Third, the source of trouble can be "personal enemies" (v. 7). But the psalmist knows that they cannot hurt one who walks under the steadfast love of the Almighty. "With Your right hand, you save me." God stretches out His hand against those who dare to stretch out theirs against God's servants.

Earlier, the psalmist declared, "He who sacrifices thank offerings honors me" (Ps. 50:23). Psalm 138 is one such honorable sacrifice. It is a prayer that help will come, and a thanksgiving for help already received. This psalm has led worshipers to know that their praises, sung with a whole heart, echo far beyond the place of worship, touching hearts in many lands, and rising to join the praises of heaven. Thanks to the LORD for His steadfast love for us.

> *Almighty God, who honored Your Word in the resurrection of Jesus Your Son, stretch out Your hand and save me from all my troubles, that I may with all my heart bear witness to Your salvation, with praises that extend to all the earth and join the music of the heavenly host. AMEN.*

Psalm 139

The Omni Psalm

Psalm 139 is one of the most profound meditations on God in the entire Psalter, yea the entire Bible. The psalmist glories in the majesty and the perfections of the One who is the God of Israel and of the whole earth, but he also marvels in fear at His character. And yet it is at that very point that some treatments of this psalm fall short. Too often it is theologized and removed from its context to become a textbook treatment of the **omniscience**, **omnipresence**, and **omnipotence** of God. This sort of treatment falls short of what the writer is really saying.

For the Choir Director. A Psalm of David.

139:1 O LORD, You have searched me and known me.
2 You know when I sit down and when I rise up; You understand my thought from afar.
3 You scrutinize my path and my lying down, And are intimately acquainted with all my ways.
4 Even before there is a word on my tongue, Behold, O LORD, You know it all.
5 You have enclosed me behind and before, And laid Your hand upon me.
6 Such knowledge is too wonderful for me; It is too high, I cannot attain to it.
7 Where can I go from Your Spirit? Or where can I flee from Your presence?
8 If I ascend to heaven, You are there; If I make my bed in Sheol, behold, You are there.
9 If I take the wings of the dawn, If I dwell in the remotest part of the sea,
10 Even there Your hand will lead me, And Your right hand will lay hold of me.
11 If I say, "Surely the darkness will overwhelm me, And the light around me will be night,"
12 Even the darkness is not dark to You, And the night is as bright as the day. Darkness and light are alike to You.
13 For You formed my inward parts; You wove me in my mother's womb.
14 I will give thanks to You, for I am fearfully and wonderfully made; Wonderful are Your works, And my soul knows it very well.
15 My frame was not hidden from You, When I was made in secret, And skillfully wrought in the depths of the earth;

16 Your eyes have seen my unformed substance; And in Your book were all written The days that were ordained for me, When as yet there was not one of them.
17 How precious also are Your thoughts to me, O God! How vast is the sum of them!
18 If I should count them, they would outnumber the sand. When I awake, I am still with You.
19 O that You would slay the wicked, O God; Depart from me, therefore, men of bloodshed.
20 For they speak against You wickedly, And Your enemies take Your name in vain.
21 Do I not hate those who hate You, O LORD? And do I not loathe those who rise up against You?
22 I hate them with the utmost hatred; They have become my enemies.
23 Search me, O God, and know my heart; Try me and know my anxious thoughts;
24 And see if there be any hurtful way in me, And lead me in the everlasting way.

(Psalm 139, NASB)

A favorite treatment of Psalm 139 divides it into a discussion of God's omniscience in verses 1–6 ("Lord you have known me"); of God's omnipresence in verses 7–12 ("Where shall I go from your Spirit?"); and God's omnipotence in verses 13–16 ("You formed me"). These three omni-words are not the psalmist's words but are modern theological terms. It is not wrong to invent such words to convey Biblical truths but the danger in doing so is that when we speak about God in such terms we turn Him into an object to be analyzed and theorized about rather than the Lord to be worshiped and served. We run the danger of examining God rather than allowing Him to examine us! This approach abstracts the composition out of the real life situation of the writer and neglects **the intensely personal expressions that culminate not in a theoretical knowledge of the Deity but in a passionate plea for forgiveness at the end ("Search me O God ...") in verses 23 and 24.**

The psalmist focuses rather on what these great Divine perfections mean for him personally. The pronouns *I, me,* or *mine* appear over fifty times in twenty-four verses! That is not because the psalm is self-centered, it is because the psalmist is personally overwhelmed as he sees himself in relation to the Almighty's character perfections. Yes, this is a psalm about God, but it is more about my personal response to what I know to be true about God!!

This recognition also will help us to understand verses 19–22 where the psalmist prays for judgment on God's enemies, which makes it one of those perplexing *imprecatory* psalms. Simply put, we have a hard time understanding these prayers for judgment because we have such a low view of God in our modern mindsets.

So, yes, this is a psalm about the attributes of God, but not in the way that those attributes are usually studied. They can and should be studied, but our response should be the psalmist's: "How precious to me are your thoughts, O God! How vast is the sum of them! If I would count them, they are more than the sand. I awake, and I am still with you" (vv. 17, 18).

This is a response that is *doxological*, not *theological*. Read the psalm again in this manner! And then pray the last two verses with me, as I pray them every morning:

> *Search me, O God, and know my heart; Try me and know my anxious thoughts; And see if there be any hurtful way in me, And lead me in the everlasting way. AMEN.*

Psalm 140

"That's Not True"

Receiving slander and the spreading of untruths about you will definitely take place—especially if you are in the Lord's work. This psalm of disorientation is all about slander against David and his reaction to it. Don't get tired of reading these "lament" psalms. If you do, then suddenly someday you will need one like Psalm 140 to give voice to your prayers.

For the Choir Director. A Psalm of David.

140:1 Rescue me, O Lord, from evil men; Preserve me from violent men
2 Who devise evil things in their hearts; They continually stir up wars.
3 They sharpen their tongues as a serpent; Poison of a viper is under their lips.   Selah.
4 Keep me, O Lord, from the hands of the wicked; Preserve me from violent men Who have purposed to trip up my feet.
5 The proud have hidden a trap for me, and cords; They have spread a net by the wayside; They have set snares for me.   Selah.
6 I said to the Lord, "You are my God; Give ear, O Lord, to the voice of my supplications.
7 "O GOD the Lord, the strength of my salvation, You have covered my head in the day of battle.
8 "Do not grant, O Lord, the desires of the wicked; Do not promote his evil device, that they not be exalted. Selah.
9 "As for the head of those who surround me, May the mischief of their lips cover them.
10 "May burning coals fall upon them; May they be cast into the fire, Into deep pits from which they cannot rise.
11 "May a slanderer not be established in the earth; May evil hunt the violent man speedily."
12 I know that the Lord will maintain the cause of the afflicted And justice for the poor.
13 Surely the righteous will give thanks to Your name; The upright will dwell in Your presence.

(Psalm 140, NASB)

The psalm develops a portrait of David as the righteous sufferer who is content to leave the wicked in God's hands for judgment. It is a good example of the true spirit of those harsher imprecatory psalms which sometimes raise questions among Christian readers. Actually verse 10 is recalled by Prov. 25:21–22 and Rom. 12:19–21 as the proper response to slanderers. In this regard, Psalm 140 should serve as a key to interpreting the imprecatory psalms.

The enemy has two favorite weapons that he uses against God's people: **poisonous tongues (vv. 1–3) and hidden traps (vv. 4–5).** He slanders God's leaders (sometimes using the lips of professed Christians), and he sets traps for them, hoping to trip them up.

David's response should be ours also. **He depended on prayer (vv. 6–11), God's promise (v. 12), and praise (v. 13).** God hates a lying tongue (Pr. 6:17) and will one day judge slanderers. Meanwhile, maintain your character before God and let Him take care of your reputation. So live that when people hear lies about you, they will not believe them.

When the righteous are afflicted and the needy exploited and have no advocate, they can count on the Lord to maintain their cause and execute justice for them (v. 12).

I thank You, Lord, that You are on the side of the slandered. Just as You vindicated Your Son, so uphold me by Your righteousness.
AMEN.

Psalm 141

Set a Guard for My Mouth

Speech ethics play a large role in the wisdom literature in the OT and in the pre-eminent wisdom writing of the New Testament (Jas. 3:1–12). David is keenly aware that the words he utters in these lament psalms can be understood wrongly as the spiteful response of a bitter soul. He writes carefully about the wicked, so don't misunderstand him. This Psalm continues the themes of the previous one.

> *A Psalm of David.*
> 141:1 O LORD, I call upon You; hasten to me! Give ear to my voice when I call to You!
> 2 May my prayer be counted as incense before You; The lifting up of my hands as the evening offering.
> 3 Set a guard, O LORD, over my mouth; Keep watch over the door of my lips.
> 4 Do not incline my heart to any evil thing, To practice deeds of wickedness With men who do iniquity; And do not let me eat of their delicacies.
> 5 Let the righteous smite me in kindness and reprove me; It is oil upon the head; Do not let my head refuse it, For still my prayer is against their wicked deeds.
> 6 Their judges are thrown down by the sides of the rock, And they hear my words, for they are pleasant.
> 7 As when one plows and breaks open the earth, Our bones have been scattered at the mouth of Sheol.
> 8 For my eyes are toward You, O GOD, the Lord; In You I take refuge; do not leave me defenseless.
> 9 Keep me from the jaws of the trap which they have set for me, And from the snares of those who do iniquity.
> 10 Let the wicked fall into their own nets, While I pass by safely.
>
> (Psalm 141, NASB)

Not only his mouth but every part of David's body comes into view in this Psalm.

"My voice… my hands" (vv. 1–2). His prayer would be like the incense on the golden altar (Ex. 30:1–10), and his praise like the burnt offering on the brazen altar (Ex. 29:38–41; Heb. 13:15). No matter where you are, worship the Lord!

"My mouth… my lips" (vv. 3–4). When evil is near you, and evil people tempt you, it is very easy to say the wrong thing. It is actually our hearts that need protection, because words come from within (Matt. 12:34–37).

"My head" (vv. 5–7). "Faithful are the wounds of a friend" (Pr. 27:6). They may hurt, but like oil, they heal. Watch out for the kisses and delicacies of the enemy. "When we can give good men nothing more, let us give them our prayers, and let us do this doubly to those who have given us their rebukes" (Spurgeon).

"My eyes" (vv. 8–10). Keep your eyes of faith on the Lord, and He will direct and protect your steps. David gave the Lord every part of his being (Rom. 12:1–2).

> *O LORD, may my prayer be set before You as incense, and the raising of my hands as the evening offering. Keep me from the corruption of evil temptations and set a watch before my lips, and through the intercession of my Great High Priest, give ear to my cries before Your throne. AMEN.*

Psalm 142

In The Cave With Dave, Again!

Psalms 57 and 142 are referred to as the "Cave Psalms." The Cave of Adullam could be the setting, if not the Cave of En Gedi (1 Sam. 22:1, 24:1–3). The two psalms give us some idea of the changing state of David's emotions when he was a fugitive from Saul. Psalm 57 is bold and animated, almost enjoying the situation for the certainty of its outcome. In the present psalm the strain of being hated and hunted is almost too much and David's faith is at its limit. That faith, however, is undefeated, and in the final words it is at last joined by hope (Kidner).

> *Maskil of David, when he was in the cave. A prayer.*
> 142:1 I cry aloud with my voice to the LORD; I make supplication with my voice to the LORD.
> 2 I pour out my complaint before Him; I declare my trouble before Him.
> 3 When my spirit was overwhelmed within me, You knew my path. In the way where I walk They have hidden a trap for me.
> 4 Look to the right and see; For there is no one who regards me; There is no escape for me; No one cares for my soul.
> 5 I cried out to You, O LORD; I said, "You are my refuge, My portion in the land of the living.
> 6 "Give heed to my cry, For I am brought very low; Deliver me from my persecutors, For they are too strong for me.
> 7 "Bring my soul out of prison, So that I may give thanks to Your name; The righteous will surround me, For You will deal bountifully with me."
>
> (Psalm 142, NASB)

What can we learn about God when we are "in the cave with Dave"?

He hears our prayers (vv. 1–2). There are times when prayer is worship (v. 1), and there are times when prayer is warfare. In the heat of the battle, pour out your heart to the Lord. Turn the cave into a Holy of Holies.

He knows our path (v. 3). David walked in God's will, but the enemy lied about him and set traps to catch him. Walk with the Lord one step at a time and He will always see you through (Pr. 3:5–6).

He feels our pain (v. 4). David felt completely abandoned, but he knew the Lord was with him. When you feel like nobody cares, remember that "He cares for you" (1 Pet. 5:7).

He becomes our portion (v. 5). If you have God, what more do you need? One with God is a majority in any community.

He can still be praised (v. 6–7). It may not look like it now, but one day your trials will turn out for your good and for God's glory (Jam. 1:2-15). If you praise him now, you will be in tune when the answer comes.

David visualizes the day when he is no longer hunted, but thronged by his righteous followers. He looked forward to bringing a thank-offering during public worship when he would be a free man again. He already knew himself to be the future king (1 Sam. 16:13).

> *To You, O Lord, who walked the way of suffering for me, I lift up my voice. I pray that You will free my soul from any frailty of doubts, that I may bear witness to Your name, and know You as my portion while I remain here in the land of the living. AMEN.*

Psalm 143

In Your Righteousness

Sometimes Church tradition is helpful in the Psalter and sometimes it isn't! This is the last of the seven penitential psalms in the liturgical approach to the Psalter, but only verse 2 makes a passing reference to sin or forgiveness. If his concern at first is mainly with his own troubles, by the end of the psalm he is largely concerned with finding and following God's way ahead. How many of the lament psalms are like this! They often begin as a **psalm of disorientation** and end up being a **psalm of re-orientation!** Follow that development in Psalm 143:

A Psalm of David.

143:1 Hear my prayer, O Lord, Give ear to my supplications! Answer me in Your faithfulness, in Your righteousness!

2 And do not enter into judgment with Your servant, For in Your sight no man living is righteous.

3 For the enemy has persecuted my soul; He has crushed my life to the ground; He has made me dwell in dark places, like those who have long been dead.

4 Therefore my spirit is overwhelmed within me; My heart is appalled within me.

5 I remember the days of old; I meditate on all Your doings; I muse on the work of Your hands.

6 I stretch out my hands to You; My soul longs for You, as a parched land. Selah.

7 Answer me quickly, O Lord, my spirit fails; Do not hide Your face from me, Or I will become like those who go down to the pit.

8 Let me hear Your lovingkindness in the morning; For I trust in You; Teach me the way in which I should walk; For to You I lift up my soul.

9 Deliver me, O Lord, from my enemies; I take refuge in You.

10 Teach me to do Your will, For You are my God; Let Your good Spirit lead me on level ground.

11 For the sake of Your name, O Lord, revive me. In Your righteousness bring my soul out of trouble.

12 And in Your lovingkindness, cut off my enemies And destroy all those who afflict my soul, For I am Your servant.

(Psalm 143, NASB)

The psalm is bracketed by two very similar requests:
"In Your righteousness, answer me" (v. 1).
"In Your righteousness, deliver me" (v. 11).

Richard Hays in *Echoes of Scripture in Paul*, views this psalm as providing Old Testament background for Paul's explanation of salvation in Romans 3. *Righteousness* is the key word that is the bridge between the testaments here. But this is no abstract doctrine of soteriology for either the psalmist or for Paul. God's faithfulness to His covenant promises to David and his descendants permeate this writing. God's righteousness is both the grounds and the means for answering the cry of His servant and delivering him from both sin and sinners. There is nothing abstract here. It is life where it is lived, and the psalms are permeated with both a this-world context as well as a life-to-come hope.

Jesus the Messiah is our righteousness—forensically, yes, but practically also. James tells us that certain sins do not promote the righteousness of God (Jas. 1:20). May the Lord deliver us from that type of behavior—in His righteousness!

Finally, this psalm adds significantly to our understanding by its reference to Divine leading by God's "good Spirit" (v. 10). David is a model of dependence on Divine Spirit-guidance. These concepts are clearly anticipating the blessings of the new covenant (Ezek. 36:27).

> *God of faithfulness and goodness, I hold before You the sufferings that sometimes drain away my joy. O come quickly, Lord, to save me, and by Your Spirit lead me into Your holy and pleasant land.* AMEN.

Psalm 144

A King's Song

Derek Kidner has been a valuable companion in this journey through the Psalter. Such is the case in his introductory comments on Psalm 144: "The Psalm is a mosaic, not a monolith; most of its material, short of the final verses, is drawn from other psalms of David, most substantially Psalm 18. But occasionally other parts of the Psalter can be glimpsed here, (so it seems) that a later author has compiled the Psalm for David's heirs, whereby on state occasions they might wear, so to speak, his mantle and invoke a renewal of the blessings and victories he enjoyed."

A Psalm of David.

144:1 Blessed be the LORD, my rock, Who trains my hands for war, And my fingers for battle;
2 My lovingkindness and my fortress, My stronghold and my deliverer, My shield and He in whom I take refuge, Who subdues my people under me.
3 O LORD, what is man, that You take knowledge of him? Or the son of man, that You think of him?
4 Man is like a mere breath; His days are like a passing shadow.
5 Bow Your heavens, O LORD, and come down; Touch the mountains, that they may smoke.
6 Flash forth lightning and scatter them; Send out Your arrows and confuse them.
7 Stretch forth Your hand from on high; Rescue me and deliver me out of great waters, Out of the hand of aliens
8 Whose mouths speak deceit, And whose right hand is a right hand of falsehood.
9 I will sing a new song to You, O God; Upon a harp of ten strings I will sing praises to You,
10 Who gives salvation to kings, Who rescues David His servant from the evil sword.
11 Rescue me and deliver me out of the hand of aliens, Whose mouth speaks deceit And whose right hand is a right hand of falsehood.
12 Let our sons in their youth be as grown-up plants, And our daughters as corner pillars fashioned as for a palace;
13 Let our garners be full, furnishing every kind of produce, And our flocks bring forth thousands and ten

> thousands in our fields;
> 14 Let our cattle bear Without mishap and without loss, Let there be no outcry in our streets!
> 15 How blessed are the people who are so situated; How blessed are the people whose God is the LORD!
> (Psalm 144, NASB)

David utilizes warfare metaphors here and it is possible to see three stages in David's spiritual battle that are helpful to us in our spiritual warfare.

God will train you *before* the battle (vv. 1–4). God equips you for what lies ahead. He has a number of ways to do that, so accept by faith the disciplines in His boot camp. David fought a lion and a bear before God let him fight a giant. Each morning, put on the whole armor of God and be ready for the call to battle (Eph. 6:10–18).

God will help you *during* the battle (vv. 5–8). God's hand is there to strengthen and deliver you, so do not be afraid to engage the enemy. You are fighting the Lord's battles and He will not abandon you (2 Chron. 20:14–19).

God will be praised *after* the battle (vv. 9–15). Thank Him for all He has done for you *personally* (vv. 8–11), for your *family* (v. 12), and for your *nation* (vv. 13–15). When your God is Yahweh, then you will know true happiness (v. 15).

> "When gratitude dies on the altar of a man's heart, he is well nigh hopeless" (Bob Jones Sr.).

Lord Jesus, my exalted King, grant to me and to all Your people the pure happiness of being ever bound to You in love, that through our prayer and faithful witness Your blessings may flow to all peoples. AMEN.

Psalm 145

Who He Is and What He Does

This is the only psalm titled by the specific words, "a praise psalm." In its plural form, this is the title of the entire Psalter: *tehillim* or "praises." The psalm opens (vv. 1–2) and closes (v. 21) with David blessing the Lord in the first person singular ("I"). These verses comprise an *inclusio* bracketing the rest of the psalm's praises.

A Psalm of Praise, of David.

145:1 I will extol You, my God, O King, And I will bless Your name forever and ever.
2 Every day I will bless You, And I will praise Your name forever and ever.
3 Great is the Lord, and highly to be praised, And His greatness is unsearchable.
4 One generation shall praise Your works to another, And shall declare Your mighty acts.
5 On the glorious splendor of Your majesty And on Your wonderful works, I will meditate.
6 Men shall speak of the power of Your awesome acts, And I will tell of Your greatness.
7 They shall eagerly utter the memory of Your abundant goodness And will shout joyfully of Your righteousness.
8 The Lord is gracious and merciful; Slow to anger and great in lovingkindness.
9 The Lord is good to all, And His mercies are over all His works.
10 All Your works shall give thanks to You, O Lord, And Your godly ones shall bless You.
11 They shall speak of the glory of Your kingdom And talk of Your power;
12 To make known to the sons of men Your mighty acts And the glory of the majesty of Your kingdom.
13 Your kingdom is an everlasting kingdom, And Your dominion endures throughout all generations.
14 The Lord sustains all who fall And raises up all who are bowed down.
15 The eyes of all look to You, And You give them their food in due time.
16 You open Your hand And satisfy the desire of every living thing.
17 The Lord is righteous in all His ways And kind in all His deeds.
18 The Lord is near to all who call upon Him, To all who call upon Him in truth.
19 He will fulfill the desire of those who

fear Him; He will also hear their cry and will save them.
20 The Lord keeps all who love Him, But all the wicked He will destroy.
21 My mouth will speak the praise of the Lord, And all flesh will bless His holy name forever and ever.

(Psalm 145, NASB)

David praises the Lord by extolling **who He is** and then **what He does**. The first is done by the form "Yahweh is _____."

There are eleven such statements, with the second line restating the first line.

1. Yahweh is great (v. 3)
2. He is highly praised (v. 3)
3. He is gracious (v. 8)
4. He is compassionate (v. 8)
5. He is slow to anger (v. 8)
6. He is great in steadfast love (v. 8)
7. He is good to everyone (v. 9)
8. He is faithful in His works (v. 13)
9. He is gracious in His deeds (v. 13)*
10. He is righteous in His ways (v. 17)
11. He is gracious in His acts (v. 17)

(*An extra verse appears in the ancient translations of this psalm.)

The second thrust of the psalm is telling us **what God does** (vv. 14, 19, 20). This is expressed by seven statements in the form: "Yahweh _____ those."

1. Yahweh helps those who fall (v. 14)
2. He raises up the oppressed (v. 14)
3. He fulfills the desire of those who fear Him (v. 19)
4. He hears their cry (v. 19)
5. He saves them (v. 19)
6. He guards those who love Him (v. 20)
7. He destroys the wicked (v. 20).

Is your problem that you need more faith or that you need a greater vision of who God is and what He does? The title of a recent book that I read expresses it this way: *Small Faith—Great God*. I think that sums it up well.

PSALM 145

More than one person has told me that Psalm 145 is their favorite psalm. I can see why! What a way for the sweet psalmist David to crown his contributions to the Psalter.

> *O Lord, eternal King, lead me through moments of struggle to a continuing faith in Your promises. May I bless You every day and, through all I do and am, pour out the story of Your abundant hesed.*
> *AMEN.*

Psalm 146

Faith, Hope, Love

The final five psalms of this wonderful "book" we call the Psalter each begins and ends with "Hallelujah." Thus these psalms form an extended benediction of praise that concludes this entire collection of praises, prayers, petitions, thanksgivings, laments, and descriptions of God, His word, and His world. But each of the final five is still a unique composition of its own. Psalm 146, for example, is an encouragement toward faith, hope, and love—the triad of Christian virtues lauded as the "Great Three" by the Apostle Paul (1 Cor. 13:13).

146:1 Praise the Lord! Praise the Lord, O my soul!
2 I will praise the Lord while I live; I will sing praises to my God while I have my being.
3 Do not trust in princes, In mortal man, in whom there is no salvation.
4 His spirit departs, he returns to the earth; In that very day his thoughts perish.
5 How blessed is he whose help is the God of Jacob, Whose hope is in the Lord his God,
6 Who made heaven and earth, The sea and all that is in them; Who keeps faith forever;
7 Who executes justice for the oppressed; Who gives food to the hungry. The Lord sets the prisoners free.
8 The Lord opens the eyes of the blind; The Lord raises up those who are bowed down; The Lord loves the righteous;
9 The Lord protects the strangers; He supports the fatherless and the widow, But He thwarts the way of the wicked.
10 The Lord will reign forever, Your God, O Zion, to all generations. Praise the Lord!

(Psalm 146, NASB)

As was mentioned above, this psalm is **a practical encouragement (1) to demonstrate faith in God, not men (vv. 3–4); (2) to encourage hope in the Maker of all who keeps faith (vv. 5–7); and (3) to manifest love** toward the unfortunate around us (vv. 8–10a). And it is the praise of Yahweh that surrounds this faith, hope, and love both before (vv. 1–2) and after (v. 10b).

Praise is, therefore, quite practical, and issues forth in a lifestyle that **shows** his praise and does not just **shout** his praise. One might paraphrase both Paul and James that when our praise of God is not accompanied by works of love and mercy, we are just a clanging cymbal—making noise that ends when the noise ceases, or worse yet, our faith is dead!

Practical praise is the praise that honors God by believing Him enough to follow Him, by hoping in Him although you don't see Him, and by loving those whom God loves—the poor and the helpless. Praise is an evidence of life, not just physical life, but the life of God in the heart. And that life manifests itself in behavior that also brings praise to Him.

> "My days of praise shall ne'er be past, While life and thought and being last, Or immortality endures" (Isaac Watts).

Lord God, Creator and King, help me in every trial to put my trust and hope in You, that I may know the happiness of Your salvation, and for all my life long make music to Your name. AMEN.

Psalm 147

No Other Nation

If you have ever pondered the Lord's rhetorical questions in Isaiah 40 or His equally powerful questions to Job (Job 38–41), then you will marvel also at the way in which He addresses us about the wonders of His powerful creation and His providential care in Psalm 147.

Read it as you recall Isaiah and Job, as the psalmist was likely doing:

> 147:1 Praise the LORD! For it is good to sing praises to our God; For it is pleasant and praise is becoming.
> 2 The LORD builds up Jerusalem; He gathers the outcasts of Israel.
> 3 He heals the brokenhearted And binds up their wounds.
> 4 He counts the number of the stars; He gives names to all of them.
> 5 Great is our Lord and abundant in strength; His understanding is infinite.
> 6 The LORD supports the afflicted; He brings down the wicked to the ground.
> 7 Sing to the LORD with thanksgiving; Sing praises to our God on the lyre,
> 8 Who covers the heavens with clouds, Who provides rain for the earth, Who makes grass to grow on the mountains.
> 9 He gives to the beast its food, And to the young ravens which cry.
> 10 He does not delight in the strength of the horse; He does not take pleasure in the legs of a man.
> 11 The LORD favors those who fear Him, Those who wait for His lovingkindness.
> 12 Praise the LORD, O Jerusalem! Praise your God, O Zion!
> 13 For He has strengthened the bars of your gates; He has blessed your sons within you.
> 14 He makes peace in your borders; He satisfies you with the finest of the wheat.
> 15 He sends forth His command to the earth; His word runs very swiftly.
> 16 He gives snow like wool; He scatters the frost like ashes.
> 17 He casts forth His ice as fragments; Who can stand before His cold?
> 18 He sends forth His word and melts them; He causes His wind to blow and the waters to flow.
> 19 He declares His words to Jacob, His statutes and His ordinances to Israel.
> 20 He has not dealt thus with any nation; And as for His ordinances, they have not known them. Praise the LORD!
> (Psalm 147, NASB)

The psalm asks us to praise God three times (vv. 1, 7, 12), and each time it is because of another of His wonderful acts toward His created world of men and things.

Praise for the God who creates (vv. 1–6). Scholars call it *intertextuality*. Normal folks just call it scripture citing scripture. It seems that a text like Isaiah 40 was in the mind of the psalmist as he reflects on God's physical creation and His redemptive creation of Israel as God's people.

Praise for the God who cares (vv. 7–11). It appears that the psalmist has been challenged by that truly awesome vision granted to Job in chapters 38–41 of his book. Clouds, storms, grass, beasts, ravens, and then mankind! All owe their existence to the *hesed* of Yahweh!!

Praise for the God who commands (vv. 12–20). God's command, His word, His statutes, His rules (vv. 14, 19)—this sounds like an echo of Psalm 119. It is the Divine word in its various modes that communicates His *hesed* to His people. A final point is that God gave His commands to no other nation than Israel. His commandments are not a burden but are part of the privilege of being His people (Deut. 7:6–8).

As important as praise is, it must never become simply a pragmatic device for getting blessings from God. When you sincerely praise Him, the blessing will come without your asking for it. Praise changes things—and people.

> *O God, You declared Your Word in Jesus the Messiah and are ever building Your Church by bringing home the outcast and healing the broken-hearted. Strengthen me with the delight of Your praise, and grant me to be at peace amid all the wonders of Your creation. AMEN.*

Psalm 148

A Choir of Creation

Beginning with the host of angels, and then descending through the heavens to the creatures of earth, finally encompassing the people of Israel and all peoples of earth, this psalm unites the whole of creation in an oratorio of praise to the Almighty.

Read it and watch this progression develop:

> 148:1 Praise the LORD! Praise the LORD from the heavens; Praise Him in the heights!
> 2 Praise Him, all His angels; Praise Him, all His hosts!
> 3 Praise Him, sun and moon; Praise Him, all stars of light!
> 4 Praise Him, highest heavens, And the waters that are above the heavens!
> 5 Let them praise the name of the LORD, For He commanded and they were created.
> 6 He has also established them forever and ever; He has made a decree which will not pass away.
> 7 Praise the LORD from the earth, Sea monsters and all deeps;
> 8 Fire and hail, snow and clouds; Stormy wind, fulfilling His word;
> 9 Mountains and all hills; Fruit trees and all cedars;
> 10 Beasts and all cattle; Creeping things and winged fowl;
> 11 Kings of the earth and all peoples; Princes and all judges of the earth;
> 12 Both young men and virgins; Old men and children.
> 13 Let them praise the name of the LORD, For His name alone is exalted; His glory is above earth and heaven.
> 14 And He has lifted up a horn for His people, Praise for all His godly ones; Even for the sons of Israel, a people near to Him. Praise the LORD!
> (Psalm 148, NASB)

Two similar expressions clearly divide this song into two stanzas. "Praise the Lord from the heavens" (v. 1) and "Praise the Lord from the earth" (v. 7).

From ancient times people have tended to worship angels in heaven and the stars in the sky. The Bible calls both of these at different times "the host of heaven" (vv. 2–3; Deut. 4:19). This psalm, however, shows the folly of such worship by declaring that each group was created by the Lord of Hosts,

PSALM 148

the Almighty (vv. 5–6; Ps. 24:10). This calls to mind Paul's statement that idolaters worship the created things rather than the One who created them (Rom. 1:25).

The second part of the psalm (vv. 7–11) emphasizes praise **from the earth** (v. 7). Sea creatures and storms, mountains, mammals and birds, and finally all kings and commoners each sing their parts in this oratorio that inspires and surpasses Haydn's "Creation." The Genesis account and Job's whirlwind are both echoed within this *panoply of praise.*

This psalm reminds us that people will not praise until they acknowledge that they are created beings who derive their lives from a benevolent Creator. It is the first step toward their ultimately worshiping Him as Redeemer.

A little boy lost the toy boat he had made, and then later had to repurchase it from a lost and found store. He then said, "It is twice mine now. I made it and I bought it!" Angels can sing a song of creation, but believers sing a song of both creation and redemption! (Rev. 4:11, 5:9).

> *Almighty Father, Creator, and Redeemer, bring me so close to You that I also grow closer to all Your people. May I be ready to join in the future hymn of all creation, to the praise of Your glorious name. AMEN.*

Psalm 149

Sing Along

I reveal my age when I tell you that I remember watching the black and white TV program, "Sing Along With Mitch." In this psalm we are also invited to "sing along with the psalmist"—and also with a multitude of believers through the ages.

I will also be honest with you. Since I have never been involved in a congregation that sings the psalms, I feel like I have been cheated out of a great worship experience. Paul tells us that in our corporate worship we should sing "psalms, hymns, and spiritual songs" (Eph. 5:19). That sounds to me like a balanced diet of singing! Paul was simply following the advice of the psalmists themselves. Psalm 149 exhorts us to "sing to the Lord."

Read it, or should I say, sing it!

> 149:1 Praise the Lord! Sing to the Lord a new song, And His praise in the congregation of the godly ones.
> 2 Let Israel be glad in his Maker; Let the sons of Zion rejoice in their King.
> 3 Let them praise His name with dancing; Let them sing praises to Him with timbrel and lyre.
> 4 For the Lord takes pleasure in His people; He will beautify the afflicted ones with salvation.
> 5 Let the godly ones exult in glory; Let them sing for joy on their beds.
> 6 Let the high praises of God be in their mouth, And a two-edged sword in their hand,
> 7 To execute vengeance on the nations And punishment on the peoples,
> 8 To bind their kings with chains And their nobles with fetters of iron,
> 9 To execute on them the judgment written; This is an honor for all His godly ones. Praise the Lord!
> (Psalm 149, NASB)

God's people should sing His praises. **First, they should sing in the sanctuary (vv. 1–4)** because God is their Savior (v. 1), their Maker, and their King (v. 2). Dancing and tambourines (v. 3)? What would my strict college alma mater say? Maybe we need to learn something from these ancient Hebrews! Praise pleases God and beautifies His people (v. 4; Ps. 147:1, 11).

Second, God's people should also sing at home (v. 5), even when in bed! How often I have read this to the bed-ridden and suffering, but the verse is also for the healthy! Sing when you wake up in the morning, sing when you take a nap, and sing when you go to bed at night. If it is a bed of illness, sing to the Lord even more.

Third, God's people should sing to the Lord on the battlefield (vv. 6–9). God's Word is your sword (Eph. 6:17; Heb. 4:12), and it should be on your lips as well as in your hand. Praise is THE weapon to defeat the enemy. Jehoshaphat exhorted his troops to sing praises in the face of their enemies, and when they did so, they were victorious (2 Chron. 20:20–23).

The psalm calls the Lord's people to the song that acclaims His new creation and to the praise that responds to its light and reflects it with saving power toward all that hinders God's kingdom. This psalm is the penultimate pattern for praise!

> *Help me, Lord, to grasp the power not only of prayer, but also of praise, that I may overcome evil by lifting my heart and voice in thanksgiving for Your salvation and the sure hope of Your world to come.* AMEN.

Psalm 150

What a Way to End!

Scot McKnight chose *The Paraclete Psalter* as his "Book of the Year" for 2010. I agree with his choice and have used this Psalter as a prayer manual for the past year. The thin volume also includes devotionals on selected psalms, and I recommend its use if you want to make these psalms part of your daily walk.

What more can be said about the Lord God after one hundred and forty-nine psalms that celebrate His character? The book we call the *Psalms* is actually a collection of five books, each of which ends with a brief doxology (Ps. 41:13, 72:19, 89:52, 106:48). In Psalm 150 all the previous doxologies have combined and expanded into one glorious eruption of jubilant praise.

> 150:1 Praise the LORD! Praise God in His sanctuary; Praise Him in His mighty expanse.
> 2 Praise Him for His mighty deeds; Praise Him according to His excellent greatness.
> 3 Praise Him with trumpet sound; Praise Him with harp and lyre.
> 4 Praise Him with timbrel and dancing; Praise Him with stringed instruments and pipe.
> 5 Praise Him with loud cymbals; Praise Him with resounding cymbals.
> 6 Let everything that has breath praise the LORD. Praise the LORD!
> (Psalm 150, NASB)

Including the opening and closing Hallelujahs, this psalm consists of 13 commands to "praise the Lord." Its genius is in how much it says with so few words. It is a psalm to be sung! It is praise in practice! There is a growing sense of urgency as each new instrument is cued to add its voice to the symphony of sound. Ironically, it feels as if one is breathless by the time "everything that has breath" is invited to join in.

I recently saw a video of church musicians playing Christmas music on their iPads. A dear brother thought that this was simply taking technology

PSALM 150

too far. I disagreed and thought about the variety of instruments used in this psalm to praise the Lord. More power to them!

If praise is the joyful recognition that we are not the center of the universe, and the grateful acknowledgment that Someone Else is and always will be, then Psalm 150 is praise at its best.

> *Almighty and gracious Lord, lead me through all doubts and sufferings into the world that is ignited by Your glory. May I join there with full heart in the music of all Your creatures, in praise and thanksgiving to Your holy name. AMEN.*

What I've Learned During My Journey Through The Psalms

This is the first time in my life that I have systematically worked through the Psalter by writing down what each psalm has spoken to my heart. Then there has been the added spiritual exercise of composing and adapting personal prayers for each of the psalms. I saw things in a way that I had NEVER seen before, and it is easy to list some features of the Psalms that play a more prominent role that I had realized previously. Here are some truths that have struck me with a fresh force as I have meditated my way through the Psalter.

1. The **prominent role of Exodus 34:6** as the control theme text for the Psalmists' doctrine of God. In that passage God's attributes, especially His *hesed*, provide the theological framework for the Psalmists' observations both about God and about His world. Psalms 89 and 103 are great examples of this. The combination of *hesed* (steadfast love) and *emet* (truth) also is quite powerful (twenty-five times!). Doesn't this also point to John 1:14 ("full of grace and truth")?

2. The **prominent role of the Davidic Covenant promises** as the channel of blessing for David and His Descendant, the Messiah (2 Sam. 7:12–16). It is primarily this connection with David that makes the Psalms *Messianic* (Luke 24:44). Psalms 89 and 132 are great examples of this, but I now have a much broader understanding of the Messianic thrust of the entire Psalter.

3. The **prominent role of the Gentiles** in the saving purposes of God as a further elaboration of the Abrahamic Covenant (Gen. 12:3). We do not have to wait until the New Testament to discover God's saving purposes for the Gentiles. What I always had recognized as being promised in the Prophets is portrayed far more in the Psalms than I had realized before. Psalms 97 and 117 are great examples of this.

4. The **prominent role of the Lament Psalms**, alongside the Psalms of Praise, as vehicles of honest prayer when we just don't understand the ways of God. Psalms 39 and 89:38–51 make me wonder if *Lament* should be added to *Adoration, Confession, Thanksgiving* and *Supplication* as the regular components of my prayers. (Remember the *ACTS* prayer meeting?)

I just realized that all of these great truths are actually developed from previous revelation—in Genesis and Exodus and 2 Samuel and Job. What a wonderful illustration of *intertextuality*—the use of Scripture by Scripture writers, looking back. When we join that with the Messianic promises, we then see that the psalmists are also looking forward—to the New Testament!

What a blessed portion of the entire Word of God that we have in this inspired prayer and praise book!

> *My final prayer to you, O God of praise, is one of thanksgiving for allowing me the time and providing me the grace to praise You in this cathedral of worship, Your prayer and praise book—the Psalms. AMEN and AMEN.*

About the Author

William Varner is Professor of Bible and Director of the Israel Study Program (IBEX) at The Master's University in Santa Clarita, California. He also pastors the Sojourners Fellowship at Grace Community Church.

Made in the USA
Columbia, SC
20 August 2018